The French Communists

The French Communists

Profile of a People

Annie Kriegel

Translated by
Elaine P. Halperin

Foreword by
Aristide R. Zolberg

The University of Chicago Press
Chicago and London

Originally published in 1968 as *Les communistes français,*
© Éditions du Seuil, 1968

The University of Chicago Press, Chicago 60637
The University of Chicago Press, Ltd., London

© 1972 by the University of Chicago
Published 1972
Printed in the United States of America

International Standard Book Number: 0–226–45290–5
Library of Congress Catalog Card Number: 72:171346

Contents

Foreword

In half a century, the enfant terrible of the Komintern has grown up into the eldest daughter of the orthodox Bolshevik church. Of all the Communist parties launched after World War I in countries where universal political citizenship was already firmly established, the French alone was able to eventually incorporate into its own world a substantial part of the working class. In some Paris suburbs, to grow up communist is as natural as to grow up French. Except for the brief interruption of World War II, communist representatives have sat in the parliaments of three successive republics, where they constituted for a time the largest single partisan bloc. Through over twenty thousand municipal councilors, the party's roots are firmly anchored into the local soil of France; in recent years, one city out of every five has steadily renewed the mandate of its diligent Communist mayor. Intellectuals come and go, but at any one time the party can point with pride to the presence of illustrious artists, scientists, and scholars in its midst.

The eldest is also a dutiful daughter. In recent years, while much of the world deplored the French Communist party's "immobilism," the heads of the family could rejoice in the party's "steadfastness." Unlike other Western European communists who make a spectacle of their difficulties, the French know how to behave in public. With nary a loss of bearing, they successfully weathered the squall of May and the storm of August, 1968. Providence, which helps those who help themselves, even intervened to minimize the difficulties of succession. From the vantage point of Moscow as well as from that of Paris, the life of the French Communist party is a success story unique in the West. In half a century, this revolutionary creature has even learned to live without revolution.

Or has it? In the absence of revolution, the party has become an enduring and familiar landmark of the French political landscape. Too familiar, perhaps, like an aging house. The party's impending move into new headquarters designed by the communist architect of Brasilia, one of the few concessions to contemporary architectural taste to be seen in the heart of popular Paris, is but one indication of a desire to bring its image up-to-date. But the explicit manifestation of that concern provides an ironic echo to the fundamental question Professor Kriegel raises in her book: not *whether* the party has changed, but *how* it can change.

The method set forth is that of disciplined experience. It is stated most explicitly in the French subtitle, "An Experiment in Political Ethnography." That is not metaphoric allusion. The author writes from the vantage point of a participant observer who lived among those she studies, experiencing the joy of action, the pain of doubt, and the mysteries of initiation. At the end, she presents the complex answer she believes to be correct. But, more important, between the question and the answer, Professor Kriegel organizes the ethnographer's personal experience into a framework of analysis which enables the reader to share that experience. Social science, as she conceives it, is a tool for sharpening our understanding. That understanding can be put to work on the data she provides as well as on other data to progress beyond her own conclusions.

The present subtitle emphasizes the word "people." That is not a metaphor either, but a reference to one of the book's major propositions. This "people" was not merely born out of the matrix of history; it was created, out of existing materials, by means of and as a logical extension of the strategy which Professor Kriegel identified in her pioneering work, *Aux Origines du Communisme français* (Paris: Éditions Mouton, 1964), as the essence of communism. The present study, published in the original French in 1968, examines how that strategy, devised after World War I to carry out a proletarian revolution, has been conducted amidst changing circumstances in France and abroad during the half-century that followed. It helps us understand how the French communists constitute not merely an ideological aggregate or a political organization, but a "countersociety" within France which partly replicates the society erected by the Bolsheviks at home.

A minority Bolshevik society which exists within the confines of a liberal polity: it is the fundamental ambiguity of that phenomenon and its implications for the question of change which are both difficult to understand and which are the most important thing to understand. The necessary starting point is the acceptance of a distinction between the outer and inner aspects of the communist phenomenon, between the "profane" and the "sacred." Going beyond cold-war identifications of the one as "façade" and the other as "reality," Professor Kriegel establishes the reality of both aspects and analyzes the relationships between them, leaving no doubt, however, concerning the intention which has always guided the project. As is always the case, the profane exists on behalf of the sacred. In ordinary times, each is guided by a distinct set of norms, but the profane is clearly subservient; in times of extreme crisis, the one is unhesitatingly sacrificed to the survival of the other. Starting with a presentation of the "outer circle" of the communist world, voters and readers of the communist press, the Dantesque ethnographer guides us into the first circle, still profane, of ordinary members and militants. We are then prepared to penetrate into the inner world. Part III, the book's most innovative contribution to the literature, is devoted to the *permanents* who constitute for the communists "what the clergy are to the Christian people."

Does Marx plus Weber equal Lenin? The invention of a bureaucracy of professional revolutionaries is an elegant design for the routinization of the sacred. Once again, Professor Kriegel takes us beyond previously established views. Communist leaders abroad serve *the* revolution, not as mere "agents" or "puppets" of Moscow, but as professionals who, like any other kind, naturally do the right thing at the right time, more often than not. But although the design was perfected at great cost over several generations, it suffers from the inherent defect of all such designs: it generates the temptation to play ostrich with history, to make believe that history has finally stood still. Hence the apparent paradox of a strategy designed for fundamental change but wielded by human beings who hope that change will not occur.

Beyond its contributions to our knowledge of France and of communism, this work challenges important aspects of political sociology and of comparative politics more generally.

First of all, concerning France, we are now better equipped to analyze the political game since we have gained access to the game-plan of one of the major, and for the predictable future, permanent actors. Rather than make predictions, Professor Kriegel gives us exercises in the application of the more general propositions concerning the party to particular circumstances and situations. Much as Nathan Leites did in *Operational Code of the Politburo* (New York: McGraw-Hill, 1951) she teaches us how to decode language and behavior, and to analyze a *conjoncture* as the leadership might do. The results are sometimes startling: for example, it is difficult for most political scientists to conceive that an organization which bears the label "party" and which normally engages in electoral competition will, under certain circumstances, attribute a low priority to the maintenance of its electoral position. Our working assumptions do not prepare us either for the fact that, like a snake shedding its skin, the French Communist party regularly protects itself by losing members. In turn, our understanding of the party helps us distinguish the choices available to the noncommunist French left in the foreseeable future, and through this, the evolution of political processes in the post-Gaullian Fifth Republic.

Second, the analysis of this particular case sheds greater light on the dilemma of contemporary communism more generally. The problem of the French party—how to change—is shared by all the children of Lenin, as Professor Kriegel pointed out forcefully in the lectures she delivered as visiting professor of political science at the University of Chicago in 1970. The fate of each member is a critical learning experience for the others. It is obvious that the possibilities open to the party are dependent on the future of the Soviet Union; it should be equally obvious that the narrow limits of tolerable change were sharply delineated in August, 1968. But the greater visibility of internal processes within the party, which is a consequence of the party's existence in an open society, enables us in turn to catch a glimpse of that which is better hidden in Moscow. Is it, Professor Kriegel wonders, "a chronic illness, a long, long illness: an irksome old age which never ends . . . irksome for everyone around as well"?

Third, this study reminds us that the more general analysis of parties and party systems cannot, without severe risk, be reduced to the analysis of formal coalition games. Much progress has been made in political science since textbooks emphasized the fundamental distinction between "two-party" and "multi-party" systems. But we must also learn that the presence or absence of a successful realization of the Bolshevik strategy constitutes an irreducible independent variable. Since only two Western European countries possess this characteristic and since— for reasons which are not made explicit in the present work —the French Communist party differs significantly from the Italian, this forces us to reinstate the particular and the unique into political analysis. The same could be said about the study of voting behavior since, among other things, this study demonstrates that the voting of one-fifth of the French population cannot be understood as a "free-market" phenomenon or as the mere projection onto the electoral stage of an aggregate of attitudes. These caveats do not entail a reaction against the trends which have brought the study of politics closer to its scientific aspirations. They do suggest, however, that much as the French Communist party "is not a party like all the others," political science is inherently different from other disciplines. If it is true that the party cannot be reduced to ordinary components without losing that which is most important, then political science more generally should avoid the temptation of reductionism as well.

Fourth, Professor Kriegel's emphasis on the ineluctable ties between the French party and the Soviet Union illustrate the need to reunite two subfields which have grown apart in recent years, comparative politics and international relations. That requirement is obvious in the case of studies of communism, which, as the result of specialization, have tended to divide scholarship on the Soviet Union as a national system from studies of communism in other countries, to divide the study of communism in countries where it is a dominant feature from others where communists constitute a minority, and to divide all of these from studies of the international system within which communists operate. But the point can be extended to the more general tendency in political science to consider "national systems" as "whole systems." True, at the theoretical level systems-analysis includes "other political systems" in the environment, or, if the emphasis is on the international level, "actor characteristics" which can comprise idiosyncratic features of a country's regime. In practice, however, "national systems" are viewed as more or less self-sufficient units. Nowhere is that clearer than in the study of political development and modernization, whether of the contemporary Third World or of earlier cases including Europe. The existence of the Soviet Union has been a factor *of* French politics during the last half-century; the existence of Fascist Italy was a factor *of* French politics during nearly half of that time; the Holy See was a political actor *in* most European countries for centuries; England persuaded the European powers to tolerate the Belgian Revolution of 1830 while no such protection was available to Poland; the United Nations on the whole decided to reestablish the integrity of the Congo in the early 1960s; and comparisons of the development of individual countries of the Western world since the Middle Ages cannot with impunity ignore the fact that the alignment at the starting post was not the same as at the finish, any more than they can conclude a list of crucial factors with a "last but not least, England is an island."

Finally, it is perhaps paradoxical that the study of a party founded on the doctrine of historical materialism provides a major challenge to a particular form of historical materialism which has pervaded, of late, much of political science and political sociology. It has taken the form of an emphasis on social cleavages as the independent variable, and of parties (and party systems) as the dependent variable. More generally, "politics" has come to be viewed as epiphenomenal to "society." If cleavages "produce" parties then, for example, the most likely explanation of the emergence of the Communist party in France is that the cleavage between the bourgeoisie and the working class was more acute there than, let us say, in Belgium, where the Communist party remained very small. How do we know that social cleavage was sharper in France? In the absence of independent measurement, we can only surmise that it was obviously the case—because the French Communist party in fact appeared. That, of course, is not how the case is presented: we are merely given, from the vantage point of the nineteenth century, the post-diction of an eventual split in the French working class into a socialist and a communist camp.

Although Professor Kriegel does not address herself directly to this question in the present book, her earlier work on the origins of the French Communist party on which *The French Communists* rests, as well as other recent studies of the party's early years, such as Robert Wohl's *French Communism in the Making, 1914–1924* (Stanford: Stanford University Press, 1966), illustrate what is wrong with the above view. Searching for a thread to guide them through the labyrinth of events, both scholars ultimately emphasize the relative independent effects of political strategy on major political outcomes. The French case demonstrates that even where, as the result of conflicting traditions within the working class, and as a consequence of World War I, a majority of labor militants favored joining the Third International, this decision did not "found" a Communist party. The best evidence is that those who brought the organization into the sphere of Bolshevik influence were on the whole removed from leadership positions within a relatively short time in order to facilitate transformation of their organization into a genuine Communist party. The story of the harrowing difficulties encountered by the Bolsheviks in France throughout the 1920s dispels any notion we might entertain that the French party was a "natural" outcome of French political development. Furthermore, it is not clear *what* the pattern of cleavages attributed to France is supposed to account for. Is it the decision of a majority at the Tours Congress (1920) to join an ill-defined Third International, or the much later success of Moscow in establishing a reliable proconsulate in France? Can the same factor explain why the French party obtained as little as 8.4 percent of the valid votes cast in 1932 and as much as 28.6 percent in 1946? Must we infer that the intensity of class conflict grew by a factor of more than three between those two dates? It becomes clear that even if we could operationalize "social cleavages" into a variable, it would account for only a small part of the variance existing at any one time among European party systems.

It is not by accident that the several reflections prompted by the pleasurable assignment of introducing *The French Communists* can be summarized as a plea for the reinstatement of historical understanding into political science. Adopting the ethnographer's stance to write a

book on politics while heading the Department of Social
Science at the University of Paris-Nanterre, Annie Kriegel
remains faithful to her identity as an historian. On her
achievement the defense rests.

ARISTIDE R. ZOLBERG

Preface

Two years ago my friend, Jacques Julliard, asked me to write for his political series a book about the French communists that would be the counterpart of André Philip's volume on the socialists. My first impulse was to refuse. I did not want to become wedded to a subject that had already consumed several years of my life. I hoped to test my strength on a topic altogether different from the one treated in my doctoral theses. Futhermore, rightly or wrongly, Sovietologists and specialists on communism enjoy a dubious reputation in a world where communism and its variants elicit a highly charged response. Finally—and this in itself was reason enough—my friends were urging me to turn to other subjects.

Nevertheless, I accepted.

My reasons had to do, first, with the kind of researcher I am. Unfortunately, workers in this domain can no more change their image than boxers can alter theirs.

There are researchers, of course, who like to plumb the depths and describe the various wonders they encounter along the way. These are the explorers of boundless horizons. I am not one of them. Initially, to be sure, they delude themselves into thinking that they will soon penetrate to the very heart of the subject; but it escapes them. Meanwhile they have to surface and draw another deep breath, thus inevitably returning to familiar places.

As you will see, I have not attempted to conceal this need on my part. For example, in order to make sure that my students and my children do not accuse me of unconsciously repeating myself, I frankly confess that I have copied what I wrote about developments previously examined elsewhere.

I believe, however, that this book is in essence not a mere rehash; it is based—and the credit for this must first go to the editor of the series—on a problematical question that was not discussed in my earlier works.

Actually, this book presents neither a chronological account nor even an historical outline. The reason is not that we already have a reference work written from such a point of view. Rather, the explanation is to be found in the fact that under present circumstances it seems scarcely possible to improve on what has been done not so long ago.[1]

My purpose, then, is quite different. It took shape in the heat of the debate during the past few years over the question of whether the French Communist party has or has not "changed." I quickly realized that the discussion was altogether misleading because it contained a basic ambiguity. When people exclaim that the Communist party has obviously changed, should this be interpreted as referring to the kind of change that occurs when any living thing ages as it continues on its way? Or should we look upon the party as having been transformed into a rabbit or a fish—in other words, as having abandoned its original loyalty to one order to give its allegiance to another?

This uncertainty led me to find out *how* the Communist party might have changed rather than *whether* it had done so. What mechanisms, what interactions are involved?

1. See below, the Bibliographical Note.

How far has the communist phenomenon evolved even while remaining true to itself? When did the adventure begin that caused the Communist party to deviate from its original pattern?

But we must first assess with precision the nature of the Communist party. In an effort to do so, I have resorted to the techniques of the ethnographer. Throughout, my object has been to scrutinize the communists as one would examine any closed microsociety characterized by the exercise of a political role which enables us to distinguish without risk of error those who belong to it and those who do not.

The fact that the French communists constitute a closed society does not mean that they fail to maintain ties with society as a whole, or that an indeterminate area around the fringes of the party does not exist. Quite the contrary is true. Any minority society must be capable of becoming self-enclosed in order to avoid fragmentation or abdication. It must prevent alien influences from penetrating it, yet remain sufficiently open and aggressive to draw from the outside whatever it cannot itself produce. It must pursue the dream of ultimately becoming a majority. The fact that it is a minority countersociety explains the dual, contradictory aspirations that inhere in its traditional slogans. It struggles to demolish the old society while at the same time hoping to become heir to that society. The drama that is lacerating the entire communist world is concentrated between these two poles: radical destruction on the one hand, preservation for the sake of a radically new order on the other.

This book should not be read in the context of the events of May, 1968. However, it cannot of course be truthfully said that those events are totally unrelated to the writing of the book. Had things worked out differently, either the book could not have been published or else the timing of its appearance would have been most unfortunate. But since things worked out as they did, at least this time, the reader must make a genuine effort to abstain from classifying the author in terms of the polemics precipitated by the outbreak of the May riots.

Today it is very fashionable to write and publish a book composed within the space of a week. I am probably quite out of style because this book has been in the works for two years. It is based, moreover, on information and reflection that span an even longer period of time. This should in no way be taken to mean that the mere passage of time will improve the image of the May affair. It signifies only that my book cannot *reflect* events that occurred after it was undertaken.

Finally—and it is definitely hazardous to terminate a book on French communism in 1968—the "surprise and disapproval" expressed by the political bureau of the French Communist party in regard to the Soviet Union's military intervention in Czechoslovakia should not be construed in tactical terms or as a reversal of policy. Rather, this reaction represents the culmination of a long process and the beginning of a new phase in the course of which no one knows what delays, splits, compromises, ideological accommodations and shifts will take place.

Punta Sardegna
August, 1968

Explanation of Abbreviations

AEAR   Association des écrivains et artistes révolution-
        naires (Association of Revolutionary Artists and
        Writers)

ARAC   Association républicaine des anciens combattants
        (Republican Association of War Veterans)

BP   Bureau politique (Political Bureau)

CC   Comité central (Central Committee)

CCCP   Commission centrale de contrôle politique (Cen-
        tral Commission of Political Control)

CDH   Comité de défense de *l'Humanité* (Committee to
        defend *l'Humanité*)

CE   Comité exécutif (Executive Committee)

CGT   Confédération générale du travail (General Labor
        Confederation)

CGTU   Confédération générale du travail unifiée (United
        General Labor Confederation)

FDIF   Fédération démocratique internationale des fem-
        mes (International Democratic Women's Federa-
        tion)

FISE   Fédération internationale syndicale de l'Enseigne-
        ment (International Trade Union Federation of
        Education)

FMJD   Fédération mondiale de la jeunesse démocratique
        (World Federation of Democratic Youth)

FSM   Fédération syndicale mondiale (World Trade
        Union Federation)

IC   Internationale communiste (Communist Interna-
        tional)

ICJ   Internationale communiste des Jeunes (KIM)
        (Communist Youth International)

ISR   Internationale syndicale rouge (Red Trade Union
        International)

JC   Jeunesse communiste (Communist Youth)

OMS   Otdiel Mejdounarodnoi Sviazi (International
        Liaison Section)

PC (SFIC) Parti communiste (section française de l'IC) Communist Party (French Section of the Communist International)

PC (b) Parti communiste bolchévik (Bolshevik Communist Party)

PCUS Parti communiste de l'Union soviétique (Communist Party of the Soviet Union)

SRI Secours rouge international (International Red Aid)

UD Union départementale (des syndicats) (Departmental Union of Trade Unions)

UFF Union des femmes françaises (Union of French Women)

UIE Union internationale des étudiants (Students International Union)

UJRE Union des Juifs pour la résistance et l'entraide (Union of Jews for Defense and Mutual Aid)

UJRF Union de la jeunesse républicaine de France (Union of French Republican Youth)

USTICA Union syndicale des techniciens, ingénieurs et cadres (Trade Union of Technicians, Engineers and Cadres)

USTM Union syndicale des travailleurs de la métallurgie (Trade Union of Metallurgical Workers)

WEB The antenna of the Komintern established in Berlin prior to 1933. This "Bureau for Western Europe" controlled the communist parties of Western Europe for the Communist International.

I | The Outer Circle

The French Communist party quite literally consists in the community of its members. But it is, as it were, surrounded, safeguarded, and shielded from curiosity, pressures, contagions, defections, and at the same time nurtured, animated, and permeated by several intermediate groups that firmly link it to the outside world, the world of "others."

There are two groups, different in size, makeup, and nature, that afford an initial glimpse of the communist phenomenon: the people who vote for communist candidates, and those who read the communist press. Not included of course is the motley crew of fellow travelers, a picturesque lot indeed: the clever, naive, cautious, modest, unselfish; the true communist believers and the false radicals, the ex-everythings; the awesome experts and the frivolous dilettantes, those who seek the limelight and those who work behind the scenes; the discreet go-betweens who render service and the others who do not.

It is by means of these two groups that the entire communist community communicates with and penetrates into larger and quite different kinds of entities such as, for example, the working class, the constellation of the left, the national community.

1 | The Communist Electorate

The offspring of a political technique which for two centuries has derived from the solid foundation of elections at all levels, French political science has concentrated much of its attention on the voters. My readers should not expect to encounter anything new in this regard. I shall content myself with a faithful recapitulation of the analyses and conclusions presented by the most qualified specialists on the communist electorate. Jean Ranger heads the list.[1] This chapter, then, should be read for the essential facts it contains.

Between the Two Wars

The four legislative elections—1924, 1928, 1932, 1936—that took place between the two wars and after the French Communist party was founded reveal that the people who voted for communist candidates were not very numerous. Prior to 1936, the year in which they amassed 12.7 percent of the vote, they did not exceed the prophetic 10 percent of the French electorate. Only two times out of

1. See especially Jean Ranger, *l'Électorat communiste*, a report to the colloquium of the Fondation nationale des sciences politiques on "Le Communisme en France et en Italie" (March 1968). Also to be consulted are the exceptionally good articles published in the special issues of the *Cahiers du communisme* (December 1967, January 1968). Also indispenable is the *Revue française de science politique*.

four did they succeed in gaining more than 10 percent of the total vote.

There is no work of synthesis that sheds light on the mechanisms involved in the division of former socialist voters, a solid bloc in 1919, between the two rival factions —Socialist party, SFIO (Section Française de l'Internationale Ouvrière) and the Communist party, SFIC (Section Française de l'Internationale Communiste).

The only thing we do know is that once the socialists achieved unity, their union proved permanent. The various localities where cells were first established—villages or suburban communities—developed a solid *tradition* which for some unknown reason perpetuated itself as an autonomous force. This is the only satisfactory explanation for the differential persistence of the communist vote. In 1958, for example, all the figures on comparative growth indicated that the regions where communists had obtained a foothold as early as 1924—the Paris region, the department of Nord, Pas-de-Calais, the rural areas north and west of the Massif Central—held out better than areas such as the Lorraine basin where the communists were victorious after 1945.

Similarly, it is clear that the fluctuations in nationwide electoral support, however slight (even in 1936 the actual gains made by the communists in the first balloting were, all things considered, quite modest),[2] have no direct or immediate bearing on either the growth of the party or its policy at that time. On the one hand, in point of fact, the electoral results in no way coincide with the size of the party's membership. The latter decreased steadily from 1924 to 1932, whereas the elections of 1928 showed an increase of 190,000 votes in the first round while those of

2. G. Dupeux, *Le Front populaire et les Élections de 1936* (Colin, 1959).

1932 registered a drop of about 30 percent. This could not be attributed to communist policy because the party's electoral strategy had not changed from 1928 to 1932. In 1928 communist tactics caused an outcry, deviating as they did from the "republican tradition." The Party asked its supporters not to vote for candidates of the leftist bloc in the second round of balloting, even at the risk of insuring the election of reactionaries. The object of this "class-against-class" strategy was to force SFIO candidates to choose unequivocally between the leftist bloc, which was viewed as indifferent to the principle of class collaboration, and the worker and peasant bloc of proletarian unity. Actually, these tactics failed because they were misinterpreted and unacceptable in a country accustomed to thinking of conflict between white-collar and blue-collar people, a country at once republican and moderate, leftist and rightist, clerical and lay. An overwhelming number of communist voters disobeyed orders in the second round of balloting. Even the party's functionaries made the following admission in 1928: "Eighty-one voters followed instructions properly [the Party retained 80 percent of the vote in the first round]. In seventy-one instances instructions were followed in a very slipshod fashion [the party retained 47 percent of the vote]; in sixty-one cases the strategy was implemented poorly [the PC retained only 24 percent of the vote]; in fifty-two cases the strategy was literally sabotaged [the PC retained only 6 percent of the vote]." It is clear from this that the famous discipline of the communist electorate was not built in; rather, it represented an achievement that doubtless called for a revision of the electoral strategy. Above all, it was ultimately founded on a true community of opinion. This should not be overlooked in regard to a period when, as we shall see, the party was confronted with a new crisis that challenged the confidence of its members and found expression in a substantial severance of the ties that bound the party to its electorate.

Yet, although the relationship between the electoral clientele and the party structure was not direct, it was nonetheless real. In 1932 the losses were especially evident among former communist deputies who had been excluded because of their refusal to follow the disastrous "class-against-class" strategy. These dissidents, who formed an ephemeral Party of Proletarian Unity, were dubbed *pupistes*. In the Loire, Aube, Paris, the lower Rhine, Moselle, and Indre, the orthodox candidates received a ridiculously small number of votes whereas all the *pupistes* were elected.

By the same token, the growth of the communist electorate in 1936 cannot be attributed merely to better grass roots organizational activity or to better party "work." The explanation lies in the initial response to the political initiatives of 1934. The experience of 1936 also shows that the correlation between the electorate and the party is not unilateral. Although changes in communist policy contributed to an appreciable electoral success for the party, the victory at the polls won by the Popular Front resulted in a tidal wave of new members. We therefore suspect that communication between the party and its electoral clientele is something very complex indeed.

The Persistence of the Communist Vote

Jean Ranger, who has studied communist voting support since 1945, emphasizes its persistence as evidenced by both *size* and *situation*.

As a matter of fact, ever since 1945 the communist electorate has been more stable than that of any other party in numbers and allegiance.

Proof of its nationwide stability lies in the fact that the party's electoral percentage has fluctuated less than that of other political groups, or even, if one disregards superficial changes in party labels, less than that of the great political families.[3]

Its geographical stability is such that we can still affirm the existence of the "three bastions" which François Goguel alluded to in the early 1950s: "Northern France, from the Belgian frontier to the Paris region; the Center, from Berry to Agenais; the Midi, especially the Meridional and Rhône regions."[4] The three "deserts" or areas of weakness also persist: the West, the East, and part of the Massif Central. It is very instructive to note that nationwide variations in its voting strength affect the stability of the movement and operate through certain mechanisms in much the same way that nationwide fluctuations in membership affect the permanence of local communist organizations. During periods of expansion, an increase in voting strength as well as in membership tends to attenuate the contrast between "bastions" and "deserts." The weak or intermediate regions expand at a relatively greater rate than the strong ones. But in periods of contraction, both communist voters and party members become more loyal and less susceptible to outside enticements because they form part of well established, homogeneous sections of long standing. The weak or intermediate regions, which represent a more recent tradition and are more widely dispersed, suffer more defections

---

3. The disparity in the percentage variations of the communist vote (compared to the registered voters) is 1: 1.5. It is 1: 2.1 for the socialist vote; 1: 2.4 for the radical vote; 1: 2.6 for the moderate vote; 1: 3.8 for the Popular Republican vote; 1: 9.9 for the Gaullist vote (Ranger, *L'Electorat communiste*).

4. See F. Goguel, *Géographie des élections françaises*.

than the stronger areas. Such alternations of expansion
and contraction that occur under the influence of active,
stable tightly-knit nuclei, have become obvious thanks to
the growth process of the trade union movement.[5]

Finally, the persistence of communist voting strength
is evident by the attitude of individual supporters: from
1944 to 1958 their rate of mobility (never do more than
one out of every five voters express any intention of switch-
ing), along with that of socialist voters, was the lowest.
Worth remembering in this connection because it affects
the significance of the communist vote, is the fact that vote
switches occur "mainly as a consequence of abstentions
rather than of defections to the socialist camp."[6] Here
we have the start of a development that will be the object
of much subsequent analysis and reflection: the curious
nature of the communist phenomenon, its basic lack of
communication, or at least its imperviousness to the other
world—the established, secular, profane world—and, to
put it bluntly, its solipsism. Strange too is the fact that
when there is a "break in loyalty," the disloyal voters are
dispersed throughout the electorate as if none of them

5. Compare Ranger's analyses on the electorate with those of
A. Kriegel on the membership during the interwar period
("Mouvement des effectifs et structures d'organisation," in *In-
ternational Review of Social History* 9, pt. 3 [Amsterdam, 1966],
reprinted in *Le Pain et les Roses* (Paris: PUF 1968). For the
syndicalist movement, see the graphs and statistics compiled in
A. Kriegel, *La Croissance de la CGT (1918–1921)* (Paris:
Mouton, 1964).

6. F. Goguel, A. Lancelot, J. Ranger, "Analyse des résultats,"
in *Le Referendum de septembre et les élections de novembre
1958.* Of the 176 electors who voted communist in this first round
of the legislative elections of 1958, 149 voted identically in the
first round of the 1962 legislative elections. One voted for the
PSU, one voted radical, one MRP, four voted UNR, seven
voted SFIO, and thirteen abstained. See the tables on the switch
in the voting from 1958 to 1962 published in *Le Cahier* of the
FNSP.

had any special reason to seek the favor of former communists who had already defected.

To begin with, precisely what is it that accounts for the loyalty of the communist voter? Three elements, it would seem, combine to give a *social content* to the communist vote: "The feeling of belonging to a social class; the important role played by economic and social motivations in the vote decision; the image of the communist party as the vehicle of economic and social action."[7] Although 61 percent of the voters of every shade of opinion express the feeling that they belong to a social class, this is true of no less than 75 percent of the communist electorate. Owing to the nature of the communist social code, an aura of privilege surrounds the status of membership in the working class. The proof of this is that exactly 50 percent of the communist voters regard themselves as members of this class yet, objectively speaking, only 46 percent of them qualify. On the other hand, whereas one out of every five voters of the Center can correctly be classified as belonging to the working class, only one out of eight considers himself a proletarian. Moreover, the Communist party is considered the "workers' party" by many who are not members of the party. More than half (53 percent) of all working-class voters regard the PC as a proletarian party even though less than one working-class voter out of four (24 percent) supports communist candidates at the polls.

These observations bring us to our first significant conclusion: "Despite the changes that have occurred in the French political system during the past twenty years, and above all during the past ten, despite developments in international relations and the difficulties encountered by

7. Ranger, *L'Electorat communiste,* p. 7, which particularly emphasizes the investigations of Jean Stoetzel and P. Hassner of the political attitudes of Frenchmen, published in *Sondages,* nos. 2 and 3 (1952).

the communist movement, the social roots of the communist vote have served to insure in essence the loyalty of an electorate which purely political events have affected only marginally."[8]

On the other hand, the *political content* of the communist electoral response is relatively diverse. Except for great interest in what is conventionally called politics (the communist electorate consists preponderantly of "participatory" voters),[9] it seems as if, in the stance they take and in the attitude they assume toward concrete political problems, communist voters locate their own position within a wide range extending between two poles. One pole stands quite close to the outlook and political conduct of the socialist electorate; the other probably represents a position even more radical than that of the most militant members of the Communist party.

Mutations and Breaches of Faith

However constant the communist vote may be, one should not minimize the movements, some slow, others quite violent, that affect the dimensions and patterns of this stability.

Movements that are slow present few surprises. They approximate roughly the overall changes in French society. For example, in terms of the age structure of the French population, the younger category is better represented in the communist electorate than the older,[10] but of course it too will age. On the one hand, "the younger

8. Ranger, *L'Electorat communiste*, p. 9.

9. E. Deutsch, D. Lindon, P. Weill, *Les Familles politiques aujourd'hui en France*, p. 15, point out the "participating" voters in whom one notices "a certain opening up of the individual toward society and the country," as well as "isolated" voters.

10. Cf. *Cahiers du communisme* 12 (1967).

category is the one in which the tendency to vote communist is the most marked"; but on the other, the proportion, within the communist electorate, of voters under fifty has fallen. This decrease corresponds to the decline in the proportion of individuals under fifty in the French population as a whole.[11]

Here again the social composition of the communist electorate evolved in the same way as did all of French society, although certain trends were more pronounced. When, for example, the population of urban France increased over that of rural France—from 1954 to 1962 the proportion of peasants, whether farmers or hired hands in the total population declined about 25 percent—the communist electorate in the rural areas decreased about 50 percent during the same period. In 1966 peasants constituted only 9 percent of the communist electorate whereas in 1948 they had represented one-fifth, or 22 percent.[12] Similarly, whereas nationwide the proportion of employees and middle-class people rose 25 percent from 1954 to 1962, during the years 1948–52 and 1965–66 it increased 50 percent within the communist electorate.

In addition to these slow mutations, two serious breaches of faith occurring ten years apart, in 1958 and in 1968, marked a time when, under the Fifth Republic, the communist electorate was severely shaken.

In order to pinpoint the origins and mechanisms of these upheavals, a separate study of each is necessary.

11. In the French population, the "under fifty" category changed from 43.2 percent in 1946 to 37.4 percent in 1962, a decrease of 13 percent. Among the communist electorate of that time there was a loss of 12 percent, from 75 percent to 66 percent.

12. See Joseph Klatzmann, "Géographie électorale de l'agriculture française," in *Les Paysans et la Politique* (dir. J. Fauvet and H. Mendras), 1958.

The 1958 upheaval was in its entirety the corollary of
General de Gaulle's return to power. This, it seems, has
been conclusively established. Since the upheaval occurred between May and September, 1958, it was totally
unconnected with the crises the international communist
movement experienced in 1956.[13]

According to Jean Ranger, this development crystallized four different modes of behavior: about 60 percent of the communist electorate in 1956 remained entirely loyal; approximately 20 percent broke completely
with the party. Between these unequal groups stood two
intermediate ones. The first consisted of voters who continued to cast their ballots for communist candidates in
local (municipal and cantonal) elections yet followed
General de Gaulle in referendums and general elections.
The second group showed greater loyalty, voting communist in all elections and supporting de Gaulle only in
referendums.

Perhaps each of these upheavals also provided an opportunity for closer study of the ties that bind the party to
its electorate. First it should be noted that the ratio between communist voters and members is probably about
the same today as it was before the war: roughly, one
member for every fifteen voters. But if we bear in mind
that since 1945 the national electorate has included
women, and that women constitute no more than a fourth
of the party's membership, we will perceive that the ties
between party and electorate are rather looser than they
were in the past. Are we to deduce from this that these

13. However, in November, 1956, 68 percent of those who
said they voted communist in January, 1956, expressed their
intention of voting communist again. But in March, 1957, the
rate of loyal voters once again returned to the normal 80 percent
(Ranger, *L' Electorat communiste*, p. 15).

ties were strongest during the two years that followed the Liberation, when there was reportedly one communist member for every six or seven voters? We cannot be certain. Probably the partisan community tended at that time to increase so much that it was easily confused with the electorate. If we accept the hypothesis that a growing electorate and expanding partisan structures react upon each other, may we not conclude that an increase in the electorate in a country like France serves to stimulate the growth of partisan structures? It seems altogether paradoxical that the masses that are usually the most heterogeneous—the electoral clientele—should have been relatively stable from 1945 to 1958 whereas the smallest group—the partisan community—which is generally more homogeneous, should have suffered severe shocks and the loss of more than half of its initial members. The key to the paradox doubtless lies partly in the fact that these former members continued to vote for communist candidates even after leaving the party. Did they do so because, even as members, they had regarded the party as first and foremost a powerful electoral machine?

On the other hand, although the expansion of the electorate does not lend impetus to the growth of the partisan community, the nucleus of militants nonetheless plays a definite role as a structuring agency that insures the stability of the acquired electorate. Not that this role is an easy one to assess. Differences due to the quality of the party's organizational work, to the type of election campaign the party waged, to the character of the communist deputation that emerged as a result of the campaign—all these are matters of controversy. Besides, as we know, the communist vote rests far less on the personality of the candidate than does the electoral support received by other political parties. Very rarely is the communist deputy a prominent man in the eyes of his own party, the kind of VIP for whom the voters' allegiance would justify indulgence in the event of discord or error. Yet it is this very depersonalization of the communist vote that insures the relative stability of the electorate's allegiance, even in the event of a general ebbing of the tide.

Throughout the history of the Fourth Republic, the stability of the electorate contrasted sharply with the instability of the partisan community, whereas under the Fifth the instability of the electorate contrasts sharply with the relative stability of the partisan community. This statement, to be sure, requires refinement in matters of detail, but above all it forces us to think. Are we to believe that electoral fluctuations are determined primarily by the vicissitudes of French politics, whereas the fluctuations in party membership are dictated by the situation and concerns of the international communist movement? This formulation is of course too extreme, too black and white. The international communist movement has gone through so many different phases, it has had so many ups and downs since 1945, that it is difficult to say how it could have been conducive to instability before 1958 and conducive to stability after 1958. But it is altogether plausible for communists to react in a confused and complicated way to problems that result from the party's dual role in the affairs of France and those of the international communist movement, whereas communist voters (even party members) reach decisions on their choice of candidates solely within the context of French affairs. We will revert repeatedly to this question of the party's dual role.

2 | Readership of the Communist Press

Readers of the communist press are far fewer than the number of those who vote for communist candidates. A good example is the Loire-Atlantique where *l'Humanité* is the only communist daily. Here the paper reaches only 3.5 percent of the communist voters.[1] To be sure, this percentage is unusually low. In the Alpes-Maritimes, *Le Patriote* was read by no fewer than 25 percent of the communist voters.[2] Nevertheless *l'Humanité*'s nationwide average tends to be higher. In 1954 the number of communist-inspired provincial newspapers represented only 7.93 percent of the total press, whereas communist voters at that time accounted for 22 percent of the national electorate.[3]

The Original Circle

In fact, this is the real question: should the circle of communist press readers be defined as an "external" one enveloping the nucleus of the party itself like a ring? The truth is plain: the party members themselves, although

1. Étienne Fajon, "Rapport à la conférence nationale sur les problèmes de *l'Humanité* et de la presse quotidienne communiste" (Ville-Juif, February 6–7, 1965), *l'Humanité*, February 8, 1965, pp. 5–6.
2. Ibid.
3. "La presse, le public et l'opinion," *Sondages*, no. 3 (1955).

virtually all of them vote communist (there are always a few defectors), are not always and infallibly readers of their party's newspaper. Of the twenty-one new readers of *l'Humanité* acquired in the Haute-Marne as a result of a propaganda campaign, twenty were already party members. At Saint Dizier, where the section boasts two hundred members, only eighty copies of the daily communist paper are sold.[4] These examples illustrate the kind of general situation that prevails. In 1965 it was proposed to add to article 7 of the party statutes the requirement that the communist militant read his party's press.[5]

On the other hand, a survey of the additional newspapers read by the habitual reader of a particular daily shows, curiously enough, that the communist press, although not read by all the members of the party, is read by people who are not even supporters of communist candidates. Of 1,212 readers of *l'Humanité-dimanche*, forty-five also read *Le Pèlerin;* seventy-five, *La Vie Catholique*. They also read *Confidence* (130), *Intimité* (165), *Nous deux* (283). These figures do not include those who also read *Horoscope* (48) and *Chasseur français* (169).

It seems therefore that readers of the communist press

4. Fajon, "Rapport." "Much remains to be done in order to acquire the readership of all the Party members for the daily edition of *l'Humanité*" (R. Leroy, report to the central committee, "La bataille idéologique et la propagande du Parti dans les masses" [January 17, 1968]).

5. Leroy, *"La Bataille idéologique."* Cf. the central committee of Saint-Denis' resolution in September, 1960: "Every member of the Party must read the Party's daily every day. The number of copies published shows that many communists, including those in sections where no other daily exists, read *l'Humanité* only occasionally. This situation is prejudicial to the entire party" (*Cahier du communisme,* no. 10 [October 1960]).

constitute a population which is neither the equivalent of the communist electorate nor of the community which supports the party. It is a unique population.

How Many Readers?

This is not an easy question to answer. Are we to include in our calculations occasional readers of tabloids that appear irregularly and that in some cases consist of a single page? The coverage of such papers is confined to local issues; their ultimate objective is to call attention to the vital and active presence of the party in some business or neighborhood.[6] Are we to include the readers of those weekly or monthly periodicals sold on newsstands that all the party's organizations or associations try to push in order to acquaint their members in one way or another with the communist point of view on specific issues?[7] Above all, are we to enumerate the many specialized weeklies and reviews which both explain and defend, for the benefit of various groups and specific categories of qualified readers, the party's position? Should we exclude from this list all publications designed only for domestic consumption or for assistance in the recruiting of cadres?[8]

To avoid needless difficulties, I will limit myself exclusively to a quantitative estimate of the readership of the communist press.

L'Humanité is the only communist daily that has a

---

6. Five hundred large enterprises have newspapers published by communist cells (W. Rochet, Eighteenth Congress [January 1967]).

7. For a list of this type of publication, see the *Appendix*.

8. As, for example, *France nouvelle*, a weekly of the central committee.

national audience.[9] In 1955 it sold a daily average of 169,000 copies.[10] This increased to 192,000 during the first half of 1960[11] and, after a slight decrease in January, 1964 (down to 182,000) it reached 205,000 in February, 1965.[12] The number of printed copies thus rose. But, and this the director of *l'Humanité*, Etienne Fajon, readily admitted, was rather misleading, at least so far as the number of communist readers is concerned. One must not forget that during this same decade seven provincial communist dailies totaling 250,000 copies disappeared altogether. On the other hand, the Parisian communist daily, *Libération*, likewise disappeared, and a third of its 122,000 readers switched to *l'Humanité*.[13]

The loss of audience unquestionably made itself felt. In Paris and in the region of the Seine, where *l'Humanité* had consistently been the only communist daily, its circulation fell.

9. On the history of the paper, see E. Fajon, *En feuilletant l'Humanité, 1904–1964* (Paris: presses de Paris-province impression, 1964), p. 192.

10. According to the *Officiel de l'O.J.D.*, no. 92 (April 1956), the average number of issues printed for the year 1955 was 161,911 but only 123,721 were actually distributed.

11. Resolution of the central committee (Saint-Denis, September 6, 1960), in *Cahiers du communisme*, no. 10 (October 1960), pp. 1676–78.

12. Fajon, "Rapport." This has to do with the number of copies printed. According to the *Officiel de l'O.J.D.*, no. 198, 209,736 copies were printed daily in February, 1965, but the total number distributed—25,787 to subscribers and 129,523 sold on the stands—was only 155,310. If we take, as a point of reference, the year July, 1964, to June, 1965, the average number printed was 200,741. These copies were distributed to an average number of 148,721 readers. This means that three-fourths of the total number printed were distributed.

13. Fajon, "Rapport."

This decline, however, is an old phenomenon. During the Liberation, the communist press was second only to the socialist press. At that time, thirty-four communist papers represented 20.12 percent of the total readership in the provinces. But by 1954, the thirty-four papers had dwindled to twelve with a readership of only 7.93 percent of the total.[14] In 1947 it was estimated that 2,770,000 copies of daily communist newspapers were sold.[15] The number fell to 900,000 in 1953,[16] to 800,000 in 1955,[17] and to 400,000 in 1965.[18]

This rapid decline stems primarily from the merger of several papers during the years that followed the Liberation. In 1955 there were still fourteen communist dailies; by June, 1956, five provincial dailies had abruptly ceased publication. Today, in addition to *l'Humanité*, there are only three dailies, and they circulate in fifteen different departments.[19]

14. *Sondages*, no. 3. (1955).

15. See G. Martinet, "Les maîtres de la presse française," *France-Observateur*, no. 245 (January 20, 1955).

16. *Sondages*, no. 3 (1955).

17. Ibid.

18. Fajon, "Rapport."

19. The following are the five dailies that were eliminated in 1956: *Nouvelles de Bordeaux, Le Patriote du Sud-Ouest* (Toulouse), *L'Ouest-Matin* (Rennes), *Le Patriote* (Saint Etienne), *Les Allobroges* (Grenoble). The three provincial dailies that still exist today are: *Liberté* (Lille), which covers the departments of the Nord and Pas-de-Calais and prints 95,000 copies; *L'Écho du Centre* (Limoges) which covers the departments of the Haute-Vienne, the Corrèze, the Creuse, Indre, and the Dordogne (46,000 copies); *La Marseillaise,* covering the Bouches-du-Rhône, the Vaucluse, the Gard, the Hérault, and the Basse-Alpes. *Le Petit Varois* has become a mere edition of the *Marseillaise* for the Toulon region; *Le Patriote* (Alpes-Maritimes) folded in August, 1967.

The formation of mergers is part of a trend that affects all of the national press, especially party newspapers.[20] But it has more disastrous consequences for communist newspapers whose relative position has suffered considerably:

YEAR	TOTAL DAILY PRESS	COMMUNIST PRESS
1947	11 million	2,770,000
1952	11 million	900,000
1955	10 million	800,000
1965	11 million	400,000

This decline was not commensurate, for example, with the simultaneous decrease in the communist electorate. A resolution adopted in September, 1960, by the central committee of the Communist party stated quite correctly: "The central committee believes that the disparity between the circulation of *l'Humanité* and the party's actual influence on the masses is excessive. It emphasizes the need to put an end to this abnormal situation."[21]

But how? And also why? A diagnosis of the causes may lead to suggestions of a remedy.

This was the purpose of the national conference on "the problems of *l'Humanité* and the party's daily press" that took place early in 1965. Here Fajon denounced "the monopolies' attack against the democratic press" in all its forms: the competition that newspapers had to contend with from audio-visual media not available to the party;[22] government measures that tended to deprive the "free press" of its profits by underpricing newspapers on the

20. See Maurice Frangeot, "La presse française. Étude et document," in *Nouvelle Revue politique* (January-February 1963).

21. See the complete text of this resolution in *Cahiers du communisme* (October 1960), pp. 1676–78.

22. The French Communist party had tried during the fifties to organize radio programs in Prague for French listeners, but it gave up the idea.

pretext of controlling the prices the public had to pay; the conspiracy of the big advertisers to deprive *l'Humanité* of resources that were available to *Le Figaro* to the tune of 70 percent of its total business.[23]

This analysis for popular consumption aimed at depicting the special difficulties of the communist press as the direct result of discriminatory measures taken against it by the capitalist system. Containing the usual rhetoric, the statement merely served as a reminder that the customary reprisals were available; it referred specifically to the advantages of a "militant" dissemination of newspapers.

Is it possible to sketch a complete profile of communist press readers whose numbers, it was hoped, would increase?

Profile of the Reader

To begin with, the reader of *l'Humanité* is a *he*. In 1949, four-fifths of all those who bought *l'Humanité* were men; in 1963 only two-thirds were men, but that is still a sizable proportion. The predominance of masculine readers is significant. The composition of *France-Soir's* clientele, for instance, is quite different (51 percent men, 49 percent women).

The readership is on the youngish side. More than one out of three (38 percent) is between twenty and thirty-five; almost one out of three (31 percent) is between thirty-five and forty-nine; one out of five (22 percent) is between fifty and sixty-four; finally, less than one out of ten (9 percent) is over the age of retirement. Actually, however, the preponderance of the under-fifty age group is characteristic of the readership of all the dailies. The

23. See the complete text of Fajon, "Rapport."

figures are roughly the same for *France-Soir* (34, 29, 23, 14) and even for *Figaro* (34, 27, 25, 14)—a few more young people and a few less older people read *l'Humanité*, but the difference is slight.

On the other hand, naturally enough *l'Humanité* is sold early in the morning when the first metro begins its run. More than half of the paper's readers (51 percent) were workers in 1949, almost half (49 percent) in 1963. This is not true of a popular newspaper like *France-Soir*, one-third of whose readers are workers. As for the remaining half of *l'Humanité*'s readers, they are in large part employees and civil servants (25 percent in 1949, 22 percent in 1963). It is interesting to note that from 1949 to 1963 the paper's circulation increased slightly among members of the liberal professions (7 percent and 11 percent), and more markedly among retired people (4 percent and 11 percent); but such circulation percentages are becoming more and more symptomatic of industrial society generally. The percentage of rural readers decreased in the same period from 13 percent to 2 percent. However, the communist weekly *la Terre* is a great success.[24] Furthermore, the paucity of readers among the peasants does not affect *l'Humanité* alone; in any case, the paper is not always sold in the villages. Rural readers of *France-Soir* amount to no more than 2 percent of the total.

Turning to cities—more often than not they are really suburbs—we find that less than one reader out of two (46 percent) lives in Paris, compared to more than one reader out of two (58 percent) for *France-Soir*. Also, one

24. According to the *Officiel de l'O.J.D.*, no. 191 (March 1964 to February 1965), the average number of copies of *La Terre* printed was 164,967 and of these 151,890 were distributed.

According to a subsequent count (no. 202, [April 1966]), the average number of copies printed was 179,607 and of these 158,441 were distributed during the period March, 1965, to February, 1966.

l'Humanité reader out of two (48 percent) lives in a house rather than in an apartment, compared to slightly more than one *France-Soir* reader out of three (36 percent). One *l'Humanité* reader out of four (27 percent) owns his own house.

This brings us to the conclusion that *l'Humanité*'s readership, although definitely working class, is nonetheless not without financial resources. The fact that many readers are skilled workers explains this. One *l'Humanité* reader out of four prides himself on having had a technical or primary higher education. In 1963, *l'Humanité*'s readers comprised a proportion of vacationers almost equal to that for *France-Soir*'s readers (58 percent as against 63 percent). Almost all *l'Humanité* readers own a radio (95 percent); more than a third own a television set (36 percent) and a car (35 percent); slightly less own a washing machine (31 percent), but almost half own a refrigerator (43 percent). All these figures are only a little under those for *France-Soir*'s readership (39 percent, 48 percent, 33 percent, and 57 percent, respectively). However—and this shows something rather significant about the persistence of a deeply-rooted attitude among working people —only one *l'Humanité* reader out of ten has a telephone, as compared to more than one *France-Soir* reader out of four.

Is this composite profile of *l'Humanité*'s readership likewise valid for all the readers of communist dailies? Our answer will probably be yes after we examine a similar analysis of the readership of another communist daily, the provincial *Marseillaise*. Doubtless this group comprises fewer working-class people (12 percent of the *Marseillaise*'s readership are farm owners); they are slightly older (only 59 percent are under fifty); as for the rest, the characteristics are very similar.

This information leads us to suspect that the major

difficulty of a communist daily in recruiting additional readers is the fact that it is the paper of the party's "cadres" (and of its intellectuals).

Here too lies the initial explanation of why the circulation of the communist press has steadily and sharply decreased. This decline, already described as greater than that of the electorate during the same period, corresponds in its rhythm and pattern to the steady and sharper decrease in the party's membership.

That *l'Humanité* is the paper of the party's cadres is confirmed by the fact that out of 456 *l'Humanité* readers, almost two-thirds read an evening paper even though, since the disappearance of *Ce Soir*, an evening communist paper is no longer available. Of these, 107 buy *France-Soir*, whereas twenty-five buy *Paris-Presse* and forty-eight *Le Monde*.

The point we are making here becomes clearer when we contrast our composite profile of the *l'Humanité* readership—someone in his thirties, usually a skilled worker, with a decent living standard —with a composite profile of section secretaries. The clientele of *l'Humanité* is of course not limited to this kind of readership; but the latter does influence the newspaper's spirit, style, and policy.

An analysis of the readership of *l'Humanité*'s Sunday edition illustrates the gap between ordinary working-class people and members of the party's cadres. We know that the Sunday edition has enjoyed a certain journalistic success. It is a popular publication whose avowed ambition is to bring the party closer to its voters. Its readership moreover includes women (57 percent men, 43 percent women). These readers are more "working-class" and a little less educated than those of the daily *l'Humanité*. In contrast to the readers of the daily *l'Humanité*, the readers of the Sunday edition are a little less Parisian and a bit more suburban; they also take fewer vacations (51 percent say that they take none at all), comprise fewer property owners, but possess somewhat better household equipment.

It is therefore apparent that the readership of the communist press may be subdivided, with the readers of daily newspapers representing an inner circle. In any event, the latter have direct access to the communist world, whereas the readers of *l'Humanité*'s Sunday edition constitute an outer circle only a little less remote from the inner circle than the masses of the party's voters.

The Problem of the Communist Press

The conclusions we have just reached help us to understand the difficulties encountered by the directors of *l'Humanité*. These difficulties are not specifically the result of technical problems created by fluctuations that have become more extreme as a consequence of competition from audiovisual news media and that affect the press as a whole. Several teams of editors in charge of various publications controlled by the party have demonstrated that they can meet the challenge of these technical problems.

The difficulties are really due to something else. Because *l'Humanité*, in its aims (which at regular intervals are extolled to serve as a reminder of the Leninist definition of a party newspaper), and readership, is exclusively the organ of communism's combat cadres in France, it has been undermined by the major uncertainties that plague the PCF (*Parti Communiste Français*). The troubles of *l'Humanité* do not stem from the fact that it is the newspaper of cadres. *Le Monde*, a prosperous publication if ever there was one, is also the newspaper of both the social and political elites. *L'Humanité*, on the other hand, is the newspaper of cadres whose party orthodoxy can, of course, evolve substantially but which tends nonetheless to persist unchanged.

Whenever there is an orthodoxy there is an official information bulletin but not necessarily a newspaper in the real sense of the word. And *l'Humanité* is read, quoted, and discussed precisely as if it were an official information bulletin. Furthermore, with an eye to mitigating the stiffness and formality that inevitably result from this, the party urges its editors to exercise their talents in such a way as to prevent the paper from appealing only to the inner circle. Hence the minor war usually waged against organizations and associations that seek, at least for matters that concern them, to transform *l'Humanité* into a species of bulletin board for their announcements and convocations.

When the communist administrators and editors emerge vitcorious from this small-scale war they come to the conclusion that the newspaper is not "popular" enough, that it should be made lighter, more amusing or pungent. But they are quickly stopped in their tracks because such a trend is contrary to the very nature of a party newspaper.

Hence *l'Humanité* is definitely doomed to remain the daily reflection of the inner circles into whose recesses we shall now penetrate.

II| The Communist People

A communist party is like Dante's inferno, a series of con-
centric circles. The image of the pyramid whose summit
proudly points to the heavens is too formal to accommodate
the type of structure that embraces members, cadres, and
leaders. It is a profound truth that the teeming masses—the
militants, to use the party's vocabulary—conceal the hard
and homogeneous nucleus of the intellectuals who are designated modestly as the *functionaries.*

Laymen—the comrades.

"He's a pal." There was a time, long before the era of
"Greetings, pals!" when this simple phrase (which requires
the use of the familiar pronoun, *tu,* in French) represented
an international open sesame that begot all forms of de jure
solidarity, both material and moral. A comrade is a card-
carrying member, the card in this case symbolizing allegiance
and constituting a form of recognition. The trend today is
admittedly toward an eclipse of such mystiques. The old
distinction between "our people" and all the "others" is be-

coming less definite in both theory and practice. An ever-increasing number of people have ceased to believe that a man's honor is at stake if, after thoroughly searching his own conscience, he decides to "regularize his situation." Because they are indifferent, tired, or absent-minded, members continue to accept the card handed them around January first that costs no more than the annual post-office calendar, also distributed at the same time of year. Or conversely, because they are thrifty, modest, or negligent, they continue to refuse it while considering themselves card-carrying members and conducting themselves accordingly.

To be or not to be a card-carrying member is today a subtler matter than formerly. Study of this phenomenon calls for a biographical profile and, all things considered, reveals as much capillarity between the communist and non-communist worlds as heterogeneity within the communist world.

This becomes obvious when one penetrates the first circle, that of ordinary party members or the *communist people.*

3 | A Census

Strangely enough, at a time when historians are attempting to formulate statistically items that cannot be expressed in figures—collective mentality and group sensitivity, for example—three successive histories of the Communist party containing no statistics whatsoever have made their appearance. In none of them does the question of party membership receive more than casual mention.[1]

And yet political science can neither clarify the question of power within the various parties nor the question of their role in the process of decision-making without attempting to assess the size of their membership. How does the Communist party visualize the importance of having a large membership at its disposal? Are its decisions determined by the effect they might have on the size of its membership? Does the numerical growth of the party augment its audience and its capacity to participate in a parliamentary democracy?

1. All the references and developments on the questions raised in this chapter are to be found in fuller form in A. Kriegel, "Le parti communiste français sous la IIIe République (1920–1939). Évolution de ses effectifs," *Revue française de science politique* 16, no. 1 (February 1966): 5–35. Idem, *Le Socialisme français et le Pouvoir* (in collaboration with Michelle Perrot) (Paris: E.D.I., 1966), pp. 196–202.

A Party Secret

It is true, of course, that unlike the liberal practice of the
pre-1914 Socialist party, the communists believed that
their membership should remain a "party secret."[2] During the past twenty years official figures have been very
rarely given. But such "secrecy" is perhaps the result of
circumstances rather than a matter of doctrine.

According to communist doctrine, fluctuations in the
size of the party's membership represents one of many
signs indicating the extent to which its policies are being
accepted by the industrial masses. But of and by itself this
index is not enough to sound the alarm that could force
the party to change its "line." The phrase, "against the
current," Lenin's title for his writings published between
1914 and 1917, is often used by the communists to emphasize the point that majority opinion is not in itself a valid
criterion for judging the worth of any particular strategy.
A party should be judged not by the massiveness of its
constituents but rather by the homogeneity of its ideology, its administration, and its organization. It would
therefore be illogical to attribute too much importance to
something that is nothing more than a barometer. If a dire
emergency should arise, the communists could take the
extreme step of suppressing all information likely to raise
doubts about the extent of the party's authority.

During the early twenties, the Communist party actually paid very little heed to the compilation of exact
statistics. At that time it was still clinging to the French
socialist tradition and consequently betraying no concern about domestic politics or manpower questions. A
change occurred when the Bolshevik tradition took over.

2. See chapter 13 below.

COMMUNIST MEMBERS FROM 1921 TO 1966

YEAR	CARDS ACCEPTED	CARDS DELIVERED
1921	109,391[3]	
1922	78,828	
1923	55,598	
1924	~ 60,000	
1925	~ 60,000	
1926	55,000	
1927	~ 53,000	
1928	45– 52,000	
1929	40– 45,000	
1930	39,000	
1931	30– 35,000	
1932	25– 30,000	
1933	~ 28,000	
1934	> 40,000	
1935	86,902	
1936 (Dec.)	280,000	
1937 (Sept.)	328,647[4]	
1938 (Sept.)	320,000[5]	
1939 (Aug.)	< 300,000	
1945 (Jan.)	387,098	

3. For the years 1921 to 1939 all the references plus a detailed discussion of the figures cited here, year after year, even month by month for the years 1936 and 1937, are to be found in Kriegel, "Le Parti Communiste."

4. The figures for September, 1937, August (?), 1939 and January, 1945, are taken from the organizational report presented on January 22, 1945, to the central committee meeting at Ivry. Léon Mauvais, stated in it (his report was published in pamphlet form), p. 4: "At the last census taken early this month, on the basis of information that is necessarily incomplete, our French party had 387,098 members, a figure never before achieved. To evaluate this figure, remember that our party had scarcely 300,000 members before the war. In September, 1937, a new census was taken when our party had a good year— 328,547 members, not counting Algeria where an Algerian Communist party has since been organized."

5. Marcel Gitton, *Cahiers du communisme* (February, 1939), p. 156. Note that the curve for the membership declined *before* the serious setback of the November, 1938, strike.

1945 (June)	544,989[6]	
1946 (Dec.)	775,352	
1946	804,229	
1947 (Jan.)		809,030[7]
1947 (June)		895,130
1947 (Dec.)		907,785
1948		788,459
1949 (May)		786,855
1954 (May)		506,250[8]
1955		389,000
1956		429,653[9]
1959		425,150
1960 (Apr.)		414,100
1961 (Apr.)		407,000
1963 (Jan.)		405,492
1964 (May)		420,000
1966		425,800[10]

6. For the years 1945 and 1946 we have the official figures based on membership cards. Reference is made to this in A. Kriegel, *Le Socialisme français et le Pouvoir*, p. 197. It is interesting to note that in June, 1945, the 544,989 membership cards that were effectively *accepted* refer to the 824,757 cards delivered by the Center.

7. From 1947 on and even today the figures officially published are always for cards *delivered* by the treasury of the central committee and ordered by the treasuries of the departmental federations. These are not cards that have been *accepted* by would-be members. See Kriegel, *Le Socialisme français*, p. 197.

8. The following fact shows the sometimes enormous disparity between delivered and accepted membership cards. During this period Auguste Lecoeur was secretary of the organization and was therefore the "big boss" in matters relating to the secret membership figures. In his book, *L'Autocritique attendue*, p. 24, he wrote: "In a report presented to the Tenth National Congress in June 1945, the secretary-general announced that in 1937 we had 340,000 members. Yet we ended the year 1954 with a membership list less than that of 1937." (Note that even Lecoeur was confused by the figures. The figure of 340,000 members, cited by Thorez in 1945 but without a detailed breakdown, was for the year 1937 and referred to cards *delivered*; the actual membership was approximately 320,000, as we indicated above.)

Thereafter the French communists had to pay careful attention to problems of organization; according to Lenin, this was absolutely indispensable for the existence of a party dedicated to the revolutionary conquest of power. A few secondary factors helped to underscore the new trend. When planning was first introduced in the Soviet Union, it became fashionable to feature statistics and budgets. Following the general trend, the Communist International made ample use of tables, graphs, and curves. Each of its sections, including the French, hastened to provide material for such computations. Only after the figures had been increased by an agreed-upon percentage for foreign consumption were they made public. On the other hand, as it became increasingly evident that the political line of the international communist movement was not developed by the International itself, communist

---

Be that as it may, the actual membership for 1954, according to Lecoeur, was less than 340,000. Yet the official figure for delivered membership cards in 1954 was 506,250. Therefore the ratio between delivered and accepted cards was 66 percent, a very unstable ratio. The ratio improved during the more favorable periods, from 1945 to 1946 (almost 80 percent) and doubtless regressed during the fifties. Toward the close of 1954 the practice of compulsory distribution, which was a source of tremendous confusion, ceased.

9. M. Servin, at the Fourteenth Congress (*Cahiers du communisme*, special no. [July-August, 1956], p. 209) indicated that on July 1, 1956, 429,653 cards were delivered. He added: "In other words, 40,623 more than the total for the previous year." The number of cards delivered in 1955 was therefore 389,030.

10. "In 1966 the central treasury sent our federations 425,000 membership cards" (G. Marchais, "Un parti toujours plus fort pour mieux servir les intérêts du peuple," report to the Eighteenth Congress, *Cahiers du communisme* [February-March, 1967], p. 276). He is of course talking about the number of cards delivered.

militants tended to concentrate their yearning to serve, their penchant for discussion and innovation, on questions of organization. In this area they became enthusiastic specialists.

Throughout the prewar years, rather extensive sources of information were available. They were probably used with discretion whenever the party's fortunes appeared to be relatively bleak. But when the situation began to improve, as it did in 1936–37, everything that had been omitted was suddenly disclosed, and the extent of the party's previous difficulties became quite plain. It follows then that things are probably not going too well today, because ever since the decline that has marked the fifties one can venture only a rough estimate of the true state of affairs.

Structural Variations

Two types of variations, whose significance and consequences strike very different chords, affect communist membership.

Let us begin with the structural variations. Every social group, the joining of which involves a deliberate choice, has experienced fluctuations in its numerical strength. This is due less to circumstances than to the way in which a group mechanism functions. To join a political party, no matter which it may be, is not nearly as complicated an act as registering for a return to civilian status or taking holy orders. We will refrain from stressing the careless manner in which the party's books are kept. The complaints about this have been numerous and repeated, to judge by the criticisms and recommendations that the central committee has periodically addressed to the local organizations. It is altogether understandable that in the excitement of a political victory, people may join a polit-

ical party in a burst of enthusiasm, without having given
the matter much thought. But once emotions have sub-
sided and the time has come to renew their membership,
many of them change their minds. It is also understandable that a new member, who has viewed the cause in a
certain light and had every intention of devoting himself
to its success, may fail to find what he is seeking in the
party he has joined. Thoughtlessness? An honest mistake?
Regardless of the party, these are the twin reasons that
explain the ephemeral nature of party membership.

In the Communist party, fluctuations in membership
have been particularly marked not only from one year
to another but from one month to the next. Pierre Sémard
in 1926 was probably the first to speak of the "sieve-like
party." The phrase became popular. It was subsequently
taken up by responsible militants when they deplored not
only the proportion of short-lived memberships but also
the large number of those who joined the party, played
an active role in it for a while, and then left, usually
quietly and unobtrusively.

Various explanations have been suggested. Thirty years
ago the one most frequently advanced was the severe
repression communist militants were subjected to in the
factories. This, together with unemployment, actually did
discourage vocational ambitions as well as party membership during the 1930s. Subsequently, however, although
desertions from the party did not diminish, another explanation was put forward: the party's demands on the militants were so restrictive that the less indoctrinated members proved unwilling to lead the kind of life that afforded
them no leisure. We find a stubborn echo of these concerns in the polemics that raged within the central committee in 1937. Protests were voiced against the stern
slogan, "You have to be a communist twenty-four hours
a day."

It may be that we have put our finger on the very contradictions that undermine and endlessly revive the indestructible hope for a millenium. On the one hand the party, wishing to be radically negative toward established society, tends to confer on the mere possession of a membership card and on the status of being a communist a significance that has something of a ceremonial aura about it. It therefore tends to depreciate the many different modes of living in a Western democracy as well as the political doctrine of this kind of democracy, and to praise only one form of behavior: complete and absolute militant involvement. By and large it seems to overlook those ill-defined areas, those indeterminate frontiers which, within most political parties, separate as well as unite the mere sympathizer, the dues-paying member, and the militant. In this connection, the term "active" is used to define what every member of the party should be. But, on the other hand, such a requirement becomes artificial during periods that are flat and gray, when there is no revolution to work toward within the foreseeable future.

Fluctuations in the party's numerical strength may result from a contradiction that until now has constantly recurred, or rather from the day-to-day activity of the party which inevitably makes one increasingly aware of the incongruity between the idea of worldwide revolution —which led the individual to join the party in the first place—and the national situation which precludes any social upheaval in the immediate future.

But whatever the reasons, the consequences of the phenomenon are considerable. All this helps us to understand the French Communist party's capacity to adopt or discard a particular position—something that often leaves the observer quite perplexed. Why, indeed, should we be surprised by the incredible ignorance of the core of militant communists about the history of their own party?

Why be surprised by the success of the same old tactics in the formation of cadres and organizations? And why be surprised at the effectiveness of mechanisms employed to make people forget or overlook things? Finally, why reproach the party for its ingratitude toward former but now discredited leaders in view of the fact that even its present-day leaders have scarcely grown gray in the harness of the party?[11]

An investigation carried out as early as 1930 in a department store located in Paris's twentieth arrondissement showed that out of eighty-three members only twelve (14 percent) had more than ten years' seniority. They had been members of the Socialist party before the Congress of Tours. But forty-one, or half of the total membership, had joined the party after "Bolshevization" (1925); thirteen had actually been members of the party for less than a year. None of these people had ever known what French socialism was like in the days of Jaurès and then of Lenin. Ten years later, 1939, it was estimated that only from 3 to 4 percent knew anything at all about the period prior to the formation of the Popular Front. Today, the affiliation of almost one out of every two members dates from the period since 1959—after Stalin, the Twentieth Congress, Budapest, and de Gaulle.[12]

The fluctuations in membership have a second con-

11. This description of the mechanisms of forgetfulness is not complete. Additional aspects of it will be discussed in chapter 11 in regard to the organization of cadres.

12. Using the optimistic title, "Important renouvellement du Parti," Georges Marchais, speaking to the Eighteenth Congress in January, 1967, stressed the fact that "the percentage of communists who were party members since 1959 rose to 42.1%." He comments: "This is a very sizable number and it adds to the party's vitality" (*Cahiers du communisme* [February-March 1967], p. 272).

comitant: the considerable number of people in present-
day France who formerly were card-carrying members
of the party. It would be interesting to figure out exactly
how numerous they are, but this would be complicated. It
would be necessary to compile a correct list of dues-paying members, a list of the annual "defectors" to be crossed
off, plus the number of natural deaths (based on mortality
rates according to age). These are, in fact, the components
of a real political stratum. All in all, the large group to
which I am referring tends to be diversified, composed as
it is of men whose feelings toward their former party may
range from open hostility to indifference but which will
certainly include unreserved sympathy. There are a variety of reasons why membership cards are not renewed—
the times, a person's social and professional status, the
kinds of party activities involved, and so on. Less frequently, and especially among industrial workers, some
explicit disagreement causes the defection. Far more
often, general considerations not necessarily related to
basic ideology are responsible. This stratum, which acts
at times as an insulating agent and at others as a good
conductor of the communist current, has unquestionably
helped to *acclimatize* the communist phenomenon, to in-
vest it with the quality of *familiarity*, in much the same
way that every Frenchman is naturally open to Catholic
influence even if he is not a practicing Catholic or even a
believer.

However, a new fact—previously overlooked because
of inattention on our part, perhaps—has emerged during
recent years. Structural fluctuations apparently tend to
occur at lower levels than heretofore. They affect about
one-tenth of the party's total strength.

As a matter of fact, if for the years 1961 to 1967 we
compare the number of new adherents acquired during

an annual membership drive[13] with the net gains,[14] we see that each year the real numerical strength amounts to about 30,000 less than it would if the defections were recorded for that period.[15] In other words, in order to *compensate* for the normal number of defections, approximately 30,000 new members would have to be added each year. This is a fact about which *l'Humanité* is too vague when it announces that the party has acquired fresh strength. Without such accretions the losses would of course outnumber the gains. But the paper gives the reader no clue.

At the rate of 30,000 new members per year, it would take ten years under present conditions for the entire party membership to be renewed. Actually, since we know from experience that new adherents are the ones most likely to give way to discouragement, to second thoughts, and that they are therefore the most unreliable, we can only deduce from this that the loyalty of a large segment of the membership is doubtful. Bolshevik-type parties have not always fared so badly. The enemies of communism often deride the Communist party because of the difficulty it has experienced in retaining its membership; and communist stalwarts themselves are worried about it. But such difficulty also betokens the tensions that are bound to prevail in any truly revolutionary party. The decrease in the size of the party's structural variations, the sum of its losses, should therefore perhaps be ascribed to the change in the basic nature of the party, to the fact that it has been

13. See Appendix for fluctuations in membership during the course of each yearly campaign since 1955.

14. See Appendix for fluctuations of net gains in membership in the course of each yearly campaign since 1961.

15. See Appendix for fluctuations of membership losses in the course of each yearly campaign since 1961.

integrated, so to speak, into a global system within which it remains a distinct and recognizable entity.

Circumstantial Variations

An analysis of the fluctuations produced by circumstances brings us to considerations of a very different order.[16]

First of all, I should point out that the statistics on communist strength in France provide information that is unusually clear. They show protracted periods of decline and brief but marked periods of growth. The periods of decline (1921–34; 1938–43; 1947–60) are so protracted that they seem to represent the norm. Moreover, they proceed at two different rates: one is a brisk decline (1921–24; 1947–50); the other is slower but monotonously regular (1924–34; and the 50s). A dislocation followed the failure of an artificial attempt to reverse the trend. In 1924–25 the episode of Bolshevization constituted such an attempt. The "hard line" of 1952 played a similar role during the 1947–60 period.[17]

Fluctuations in the decline and growth of membership are so apparent to the observer that he might be tempted to treat them statistically in essaying to recount the history of the French communists' periodic cycles, particularly since these fluctuations present a twofold political aspect. To begin with, the periods of decline coincide essentially with those intervals when, whether wittingly or not, the party pursued a policy of isolation and radical externalization, whereas the periods of growth occurred when the party adopted a policy of collaboration with the

16. See Appendix for communist members since 1920.

17. On this "hard line" policy, see the interesting remarks of Louis Aragon, *Blanche ou l'oubli* (Gallimard, 1967), p. 414 and especially p. 419: "Well, then, had we become strangers to people?"

noncommunist left around a national and democratic platform. And finally, there is an obvious connection between the party's performance in elections and the vigor of party membership, which increased precisely when the election figures were made public: in 1936, in 1945–46, in 1956, and in 1967.[18] After "good" elections and after others that were even more successful, the party experienced a rapid, even a considerable influx of new members (in 1936, in 1945–46). From this point of view, the French Communist party is quite clearly correct when it claims to be the direct heir of the French socialist tradition, whose heyday had come during an earlier phase of the parliamentary republic. But this may explain why those periods that were decisive for the party were qualitatively lean. We will notice this when we study the problem of "generations" (whose very existence is the corollary of the mode of membership growth) and the problem of selecting cadres, an enormous majority of which sprang from a few promotions.[19]

By and large, the incidence of circumstantial variations that have affected the size of the party's membership tends to confirm a similar fact, one we have already stressed in connection with structural variations: the decline in numbers.[20]

And it is true that the fifties were years of slow decline. The intervention of the Gaullist phenomenon in 1958 only served to underscore this trend, but perhaps not as much as present-day communist leaders claim. They strongly emphasize the fact that the party lost 30,000 members

18. In 1967, 7,500 new members were counted after the legislative elections of March and until the end of May.

19. See below, chapters 5 and 11.

20. See Appendix for fluctuations in membership during the course of each yearly campaign since 1955.

between 1958 and 1961,[21] because they prefer to mourn the death of the Fourth Republic—something which is not actually or exclusively their affair—rather than to go back to 1956, the year of the Twentieth Congress. (To be fair to them, it is true that the year 1956 had a very complicated effect on the size of the membership since domestically it also witnessed the formation of the Republican Front in France.)[22]

On the other hand, after 1961 the party enjoyed a period of relative stability. Indeed, from 1961 to 1967 it registered a net gain of 50,000 members, thus making up for the losses of the preceding years. Nonetheless, I should call attention to the fact that this gain occurred within the space of two years—1962 to 1963—and that thereafter the increase had been more moderate. All in all, the sixties are noteworthy for the slight influence exerted by circumstantial variations on the size of the party's membership.

Here we find a second indication of the radical change

21. G. Marchais, Report given to the organizational secretaries, *l'Humanité*, January 11, 1966: "During the first three years of Gaullist rule our party had a difficult time in regard to its organization. . . . At that time our membership decreased by 30,000 members."

22. After the "good" elections of January, 1956, there was clearly a wave of new members, since from January 1 to April 15, 1956, 40,000 new members were registered (M. Servin, *France nouvelle*, April 21, 1956). In *July*, at the Fourteenth Congress, the same Marcel Servin announced 50,000 new members whereas *throughout* the entire preceding year only 10,859 had joined. (*Cahiers du communisme*, special no., pp. 207–8). Now, in an average year (30,000 members per year, as in 1963), we had attained 23,000 by the end of April (cf. 1961–64, *Du XVIᵉ au XVIIᵉ Congrès du P.C.F. Trois années de lutte*, p. 196). The "progress tables" for new members in an average year is 15,000 at mid-February (the campaign for renewal of membership subscriptions begins in November-December), and 20,000 by mid-March.

undergone by the party: the fluctuations that occurred during the "classical" interval were followed by a period of calm, as if the communist phenomenon in France had acquired a little more numerical stability.

The precise dimensions of this numerical strength are, however, a subject of contention. We know that the only official figure given is 425,800 members. But this figure is merely a matter of bookkeeping. It represents the number of membership cards sent by agencies of the central committee to the federations. In order to estimate the party's real numerical strength, we would have to know how many cards were returned because of the absence of takers.

Actually, a series of converging figures leads us to believe that the party's real numerical strength during the early sixties amounted to approximately 225,000 members. This being so, the figure for its present-day membership would be somewhere between 275,000 and 300,000.[23]

But regardless of whether the estimate comes to 400,000 or 275,000, the proportion is rather low. The PCF was inevitably affected by a traditional trait of the French people: their notorious reluctance to be identified with any massive party or organization. Although the PCF's membership is larger than that of its French rivals, it is nevertheless a small party. The unique feature of the French party is its insignificant size; this distinguishes it from the "great" parties of the international communist movement.

23. The basis for this estimate will be found in A. Kriegel, *Le Socialisme français*, p. 198, n. 58. See also Appendix, communist members in 1967–68.

4 | The Conventional Criteria

As early as 1914, the German Social Democratic party initiated a new chapter in the annals of political science by developing the modern concept of a political party. Until then political science had been confined to a study of states and governments. The German Social Democratic party contributed to the evolution of a genuine political sociology thanks to the efforts of its civil servants to assess the social composition of its organization, to ascertain the age of its members, the duration of their adherence to the party, the number of female members, and so on. Paradoxically, nothing of the sort had been done in Durkheim's time, in the era of unified socialism, or in the period that followed the founding of the Communist party. Even during the years of clandestine existence, the communist leaders were very anxious to bring out what was known in the party jargon as the "bios," fact sheets on the individual militants that resembled the very detailed career information dossiers filed away in some ministry or other. The "bios" were used for internal police purposes; for a long time no one thought of utilizing them as a basis for self-analysis or self-evaluation.

This is no doubt related to all we have said about the restricted nature of the membership; the art of census-taking was not developed in small collectives such as these, where everything is known and there is no need to resort to intricate computations. The absence of any attempt at self-evaluation was probably due even more to the image Lenin and his friends projected of the Bolshevik: a man whose intellectual and moral characteristics are less the consequence of circumstances than of a certain pedagogy adapted to revolutionary ends. This sort of pedagogy had to be so pure that individuals fashioned from a single pattern could eradicate from their original natures whatever was no longer suitable. And in effect, a certain type of man—the militant communist (uniformity does not necessarily preclude complexity) was fashioned. It is quite true that no useful purpose was served by detailing his biography. Moreover, communist parties were formed and were regarded for a long time as quasi-military detachments in an international army of proletarian volunteers. The homogeneity of such groups is considerable from the outset.

The people who composed these detachments had to be convinced that they would have to pitch their camp in enemy territory for a long time; that they in turn would have to transform themselves from a subversive apparatus acting against the established order into a separate society—therefore relatively differentiated, as is every society—so that the initial homogeneity would be attenuated. Thereafter a better understanding of this relatively heterogeneous separate society became urgently necessary. The time had come for sociological questionnaires to be used for internal purposes. Although there is only fragmentary information on the period between the wars, three much broader investigations were conducted during the past fifteen years: in 1954, in 1959, and especially in 1966.[1]

1. Of these three questionnaires, which varied in scope, the opinion polls for 1954 and 1959 covered 100,000 members; that

Age Divisions

The study made in 1966 provides the following breakdown of the party membership by age:[2]

Under 25	9.4%
26–40	33.1%
41–60	40.2%
Over 60	17.3%

A first observation is that more than one out of every two members was over forty years old. This over-forty category was slightly but constantly increasing; it constituted 54.3% of the total membership in 1954, 56.2% in 1959, and 57.5% in 1966.

On the other hand, less than one member out of ten was under twenty-five. This is a very small proportion in a country where young people from fifteen to twenty-nine constitute more than a fifth of the total population.

Such a conclusion is reinforced when computations center on age division rather than on groups of uneven numerical strength. For example, if you apply the percentages listed above to the 255,000 party members in 1966, you get the following results:

Under 25	23,970 members
26–40	84,405 members
41–60	102,510 members
Over 60	43,715 members

---

of 1967 covered 17,237 cells (a total of almost 19,000). For the data and results of these, see M. Servin, *l'Humanité*, May 6, 1954; ibid., Report to the Thirteenth Congress (June 1954), "Pour gagner la bataille de l'indépendance nationale, de la paix et du pain, renforçons sans cesse l'organisation de notre parti," p. 45. G. Marchais, Report to the Eighteenth Congress of the French Communist party, *Cahiers du communisme* (February-March 1967), pp. 263–82.

2. G. Marchais, Report to the Eighteenth Congress, p. 269.

Now, if you assume that the age groups within a given category are more or less equal, you get the following results:

Less than 25	5 age groups	4,775 units
26–40	14 age groups	5,627 units
41–60	19 age groups	6,834 units
Over 60	15 age groups	2,914 units

The older the age group within the Communist party (with the exception of the over-sixty group) the more persons it contains.[3]

Is this a legitimate cause for concern? There is every reason to think so in view of the satisfaction expressed by Georges Marchais when he pointed out that the percentage of those under twenty-five increased by 3.9 percent from 1959 to 1966, and ultimately climbed from 5.5 percent to 9.4 percent. On the basis of these figures, Marchais concluded: "The Party has regained its youth."[4] But the progress has not been very significant. Although the 1966 percentage of young members was an improvement over the figure for 1959, a year when "the war in Algeria hampered the recruitment of young people"—this was publicly acknowledged[5]—it was still below the 1954 figure (10.2 percent).

Why does the party scrutinize so attentively the percentage of its "under twenty-five" members? It is anxious to insure a sufficient number of new recruits to replace older members who leave the party because of age. It

3. I am indebted for this insight to Claude Harmel, "La composition sociale du parti communiste français et son évolution de 1959 à 1966," *Est et Ouest*, no. 378, (February 1967), p. 6.

4. G. Marchais, Report to the Eighteenth Congress, p. 269.

5. M. Servin, speech to the Fifteenth Congress of the French Communist Party, Ivry, June 1959.

knows all too well that the decision to devote one's life to the cause of communism is actually a rite, the transition from childhood to adolescence, or from adolescence to adulthood, a rite akin to a solemn communion on the religious level, or to military service on the social level. Above all, it knows that the process of transforming a revolutionary into a communist, eventually a responsible one, is quite lengthy and that it will terminate successfully only if the individual himself proves to be malleable.

It is therefore a great mistake to assume that the communists share the Western world's admiration for everything "young"; they are merely fearful that this natural reservoir of new recruits may dry up at the source.

If we examine the party's policy in this matter we are struck by the meticulous care with which the communists developed both the form and content of their approach as they set out to capture the youth, taking an interest in the problems and organizations of young people. But although they approached their task with a certain efficiency, their efforts lacked dynamism and a broad perspective.

This was especially true in regard to the question of children.

I remember how vigorously Jeanette Vermeersch, speaking in 1956 to a communist parliamentary group in the National Assembly during a general debate on birth control, pleaded for the "right of maternity."[6] The reasoning that tended to stigmatize as "petty bourgeois" any agitation in favor of reducing the birth rate—which

6. Jeannette Vermeersch, *Contre le néo-malthusianisme réactionnaire, nous luttons pour le droit à la maternité,* conference, May 4, 1956, before the French Communist party's parliamentary group at the National Assembly, supplement to *France-Nouvelle,* no. 543 (May 12, 1956), p. 16.

rightly or wrongly was associated with the influence of family planning—was in the direct line of socialism's traditional optimism, its traditional predilection for life as against death.[7] Jeannette Vermeersch opportunely reminded her listeners of Lenin's sarcastic allusion to the "petit bourgeois" who "protests as the representative of a class that is doomed to perish, who views with despair the future of a class that is defeated and timid. Since things are hopeless, let there be fewer children to experience our sufferings, our calvary, our misery and humiliations."[8]

Nonetheless, not even Leninist authority can obscure the fact that in such matters the French working-class movement (which of course may, if one insists on it, be called "petit bourgeois," although the epithet is polemical in this connection) reacted and behaved in the very opposite manner. Our labor exchanges around the turn of the century were centers of propaganda whose aim it was to disseminate contraceptive information. At that time, the trade union militants (with all they represented in the way of revolutionary faith, social protest, and determination) were obviously preaching by example, taking care to have no children themselves, or at any rate very few. The proletariat should not furnish the middle class with human cannon fodder, or with additional means of exploitation. It should save its strength to combat capitalism, not to raise a brood, with all the hardships this entails.

7. Cf. André Armengaud, "Le mouvement ouvrier français devant le néo-malthusianisme," communication to the Société de démographie historique, 1965.

8. Lenin, "The Working-class and neo-Malthusianism," *Pravda*, June 16–29, 1913 (*Oeuvres* [Russian ed.], 16: 497–99). Quoted in *La Femme et le Communisme*, anthology of great Marxist texts with an introduction by J. Vermeersch and an essay by Jean Freville (Paris: Ed. sociales, 1950, p. 119).

But of greater importance is the fact that the party's position is equivocal, futile, and inconsistent. Although today somewhat watered down and attenuated, its position remains equivocal because it tends to reinforce the effectiveness of the church's teachings. It is futile because it attempts to slow down the irresistible change in mores which scientific and technological progress necessarily involves. Above all, it is inconsistent. Women have achieved a new status by their work or by some other independent activity. This means a concomitant decrease in their reproductive activities.

The inconsistency is patent when we consider all the dedicated work that goes on in communist municipalities to administer and expand institutions offering nursery care, kindergarten activities, ski lessons, advice on child-rearing, and so on. During the nineteenth century, progressive groups had hoped to see the establishment of such institutions whose marginal usefulness is no longer questioned. However, thanks to pioneering studies we know today that they probably constitute only supplementary and secondary solutions. Should these forms of substitution or relief for the maternal function be regarded as the beginning of a socialist policy?

A Frenchman, accustomed to a type of society where, for better or for worse, children and adults dwell in close proximity to one another, cannot help but be struck by the preponderance of adults in the urban communities of the Soviet Union and the peoples' democracies. The children are certainly not neglected—far from it. Nevertheless, they are treated as if they constitute separate entities within a network of special institutions that look upon the most deserving of them in a way that is reminiscent of how French society regards the sons of peasants who have been taken from the farm, educated by the church, and prepared for the priesthood.[9]

This is doubtless a problem, and a very complex one at that.[10] It is inscribed in gigantic letters in the statistics of the demographically most fragile socialist countries, such as Hungary and Bulgaria.

Such circumspection on the part of the communists is likewise encountered in their attitude toward the young. Although they are ready to assume responsibility for everything the young might demand from established society, they reject anything which suggests that a community of interests may exist among young people, that an existential solidarity may unite them, solely because of the bond of youth. Sternly reminding young people that they are living in a class society, the communists denounce as diversionary and harmful any attempt to extract advantage from the situation produced in France by the extraordinary imbalance stemming from a twenty-year population explosion and from the henceforth inevitable coexistence of the generations.

9. I dealt with this theme in an article, "Parents et enfants en démocraties populaires," *La Nef*, no. 21 (January-April, 1965). Very important works on the subject have already appeared, especially in Poland, Hungary, and Czechoslovakia. They deal with the decrease in the urban birth rate due to women working. See especially the special number, "La Femme dans le monde moderne," *Recherches internationales à la lumière du marxisme*, no. 42 (March-April 1964), with the extraordinary texts of the Hungarian, Kalman Kulcsar, and the Czech sociologist, Jiri Prokopec. See also in *Images de la femme dans la société moderne* (Paris: Ed. ouvrières, 1964), chapter 3 by the Polish sociologists Antonina Klowska and J. Piotrowski, "Les attitudes à l'égard de la condition de la femme dans les familles ouvrières polonaises."

10. See H. Zamoyska, "Situation de la femme en U.R.S.S. (1917–1967)," *La Table Ronde* (October-November 1967).

Are we then to brand as inconsistent the party's espousal of the "unity of the young generation" thesis, which has continued to surface ever since the period of the Popular Front? I rather think that this maneuver is a tactical one. Besides, the thesis itself has not progressed from the level of practical politics to that of theory. It is merely included in the overall strategy whenever the party pushes slogans of union, unity, and united front. "The unity of the young generation" should therefore not be interpreted as a doctrinal formula but rather as the application of a circumstantial approach to the "interest group" which the young represent.

The confines to which the communists intend to relegate youth problems are, moreover, very clearly emphasized by the manner in which the Communist party organizes its own young people. The JC (*Jeunesses communistes*, or Young Communists) are an "independent organization," which means in effect that they are independent in the matter of organization: in a neighborhood, a factory, or a village, the youth groups are not to be confused with the party cells. But as the formula indicates, if only by omission, this independence is strictly limited to the organizational level. In every other regard, and because they constitute a "school for communism," the JCs can have no policy other than the one elaborated, defined, and controlled by the party's central committee. This, as well as many other factors, explains the resolution on youth questions voted by the Thirteenth Congress:

> The organization of the masses of young cannot represent a communist youth party of any kind. There is room for only one communist party, the mentor and organizer of the working-class struggle, of the people of France and the entire nation, including the youth.

And again, in the report presented at this same congress by François Billoux:

> The organization of a union of the young generation is not the special concern of such-and-such a youth organization nor is it the concern of young communists. It is a matter that concerns the Communist Party alone, the supreme spokesman of the organized working class.[11]

This doctrinal view legitimizes and requires the established practice of making sure that, at every level, the person responsible for the JCs is also a party militant; a responsible "adult" in the party is designated to "follow the activities of the young." Moreover, the secretary-general of the *Mouvement de la jeunesse communiste* is a member of the party's central committee, which means that his "youth" is a relative matter.[12]

Actually, the pattern is an ideal rather than a real one. The party often "steals" its militants from the youth organizations in order to fit them into its own cadres, and it grumbles whenever it has to "release" one of them in order to help a youth group—unless the whole thing is merely an empty gesture.

But although the principle occasionally encounters difficulties when it is applied, it is nowhere contested. Patterned after Soviet Russia's policy toward Komsomols, it is also the result of a troublesome local experience. We probably tend to lose sight of the problems encountered as early as 1920, within the framework of conflicting

11. F. Billoux, *Le P.C.F. et la Jeunesse,* Report to the Thirteenth Congress of the French Communist Party, Ivry-sur-Seine (June 3–7, 1954), p. 21.

12. Thus the present secretary-general of the communist youth movement, François Hilsum, is about forty.

trends that preceded the Congress of Tours. At that time, the creation of a communist base among the socialist youth (in the name of the socialist youth's autonomy vis-à-vis the Socialist party) and its transformation into a communist youth organization had been one means among many of splitting the unified Socialist party and its centrist majority. Similarly, within the framework of the conflicting trends that split the Communist party between 1920 and 1924, the creation of a section of young communists was often used indirectly by the "left opposition" to promote its own goals within the party.

On the other hand, none of the veterans actually in the political bureau—especially François Billoux and Raymond Guyot—will ever forget the unhappy fate of "The Group" in the thirties. In 1924 Doriot, then secretary-general of the *Jeunesses communistes*, was one of the first of his contemporaries to maintain that the aptitude for becoming a true revolutionary was guaranteed by the fact of being young. But other young men—Barbé, Célor, Billoux, Lozeray, Guyot, Ferrat, Galopin—allowed themselves to be taken in by the executive committee of the Communist International. This body, believing that the time had come to assume direction of the French Communist party, demanded in 1927 a truly "Bolshevik" leadership, including militants trained in the youth groups and in the CGTU (*Confédération générale du travail unifiée*). And so, with all the vigor of a war machine, the executive committee of the Communist International launched the youthful leaders of the *Jeunesses communistes*, who were pleased and proud of the confidence Moscow placed in them. Throughout 1927 they sent many letters to the central committee of the party bitterly protesting and criticizing its electoral and legal procedures. François Billoux even edited a brochure on the subject a

little later. Although never published, its title is significant: "The Role of the *Jeunesses communistes* in the Bolshevik Training of the Party." In it, Billoux showed how
the party, at the instigation of the *Jeunesses communistes*,
had launched a campaign against the war in Morocco;
how, influenced by the *Jeunesses communistes*, it had
organized antimilitarist commissions composed of party
militants and youth. Thus, after August, 1931, these
Jeunesses leaders were condemned personally and collectively, or told to denounce themselves for having been
responsible for a split in the party caused by their foolish
leftist activities. Yet all these youthful leaders believed
that they were interpreting in all honesty the views held
in Moscow. Those who survived the ordeal were never
taken back into the party.

Thereafter, experience having been purified by doctrine, the Communist party ceased to display toward the
Jeunesses communistes an attitude of timid and embar-
rassed paternalism. Instead, it exhibited a total confidence
in the right and duty of the adult to exercise his paternal
authority. So much the worse for the unique dynamism,
the urge to innovate, to take the lead and run risks—so
much the worse for the entire complex of qualities and
feelings that nurture the spirit of adolescents. A communist apprentice is not an adventurer; he is a good boy,
eager to learn from his betters.

Is the fatherly image which the party clings to so des-
perately the hidden cause of its irrational dislike of every
aspect of psychoanalysis, which it has been denouncing
for a long time? It is probably no accident that the party
keeps harping on the "humbug" of the generation-con-
flict thesis. Secure in the knowledge that it is in full possession of its tutelary authority, it uses and abuses it to
camouflage its fear of a confrontation with its impatient
youthful heirs.

The tough resolution which not too long ago the party issued in order to put an end to the tendency of communist students to think for themselves, to raise new questions or implement new ideas, can in nowise be attributed to an urgent immediate need to impose at all costs the influence of its leaders; rather, it is part of the party line as well as of the leaders' conception of the duties of fathers toward their sons.[13]

One of the party's slogans, "He who loves well punishes well," can hardly be called modern. It probably explains the serious difficulties encountered by the *Jeunesses communistes* in their efforts to recruit new members.[14] The

13. The problem of "fathers and sons" is a great source of anxiety to a party that doubtless feels itself growing older. On the problem of the generations within the party, see below, chapter 5. This is the leitmotif of the complaints made in opposition to the Gaullists, who "try to persuade the young people that the enemy is the father; it is better to have parties of the past than parties of the period of their father" (G. Perrimond, *France nouvelle*, no. 1121 [April 12, 1967]; see also M. Girard, *France nouvelle*, no. 1128 [May 31, 1967]).

14. The *Mouvement de la jeunesse communiste* was reorganized in 1957 (after the period, following the Liberation, when the movement expanded into the *Union de la jeunesse républicaine de France*). It included all the specialized branches (even the *Étudiants communistes* whose relative autonomy was destroyed when the crisis of the years 1961–65 was resolved). At the time of the Eighteenth Congress of the French Communist Party in January, 1967, it had 50,000 members (G. Marchais, Report to the Eighteenth Congress, p. 269). This was a slight increase over 1954 when, according to Servin, the UJRF plus the UJFF (female branch) had only 40,000 members combined. But compared to 1959 it was stagnant. At that time, according to Servin, the *Mouvement de la jeunesse communiste* had more than 50,000 members. And in reality this constituted a setback if we take into account the fact that young people in the large postwar classes had reached the age of eighteen by 1963–64. We must also remember that, according to Léon Mauvais (report on organizational activities to the central committee, January 1945, p. 5), in October, 1938, the *Jeunesse communiste* had 60,495 members and in January, 1945,

party's relations with modernity are certainly quite remote. Many people naturally assume that this remoteness
proves how outmoded and outdated the party's social
form has become, how little it has kept up. These people
also assume that the party, having failed in its initial objective, survives solely by harking back to outworn ideas.
But one can also explain the party's ironic indifference to
the most aggressively innovative approaches and policies
by the fact that it is secure in the knowledge that it alone
embraces the only modern idea that matters. This idea,
being global in scope, heralds the coming of a new world.

In this sense, the attitude toward youth is at the very
core of communist thought.[15] Young people are not
viewed as separate individuals endowed with a civil status.
They are regarded as the youth of man, of society, as har-
bingers of the day *after*, when the revolution will have
created a new order by introducing a break as radical as
the coming of the night in the flow of events. The famous
slogan, "Communism is the youth of the world," expresses
a deeply rooted conviction that nothing new can or *should*
emerge from the old worn-out world in which we live. To
acknowledge with undue haste any pre- or extra-socialist
mutations and innovations is to compromise the power of
the socialist imagination, socialist *invention*. This explains the paradoxical fact that a party which aspires to
be the most leftist of all is for the moment, in France, the
most resolutely conservative, not to say backward, in so
many areas of public policy. When people maintain that

92,919 members. In other words, although the population of this
age category is larger, the communist youth movement today is
smaller than it was not only at the time of Liberation but also
thirty years ago.

15. Whereas justice is the theme that is at the core of traditional socialist thought.

the world is changing and the party has not yet even taken it over, the leaders feel that they have been robbed of something, that the destiny of the party, its future, is being eroded.

The Chinese apparently want no part of this paradox. Isn't it true that one result of the Chinese Cultural Revolution is that it changed the relations of young people to the party and to society, and that it reduced to ashes the traditional hierarchies (we have only to remember traditional Chinese society to realize how true this is)? It did this first by establishing the Red Guards and then by defining their mission and the manner in which they were to pursue it. The crowning achievement of the Cultural Revolution was to have carried out Mao's thoughts. He told the students: "The world is as much yours as ours, but basically it is to you that it belongs" (XXX). After the revolution. But before?

Sex

Not only was Georges Marchais pleased by the increase in the under-twenty-five category; he was also delighted by the higher percentage of female members, a change shown in the following table:[16]

YEAR	MALES	FEMALES
1946	88.8%	11.1%
1954	79.8%	20.2%
1959	78.1%	21.9%
1966	74.5%	25.5%

In 1946 women constituted scarcely one-tenth of the membership, whereas today the proportion is one out of four, and in Paris one out of three. As late as 1959,

16. See M. Servin, Report to the Fifteenth Congress, *Cahiers du communisme*, special no. (July-August 1959), p. 234; G. Marchais, Report to the Eighteenth Congress, p. 267.

women constituted only 32 percent of the membership in Paris and throughout the Paris region. In 1966 the figure jumped to 37 percent.[17]

This growth is so considerable that it calls for some discussion.

The explanation, of course, seems to be that through hard work the party managed to convince more and more women that it understood their problems and aspirations and that they could trust the party to look after their interests and rights.[18] According to the official propaganda line, the party had "always been mindful of the fate of women in our country." It had constantly demanded the fullest implementation of the formula, "Equal pay for equal work." And to render the equality of the sexes less illusory, it had recently gone so far as to insist that women workers be given a special reduction in working hours without reduction in pay. It had repeatedly called for the establishment of a vast network of social organizations and accoutrements in all municipalities where the party's militants had decision-making powers. It had done everything possible to set up nurseries and procure subsidized housing for workers. At the instigation of its central commission, established at the time of the Liberation, and at

17. According to J. Thorez-Vermeersch, *l'Humanité*, November 18, 1966, the percentage of women in the Fédération Seine-Ouest increased from 24.2 percent in 1959 to 30.2 percent in 1966 and in the Fédération Seine-Sud from 34.1 percent in 1959 to 38.2 percent in 1966.

18. This was the principal idea in all Jeannette Vermeersch's writings, from her first report to the Eleventh Congress (Strasbourg, 1947), "Les femmes dans la nation." We find this same idea again in her report to the central committee in November, 1961, as well as in an article in *l'Humanité* of November 18, 1966. It would be interesting to study from this angle the successive programs elaborated by the party on questions concerning women—at the time of an election campaign, for example.

the invitation of federal work commissions for women, the party had taken special pains during political campaigns to address itself particularly to the women. It had organized meetings exclusively for women, and at a time and place that would be especially convenient for them. Finally, the party had a Union of French Women (*Union des femmes françaises*) which was useful in reaching women outside the party's immediate sphere of influence. Although this organization did not quite equal the Movement of Young Communists (*Mouvement de la jeunesse communiste*) as a "school for communism," it nevertheless did have a certain importance.

All these explanations are less satisfactory than they may seem at first glance. The increase in the percentage of female members occurred during the period from 1946 to 1954, when the national membership was falling sharply. This does not indicate that there was any genuine progress in the indoctrination of women. It merely means that fewer women were leaving the party at that time. In other words, the women were more faithful than the men.[19]

To what should we ascribe the greater loyalty of the

19. This is what Claude Harmel has shown in the article already cited. In effect, after coping with complicated figures, he compiled the following statistics on membership fluctuations according to sex:

YEAR	MEN	WOMEN
1946	100	100
1954	32	57
1959	25	49
1966	27	66

Harmel therefore concludes: (a) From 1946 to 1959, "the losses sustained by the party were less numerous for women than for men"; (b) "the increase in female members since 1959 was more marked than for males" both in terms of percentages and in absolute terms.

party's female members? One cannot help wondering
whether the real meaning of all this is to be found in the
fact that there was generally less enthusiasm about what
the party stood for. Formerly, the party was thought of as
an organization created for the purpose of waging the
class struggle to the bitter end. As it became more and
more of a closed society in which administrative tasks
predominated, perhaps its image, its style, and its pace
became increasingly assimilated to the functions women
have learned to exercise in a traditional society.

This hypothesis is confirmed when we note the evolution that has taken place within two categories of female
party members. A distinction is customarily made between *working women*, engaged in remunerated labor and
therefore exploited as much as or even more than their
male colleagues, and *housewives*—"women in the home"
is considered to be an expression used only by reactionaries. In 1966, communist housewives—a category that
was practically nonexistent in working-class or revolutionary parties during the first half of the twentieth century—constituted 46 percent of the total female membership; more than one communist female out of two was not
"in production," to use the party's phrase.[20]

This surprising change indicates a dilution of the initially "masculine nature" of the working-class movement
in general and of the communist movement in particular.
In effect, female workers participate in and become integrated into the masculine world (even though male
workers manifest a characteristic distrust of their female
comrades),[21] whereas housewives are active in a purely

20. See G. Marchais, Report to the Eighteenth Congress,
p. 267.
21. See the book by Madeleine Guilbert, *Les Femmes et
l'Organisation syndicale avant 1914*, Introduction and comments

feminine universe which they introduce as such within the sphere of communist realities.

The change, however, does not mean that women have acquired greater power or influence in the communist world. This paradoxical situation, which is observable in other societies as well—in North America, for example— is perhaps not as paradoxical as it seems. In point of fact, communism remains under masculine dominance, which is considerable; the movement is referred to as a "male collectivity," and people react to it as if it were a purely masculine social phenomenon. Although women are now more numerous, they still occupy a very modest position.[22]

---

on documents for the study of female syndicalism (Paris: Ed. du CNRS, 1966). It might be helpful to remind the reader in this connection that French revolutionary syndicalism, although it had an identity of its own, was the brainchild of Proudhon. Yet he said: "the role of woman is not in the outside world, in a life filled with contacts and agitation, but rather in domestic life: the life of sentiment and the peace of the hearth."

22. In May, 1949, Marcel Servin compiled the following statistics: 4 percent women in the party's federal secretariats, 14 percent women in the party's federal bureaus, 16 percent women in the party's federal committees. And he concluded: "These are ridiculously small numbers" (*Cahiers du bolchevisme* [May 1949], p. 575). In October, 1964, Jeannette Thorez-Vermeersch indicated in her report on "La défense des droits sociaux de la femme et de l'enfant," p. 34, that there were: 23 women in the federal secretariats, or 6.4 percent; 152 women in the federal bureaus, or 12.6 percent; 602 women on federal committees, or 16.9 percent. Lastly, Jeannette Thorez-Vermeersch (*France nouvelle*, September 9, 1966), pointed out that the actual number of women serving on federal committees was approximately 600. In view of the fact that the total number of members of the federal committees is 3,600 (G. Marchais, Report to the Eighteenth Congress, p. 264), the percentage of women members on the federal committees is 16 percent—16.6 percent to be precise. How does one explain the fact that the percentage of women communists was increasing but their say in the administration of the party was not? Simply because, just as in the

This statement will probably anger all those involved, including the feminine element. Actually, it takes enormous work and effort to get a woman elected to a Communist administrative body, no matter at what level. In 1966, almost 600 women sat on national committees and almost 150 were members of bureaus. How much effort it took to enable women to participate in the school for cadres! And how much hard work to enable sixty-eight women to become eligible to run as candidates or alternates in the legislative elections of 1966! How much energy had to be expended to send 169 women as delegates to the party's eighteenth national congress in 1967![23]

Such effort and hard work are all the more commendable because they stem from a stubborn desire to promote the establishment of female cadres despite the lack of qualified candidates for the posts. Hence the considerable fluctuations in this segment of the party's personnel: from one year to the next (1965 to 1966), more than a fourth of the female members of national committees were not reelected.

---

larger society, communist "housewives" were not very active politically. For this reason they were under-represented at the party's congresses. Although they constituted 46 percent of the communist women, they represented only 10 to 20 percent of the delegates. Fourteenth Congress—17 housewives out of 130 delegates, or 13 percent; Sixteenth Congress—11 housewives out of 72 delegates, or 15.2 percent; Seventeenth Congress—33 housewives out of 168 delegates, or 19.6 percent; Eighteenth Congress—22 housewives out of 169 delegates, or 13 percent. The increase in the percentage of women members is in large part illusory. It is a purely statistical increase; the incidence of political activity among women communists is minimal.

23. I have taken these figures from extracts of reports made by Jeannette Thorez-Vermeersch and Léon Feix at the "day of study devoted to the women's work in the French Communist party" (Bagnolet, September 1966), *France nouvelle*, no. 1093 [September 28, 1966]).

Meanwhile we must not forget that most of the women who were so laboriously recruited and trained are confined to working with other women: militants of the UFF (*Union des femmes françaises*), female municipal or trade union councillors in charge of social work, and so on. The role is politically necessary and logical to boot, often a worthy cause, but it is not far removed from the notion that traditional society holds about the place of women in social life. In any case, it was a way of preventing women from intervening in the really important political matters.[24]

All this serves to underscore the fact that at present there are only twenty-five female members of federal secretariats in the French Communist party; that only nine of the ninety-six members of the central committee are women, and that the political bureau has but one female member—Jeannette Thorez-Vermeersch.

The example was set in high places long before. If Lenin really hoped that "every female cook would be put in a position to administer the state," he showed himself to be extremely prudent in the matter, at least in practice. To be sure, a few of the women in his entourage did emerge—his wife, Kroupskaya, to begin with, together with a handful of others: Alexandra Kollontay, Clara Zetkin, Inessa Armand, Elena Stassova, Angelica Bala-

24. I must admit that this was not the doing of the French Communist party; it was the rule in almost all the parties. See Dogan and Narbonne, *Les Françaises face à la politique* (Paris: Colin, 1954); M. Duverger, *La Participation des femmes à la vie politique* (Paris, 1955); Madeleine Grawitz, "L'accès des femmes à la vie politique et la personnalisation du pouvoir," in *Le Personnalisation du pouvoir* (Paris: PUF, 1964). A good introduction to the overall question is Andrée Michel, "Les Françaises et la politique," *Les Temps Modernes*, no. 230 (July 1965), pp. 60–91.

banoff—but all of them played a marginal role, one that was always ephemeral and at times sarcastically contested. Not one of them was able to achieve the powerful autonomous position of Rosa Luxembourg, who, like Lenin, got her training in the world of the Second International. Today, in the Soviet Party, in the state apparatus of the USSR, and in all the peoples' democracies, the key positions, save for a few rare exceptions, are held by men, exactly as in our bourgeois governments.[25]

Would it be going too far to say that in some respects the real position of women in the communist world has deteriorated despite the increase in number and the toning down of the earlier masculine aggressiveness?[26]

25. At a meeting of the central committee of the Soviet Communist party, April 9, 1966, only five women out of 195 members were elected! In the new government set up on August 3, 1966, of the 84 members, only one woman was named, Madame Fourtseva, Minister of Culture (figures cited by Hélène Zamoyska, "Situation de la femme en URSS, 1917–1967," *La Table Ronde*, special no., "La Révolution russe et son destin" [October-November 1967], pp. 109–26). In the Soviet Union, as in other countries, there is a substantial proportion of professional women in the intermediate cadres, and especially in the poorly paid professions (teaching and medicine in the Soviet Union, for example).

26. We can measure this short-term deterioration by listing, for example, the percentage of women among the delegates to successive national congresses since 1950:

CONGRESS AND YEAR		WOMEN DELEGATES	TOTAL DELEGATES	% WOMEN
Twelfth,	1950	196	707	27.7
Thirteenth,	1954	174	870	20
Fourteenth,	1956	130	657	16.5
Fifteenth,	1959	67	440	13.2
Sixteenth,	1961	72	424	16.5
Seventeenth,	1964	168	776	21.6
Eighteenth,	1967	169	788	21.4

Thus, despite some gains, the percentage of women among the delegates is less today than it was in 1950.

It is true that not long ago, in the old Socialist party and then in the young Communist party, there were women party members, usually teachers, who were veritable dragons; but there were also many—pacifists, feminists, trade unionists, workers in orphanages and homes for illegitimate children—who were truly admirable persons, sensitive, gentle, energetic, clear-minded—and unhappy. Most of them were probably old maids. Their lowly life as frustrated teachers gave them little of the aura of respectability generally accorded wives and mothers. But such women contributed to the current of socialist thought by their genuine suffering, their personal initiative, and their talents.

Anxious above all to denounce the imaginary threat of a war between the sexes that might replace class warfare,

---

But even more instructive is the percentage of women among the members of the central committee (which is elected at the end of every national congress):

CONGRESS AND YEAR		WOMEN MEMBERS	TOTAL MEMBERS	% WOMEN
Tours,	1920	5	32	15
First,	1921	4	31	12.9
Second,	1922	2	32	6.2
Third,	1924	2	43	4.6
Fourth,	1925	2	41	4.8
Fifth,	1926	4	79	5
Sixth,	1929	?	?	?
Seventh,	1932	1	54	1.7
Eighth,	1936	1	45	2.2
Ninth,	1937	0	50	0
Tenth,	1945	8	69	11.5
Eleventh,	1947	8	84	9.5
Twelfth,	1950	8	77	10.3
Thirteenth,	1954	8	82	9.7
Fourteenth,	1956	11	102	10.7
Fifteenth,	1959	9	93	9.6
Sixteenth,	1961	9	99	9.1
Seventeenth,	1964	9	93	9.6
Eighteenth,	1967	9	96	9.3

the communists paid only brief and tight-lipped tribute to these feminists who dreamed of leading lives of their own and who, in the eyes of the bourgeoisie, were vulgar figures of fun. In the period between the two world wars, the communists made no attempt to conceal their total indifference to such problems. At the height of the party's success, in December, 1937, when its congress convened, the Communist party did not elect a *single* woman to its central committee.[27] When things changed in 1944, at the time of the Liberation, it was embarrassing to look back and remember how the women had been treated. Now they acquired a new importance for the party. They had become voters at a time when the communists were faced with grave parliamentary problems.

Besides, how can one fail to notice the crushing conformity of the image that is thrust upon a female communist? It's probably better to be a "working" woman—Jeannette Thorez-Vermeersch, at any rate, seems to think so. She is constantly stressing the idea that "work is a positive fact." But hers seems to be the only voice to say so.[28] If a woman wishes to acquire any kind of status

27. A further indication of the smallness of the female component of the interwar Communist party's membership is to be found in the following facts: in February, 1937, the fourth regional conference of Paris-Nord showed a female membership of 400 compared to the overall 1937 membership of 10,889, or 3.6 percent. Yet in December, 1966, in the Fédération de la Seine-Saint-Denis—which corresponds approximately to the earlier Paris-Nord federation—5,280 women (C. Coulon, *La Vie du Parti*, no. 10 [1966]) constituted 36.3 percent of the total membership (J. Vermeersch, *l'Humanité*, November 18, 1966). Thus, although the overall federation membership increased from 10,889 in 1937 to 14,500 in 1966, a gain of only one-third, the number of women members during this same period increased from 400 to 5,280, or 13 times as much.

28. When we recall Jeannette Vermeersch's vehement plea, at the Eleventh Party Congress (June, 1947), for women's right

within the party, she will find that it is not enough to play
a role in the economic and social life of her community.
It is more important for her to be married and a mother
—married to a militant fellow-communist, of course. How
much power to structure a snugly closed society those
couples possess who settle down within the party as if
they were part of a great family clan! In a middle-class
society what an embarrassing sense of déjà vu is offered
by the spectacle of these conjugal tandems, where at least
the husband but preferably the two of them set an example! Surely it is no accident that seven out of nine women
members of the central committee were or are married to
members of the central committee.

All in all, the increase in the percentage of female communist members has resulted in some serious disadvan-
tages. The woman communist in effect is subject to a twofold and contradictory social pressure. Socialist tradition
and the Soviet social model induce her to believe that
work is the road that will lead to the emancipation of
women. But established society holds that only economic
necessity can justify the employment of women. The result is that female communists are just as divided as
women are generally. Female communists who have had
professional training want to work, probably for ideological reasons but also for the same reasons that motivate
noncommunist women in similar situations. Yet female
communists who have had no professional training give
up working as soon as their husbands earn enough money

to work, and when we compare it to the nuanced explanations the
same speaker gave at the Week of Marxist Thought (January
20–27, 1965) in *Femmes du XXe Siècle* (Paris: PUF, 1965),
p. 209, we can measure the extent to which the present crisis
regarding the status of women in contemporary society is reflected, even in the French Communist party.

to permit them to do so. In other words, the politically active communist women—the working women—are for the most part members of the middle class. And so we witness an unfortunate twofold phenomenon: an increase in the number of politically inactive housewives who inject into the class struggle a "feminine" note; the presence of politically active working women who belong to a relatively high social and occupational stratum.

Status

Satisfied by the increase in the percentage of young people and women in the party, Georges Marchais was equally well pleased by the social composition, which he described as follows in the light of the 1966 study:[29]

$$
\text{Workers} \quad 60.1 \ \% \begin{cases} 43.4 \ \% \text{ from the private sector} \\ 13.5 \ \% \text{ from public service} \\ 3.2 \ \% \text{ from agriculture} \end{cases}
$$

29. See G. Marchais, Report to the Eighteenth Congress, p. 273. Theoretically, one ought also to be able to have an idea of the party's social composition based on a study of the financial reports. In effect, we know that the ratio of contributions is proportionate to the income of the members. Thus, according to the published financial report of the year 1936, and in view of the decisons made by the central committee on October 17 and 19, 1935, concerning the *decrease* in the rate of contributions, the party members are classified into four categories:

CATEGORY	SALARY	DUES (EVERY TWO WEEKS)	%
1	500 Francs	.50 F	50
2	501 to 750	1 F	37
3	751 to 1,000	2 F	9
4	1000+	3 F	3

Unfortunately, one cannot be certain that, either before or after the war, the militant paid what was expected of him according to this scale (strange as this may seem, and although this does not reflect on a militant's dedication to the cause, his attitude toward the treasury of his cell was similar to his attitude toward the tax collector!).

White-collar employees	18.57%	{	8.12% from the private sector
Farm owners	6.56%		
Intellectuals	9 %	{	4.85% teachers and researchers 1.93% engineers and technicians
Tradesmen and artisans	5.77%		

In order to assess the exact and full significance of these statistics, we must make two preliminary observations.

The first is that the victorious, dynamic sector within the party consists of militants assigned to official posts and to the public services.[30] It is probable that this sector did not figure in the 1966 statistics, whereas in the 1954 and 1959 investigations it appeared quite plainly under a rubric grouping together individuals designated in the 1966 statistics as "workers in the public services," "employees of the public services," "teachers," and "engineers and technicians."[31] But if we analyze the 1966 data in conjunction with the 1954 and 1959 figures, we immediately note that, first of all, the percentage of workers in the private sector has remained quite stable:

1954	40.1%
1959	40.3%
1966	43.4%

30. This is the conclusion Claude Harmel arrived at, after a painstaking investigation (Harmel, "La composition sociale," pp. 9–11).

31. For the year 1954, Marcel Servin, *l'Humanité*, May 6, 1954, gave the following results of a questionnaire addressed to 105,776 members: 40,370 industrial workers, 10,665 railway, postal, and electrical workers, 3,273 agricultural workers.

At the Thirteenth Congress (*l'Humanité*, June 5, 1954) he indicated that of 153,164 members, 58,657 were industrial and dock workers, or 38 percent (not including workers in the public services or agricultural workers).

By contrast, the percentages of public officials and public service workers are as follows:

1954	14.5%
1959	14.9%
1966	30.7%

Thus, we can measure the difference in the degree of dynamism within the two sectors of the party, public and private, with the public sector coming out on top.

My second observation has to do with the size of another category, that of the nonactive members. There is no heading marked "miscellaneous" in the statistics for 1966. We can only deduce from this that retired workers have been tabulated by their original occupations and "housewives" by their husbands' occupations.[32] Since the over-sixty group (comprising a large number of retired people) amounts to 17.3 percent of the total membership, and since housewives represent 46 percent of all female members (25.5 percent of the total membership), we may assume that the sector which consists of those who are not part of the "active population" represents approximately 25 to 30 percent of the total membership. One member out of three or four is not or is no longer "in production."

These two observations correct the excessively flattering impression that the 1966 figures tend to give. But, having made these reservations, I should also point out that the French Communist party is really a party that springs from the *working-class world*—a designation that is perhaps more precise than "workers' party." This of course does not mean that *all* French workers or even a majority

32. This makes the likelihood of an increase in the percentage of workers in private industry, indicated above, doubtful. In 1966 the housewives whose husbands were workers were classified under this heading.

of them are communists. On the other hand, even if one figures, for example, that 981 out of every 1,000 workers are not party members,[33] this does not mean that the Communist party is not a workers' party. It merely signifies that in France, as in other countries where social classes are averse to politics, only a small proportion of the working class is organized into a political party. The French Communist party as such is not noteworthy for its large proportion of factory workers—actually, the number of dues-paying communists in the Simca, Citroen, or even Renault factories is incredibly small. Moreover, it should also be pointed out that the official party figures for the percentage of "workers" in its ranks are somewhat contrived since there are included under this heading many thousands of party functionaries who are *former* workers. Nevertheless, even if they are no longer "in production," these militants, some of whom have not been workers for at least five years, continue to be steeped in a working-class ambiance through their contacts with relatives, young people, and neighbors.

All in all, the party is probably less working-class in composition than it was during the interwar period when obviously the most active elements of the working-class world were to be found in the central nucleus of the party. In 1926 Pierre Sémard stated that after "Bolshevization" only "about 5 percent of the middle class were members of the French Communist party whereas the former Socialist party comprised no fewer than 25 percent."[34]

33. *Le Parti communiste français en 1967* (Lille: Assises nationales de l'UNR, November 1967).

34. Pierre Sémard, Fifth National Congress in Lille, typescript, p. 12. Quoted in A. Kriegel, "Les Communistes français et le Pouvoir," in *Le Socialisme français et le Pouvoir* (Paris: EDI 1966), p. 202.

These figures may not be entirely trustworthy but they do give us an idea of the trend. "L'état de l'organisation du Parti," an appendix in *Rapport politique du comité central* of the Sixth Congress (Saint-Denis, March 31–April 6, 1929), summarizes the results of an investigation made in 1928[35] and thereby enables us to compile the following information:

Workers in the private sector	38.28%
Nationalized workers	18.67%
Functionaries and public services	3.41%
Middle classes	20.21%

And here is another suggestive indication: whereas in 1928 communists represented only .8 percent of the national population, they constituted 2.2 percent of the steelworkers and 4.3 percent of the miners.

Still another indication: in 1929–30 the committees of the fifteen *rayons* (sections) of the Seine[36] comprised eighty-two workers in the private sector (fifty-seven of whom were steelworkers) as against a total of seventeen nationalized workers.

35. Sixth Congress of the French Communist Party, *Rapport politique du comité central*, p. 98. This investigation seems to have been executed rather crudely. Because of the haphazard nature of the study, the answers, which are not very numerous, do not necessarily constitute a valid sampling. Included among workers in the private sector are those belonging to the following industries: metals, textiles, building, chemical products, transportation, lumber, food, leather goods. Under the heading of unskilled workers are listed: railway workers, book binders, miners, dock hands, and lighting workers. Lastly, classified under middle classes are peasants, artisans, small businessmen, housewives, intellectuals, and business employees.

36. The *rayons* represent what we today call sections. Cf. A. Kriegel, "Structures d'organisation et mouvement des effectifs du PCF entre les guerres," *Revue internationale d'histoire sociale* 11, pt. 3 (1966): 340–42.

The sizable increase in manpower recorded in 1936 was undoubtedly due to an increase in workers. Confirmation of this is provided by an analysis of the differences in growth patterns of the five communist regions, led ever since 1933 by the Paris region.[37]

From 1933 to September, 1938, the manpower of the city proper increased in precisely the same ratio as that of the five other Paris regions: If we take into account the social structure of the purely Parisian population and the preponderant elements of the city's economy, we will of course realize that the composition of the communist membership in this region is bound to be less working-class than elsewhere. But the number of party members

37. Under the old unified Socialist party, the four socialist federations constitute the four departments of Seine, Seine-et-Oise, Seine-et-Marne, and the Oise. During the days of the young Communist party, 1926–32, a communist Paris region stood for these four departments. But from 1933 to 1939 this Paris region was "decentralized" and cut up into five different regions, the five comprising only three departments: Seine, Seine-et-Oise, Seine-et-Marne. These five regions—Paris-Ville, Paris-Ouest, Paris-Est, Paris-Nord, Paris-Sud—equal roughly the five present departments. Since 1965 the Paris region has been officially detached from this area.

The following shows the number of communist members in each of the five regions:

YEAR	PARIS-VILLE	PARIS-OUEST	PARIS-NORD	PARIS-EST	PARIS-SUD
1933	2,884	1,300	1,676	1,660	1,560
1934	4,575	2,372	2,436	2,824	2,076
1935	8,450	5,400	4,235	5,950	4,825
1936	31,560	27,048	8,500	15,500	17,230
1937	34,530	34,448	10,889	16,500	19,000
1938	30,000	31,550	10,095	15,700	17,500

(Table compiled from statistics in *Rapports du comité central* published for the congresses of Villeurbanne [January, 1936], Arles, [December, 1937], the national conference of Grennevilliers [January, 1939], the Paris congress [March, 1945] and the Strasbourg congress [June, 1947]).

remained fairly constant here—between 28 to 32 percent of the national total.[38]

From 1933 to September, 1938, the manpower of the western Paris region increased far more, proportionately, than that of the other Paris regions: from 14 percent in 1933 it jumped to 33 percent of the party's national membership by 1938.[39] This part of Paris has, of course, an

38. The following table illustrates the relative strength of the Paris-Ville membership in comparison to the total membership of the five Paris regions:

YEAR	PARIS-VILLE	TOTAL PARIS REGION	%
1933	2,884	9,080	31
1934	4,575	14,283	32
1935	8,450	28,860	29
1936	31,560	99,838	31
1937	34,530	115,367	29
1938	30,000	104,845	28

39. For the Paris-Ouest region:

YEAR	PARIS-OUEST	%
1933	1,300	14
1934	2,372	16
1935	5,400	18
1936	27,048	27
1937	34,448	29
1938	31,550	30

There is another way to check the working-class character of the influx in membership to the Paris-Ouest region in 1936: The percentage of company cells in comparison to the total number of cells in the Paris-Ouest region increased from 41 percent in May, 1934, to 54 percent in November, 1936, according to information given at the fifth and eighth Paris-Ouest regional conferences (January 16–17, 1937, and November 19–20, 1938), pp. 35 and 44:

YEAR	COMPANY CELLS	ALL CELLS	% COMPANY CELLS
May 1934	48	115	41
February 1935	63	176	35
November 1935	87	274	31
March 1936	115	327	35
November 1936	354	692	51
November 1937	464	844	54
November 1938	454	843	53

industrial infrastructure that is more powerful than those of all the other Paris regions.

I should like to call attention to a few facts that underscore the plainly working-class nature of the expanded membership in 1936. In May, 1931, only one cell of nineteen members existed in the entire Renault-Billancourt automobile factory. By May, 1936, this pilot factory of the Paris region had only 120 communists. But in December, 1936, the fifty-five organized cells in the various factory workshops were combined into a single powerful section that boasted no fewer than 6,000 members. Finally, by 1937, 7,500 dues-paying communists were working in the Renault factory.[40] We can get a better idea of the significance of this figure if we stop to think that on January 6, 1967, a celebration was held in honor of the one-thousandth member of the plant's fifty-eight current cells.

There are many reasons why the French Communist party is today less working-class in composition than it

40. On the organization of the party in the Renault factory in 1931, see *P.C.-région parisienne, rapport d'organisation pour la conférence* (February 26–28, 1932), p. 34. On its organization during the years 1936 to 1938, see *P.C.F.-région Paris-Ouest, IVᵉ conférence de la section Renault*, Salle Lucien, Billancourt (May 28, 1938), p. 24. On the present situation, see Henri Oursin, organizational secretary of the Renault-Billancourt section, *La Vie du Parti* (January 1, 1967), pp. 6–7. Oursin points out that with the one thousandth member in January, 1967, the party had 120 more members at Renault than it had by the end of 1966, and as many members as in 1956, which gives us the following table:

YEAR	MEMBERS	TOTAL EMPLOYEES
1931	19	
1936 (Jan.)	120	
1936 (Dec.)	6,000	37,000
1937	7,500	45,000
1956	1,000	45,000
1966	880	
1967	1,000	35,000

once was. First of all, ever since World War II, the party has tended to be less narrowly confined to a few large cities. This becomes plain when we examine the variations in the relative strength of the organizations in the Paris region and the resultant fluctuations of their numerical importance in the party as a whole. In the former unified Socialist party, only one member out of five lived in the Paris region; the socialist phenomenon was thus largely a provincial phenomenon.[41] This was also substantially true of the Communist party until 1925.[42] However, as early as 1926, after Bolshevization, matters changed; more than one communist member out of four now lived in the Paris region.[43] After 1934 and throughout the entire period of the Popular Front, more than one out of three resided there.[44] But in 1945–46, after the Resistance, a phenome-

41. On December 31, 1919, the four socialist federations constituted the following departments: Seine, Seine-et-Oise, Seine-et-Marne, and the Oise. They totalled 26,701 members out of 133,327 (*Rapport du Secrétariat,* National Congress of Strasbourg, [February 1920]).

42. PC (SFIC). Congrès national de Paris, *l'Action communiste et la crise du Parti,* p. 101. In 1921, the four communist federations together had 23,535 members out of 109,391, or 21 percent; in 1922, there were 16,225 members out of 78,828, or 20 percent. In 1925, the newly constituted Paris region was credited with 13,586 regular card-holders out of the 60,000 possible card-holders, or 22 percent (National Congress of Lille, *Rapport moral du comité central*).

43. The *Rapport moral du comité central* at the national congress at Lille, June, 1926, attributed 15,000 members (on April 15) to the Paris region out of a total of 55,000 members, or 27 percent. The *Rapport d'organisation* of February, 1932, p. 5, counted 13,472 members of the Paris region for the year 1928 out of a total for that year of 45,000 or 28 percent.

44. The following is the membership count according to the figures of the central committee (cf. note 37 above):

YEAR	PARIS REGION	TOTAL MEMBERSHIP	%
1933	9,080	28,754 (?)	34
1934	14,283	42,000	34

non that occurred primarily in the provinces and therefore had the effect of stirring up the remotest reaches of the country, the proportion changed: now less than one member out of five lives in the Paris region.[45]

The party's spread into areas outside its traditional bastions cannot be easily explained. The changes in the very structure of the working world are undoubtedly an important factor. We will come to grips with this and deal more concretely with the realities involved.

Although at present the party unquestionably has a socially more diversified membership than it had in the past, it has nonetheless maintained solid ties with its working-class nucleus. But it would be a mistake to believe that this happens naturally, spontaneously, or that a policy inspired by the interests of the industrial masses is enough

1935	28,860	87,752	33
1936	99,838	275,732	36
1937	115,367	323,283	35
1938	104,845	318,549	32

45. On the Resistance, see chapter 5 below. In 1945, the three federations of the Paris region were credited with 138,652 members out of a total of 775,342; in 1946, 147,448 out of a total of 804,229.

The following table shows variations in the relative strength of organizations in the Paris region in comparison to the party as a whole:

YEAR	%
1920	21
1921	20
1925	22
1926	27
1928	29
1933	31
1934	34
1935	33
1936	36
1937	35
1938	32
1945	17
1946	18

to account for the continued existence of such ties. Constant vigilance and a variety of technical approaches are required to insure an adequate flow of new recruits.

Thus constant scrutiny accompanies the selection of candidates for the various communist schools and yields an accurate picture not only of the social composition of administrative bodies at all levels of the apparatus but also of the multiform institutions that enable the party to function in opposition to established society. Whenever necessary, the party does of course seek the help of qualified technicians, but directors or collaborators from the workers' world are assigned to these technicians—a system perfected by the Soviet republic during the early years of its existence.

The organizational measure most effective in preserving the preponderance of working-class people within the party was implemented in 1924–25. It is known as "Bolshevization."[46] At that time the Communist International stipulated that all its sections must radically change the nature of their primary electoral districts upon which the party's structure was henceforward to be based. In the earlier type of socialist parties, the primary electoral district was the *commune*, the traditional scene of electoral battles; in the young "Bolshevized" communist parties, it was replaced by the factory, a privileged terrain "where the two basic classes confront one another"

It is from the factory, the mine, the shipyard,
the office, that the outcry arises which unites

46. On the episode of Bolshevization, see A. Kriegel, "Structures d'organisation et mouvement des effectifs du PCF entre les deux guerres," *International Review of Social History* 11, pt. 3, especially the letter of the Communist International addressed to the national sections and published by the French party in 1930 under the title, *le Travail des cellules d'usine*, p. 31.

in a single struggle all those subject to capitalist rule and to man's exploitation of man. It is
in the factory, the mine, the office, the shipyard
that thousands and tens of thousands of workers are brought together by the capitalists. The
factory is the nerve center of modern society,
the very threshold of the class struggle. That
is why for you, as communists, the factory
should be the center of all your efforts, of all
your activities.[47]

This reorganization resulted in an impressive upheaval
that constitutes a highly significant episode in the history
of French communism. Moreover, this revolution in organizational procedures was remarkable for its durability.
Despite winds and storms the principle is still respected
and the regulations still observed.

But the winds and storms were violent ones. The structure of a profession (in the building industry, for example, where mobile work-teams are temporarily tied to the
existence of a shipyard or some other place of work), the
way working time was organized (with day and night
shifts, or "brigades" replacing one another), the nature
of the labor force (of relevance here was the practice of
giving bus service to those who worked in textile mills,
mines, and certain steel plants, to say nothing of the presence of large contingents of foreign, non-French-speaking
workers)—all these caused endless complications. Only
protracted experience could provide solutions to the problem of how to gather communist workers together in companies as complex as the railways or the merchant marine,
or how to reach migrant agricultural workers who are
employed only seasonally. In every instance there had to
be some precise indication of the unit that constituted the

47. Communist Party, *Au nouvel adhérent*, Pref. by J. Duclos,
p. 5.

"territory" of the cell: workshop, office, shipyard. All
things considered, the problem that proved to be the most
difficult and also the one that was the most inadequately
resolved was invariably that of organizing the unemployed.

Without even taking into account the factors that naturally contribute to instability—restrictive actions by the
employers, above all the mergers that forced the less adapt-
able plants to shut down, labor's growing mobility—
one can easily understand why, given the circumstances.
the factory cells turned out to be quite fragile. Occasionally the mere departure of a few militant propagandists
sufficed to cause the cells' demise.[48]

Subjective factors proved no less powerful. A good
many militants in charge of the sale of *l'Humanité-dimanche* arrive at their posts each Sunday with remarkable
punctuality. But they are most reluctant to draw attention
at their places of work. "The sector," Pierre Sémard conceded, "is at some distance from the employers, from
capitalism, but the cell is much closer."[49] Concern for
one's career—the humbler it is, the more precious it may
seem; a recurring anxiety whenever the labor market
shrinks, or when advancing age lessens the chances of
being reclassified; complications in time schedules where-
ever collective transportation is available only at the end
of the day's work; preoccupation about output—these

48. From 1961 to 1967 the total number of company cells
increased from 3,800 to 5,100, or a net gain of 1,300 (G.
Marchais, Report to the Eighteenth Congress, p. 281). Yet, in
a single year, 1962, the number of new company cells rose to
1,062. In other words, in the space of a single year, there were
almost as many new cells as there had been over a five-year
period.

49. Communist Party, Fifth National Congress, Lille, typescript, p. 11.

represent arguments that can be adduced against the pursuit of political activities in the shipyard or the factory. Such activities are not only quite unprotected by law; employers as well as most trade unions regard them with suspicion, sharing as they do a concern that is constant, equivocal, and characteristically French—a profound anxiety to make sure that the company does not become a political battlefield.

We have to acknowledge that the concept of company cells as an elemental form of organization is directed toward the elimination of the inherent electoral opportunism of "socialism in the French manner." It can also serve as a weapon that may eventually be used against revolutionary trade unionism. Significant in this connection is the initial discussion at the party's Third Congress (1924) in which the possibility of creating factory cells was mentioned. On this occasion, a member of the *Jeunesses communistes*, Roger Gaillard, opposed the veteran trade-unionist, Pierre Monatte. The latter very aptly maintained that the measure under consideration was designed to effect in a concrete way and in accordance with Bolshevik principles, the subordination of the trade union to the party at the very site of its indoctrination.

Yet, because of the resistance, because of the persistence of traditional ideas about trade unionism among communist militants, trade union and party activities inevitably overlapped and duplicated one another within the plant. This explains why, despite the party's emphasis on the importance of cells, the members, anxious to avoid duplication or the substitution of cells for trade unions, remained uncertain and divided.The activities of factory cells are often confined to the occasional publication of a cell newspaper which merely serves to attest the presence of the communist ideology in the very midst of the "capitalist citadel." In a recent statement that very well summarizes the problem, Léon Feix says:

> It should be noted that in quite a few companies priority is accorded to trade union responsibilities. Each new communist cadre to appear is immediately "plugged into" a trade union responsibility even though the party organization may suffer as a consequence. . . . This practice, springing unquestionably from failure to understand the party's decisive role in the plant and sanctioned by the old, oft-condemned notion that "the trade union is capable of handling everything," is most harmful.[50]

One of the permanent tasks of the leaders responsible for party organization is to convince those members who are improperly inscribed on the list of a local cell that they should have their names transferred to the factory cell. At regular intervals the party's newspapers, especially *l'Humanité*, call attention to the urgency of giving top priority to the question of how "to work within the companies."

But the effort has proved quite unrewarding. Despite a great deal of hard work, the number of factory cells never managed to exceed a third of the total, except in the very beginning and even then perhaps the figures given were merely part of the launching of a campaign that was naturally predicated on the certainty of victory. Frequently the percentage of cells fell to a fourth or a fifth of the total, as the following figures show:[51]

50. *La Vie du Parti*, no. 8 (October 1966), p. 3.
51. For the increase in the number of company cells compared to the total number of cells, see the Appendix.

	FACTORY CELLS IN RELATION
YEAR	TO TOTAL CELLS
1926	48.4%
1927	31 %
1928	27.3%
1929	29.2%
1934	21.5%
1937	31.1%
1945	20.1%
1946	23 %
1967	26.8%

Since the membership of a factory cell was often smaller than that of a local cell, it may be assumed that seldom, except during the brief period of the Popular Front, did more than one out of five communists belong to a factory cell.[52]

Inadequate, uneven, and overly optimistic as such efforts are, this stubborn push nevertheless did produce some tangible results. Thanks in the main to this special effort, the party was able to maintain its working-class makeup.

Meanwhile, of course, a new danger appeared. The factory cells attracted a special kind of worker. In the nationalized industries the cells were far more stable than those in the private sector, a fact which of course reflected the greater stability of the nationalized industries. The

52. Marcel Servin, reporting the results of a questionnaire addressed to 105,776 members, indicated that only 23,887, or 22 percent were organized into company cells (*l'Humanité*, May 6, 1954). Yet in 1966 the situation was probably no better (despite the relative as well as absolute increase in the number of cells) since George Marchais, in reporting the results of investigations made that year, refrained from mentioning a figure for the percentage of the total number of communists organized into company cells.

problems involved here resembled those of the trade-
union movement generally; the network of trade-union
sections is more populous, better structured, and above all
less ephemeral among railway or gas company workers
than among those employed in the steel or building industries. This fact was noted long ago. At the close of 1927
there were 898 factory cells. Three hundred and fifty-five
of these, with a combined membership of 7,000 were in
the public sector—railway workers alone accounted for
218 cells comprising 10,000 members. Again in 1929 railway workers represented more than 30 percent of the total
CGTU membership. There is therefore no reason to be
surprised by the phenomenon previously mentioned: the
very clear increase in the percentage of those communist
members who were employed in the public services. Yet
it must be said that even in the nationalized industries,
employees who perform manual labor and who are consequently workers in the fullest sense of the word, nevertheless represent a privileged group, or at any rate a
rather special breed.

Actually, the problem is even more general. With the
extension and multiplication of every large firm's or industry's internal regulations, the concept of the private
sector is no longer associated with the notion of freedom
of work and no longer conflicts with the idea of security
in employment, the guiding principle of all the statutes.

Then there is another complication: factory cells, even
in the "freest" sector, fail to attract representatives from
all categories of workers. Although the party is largely indebted to the cells for its deep roots in the workers' movement generally, it is likewise indebted to them for its initial spread within one specific segment of the working
class.

To regard the world of the factory as one that is en-

tirely homogeneous and equal, without structure or hierarchy, is to hold a very superficial and false notion of the
actual situation. On the contrary, the existence of hierarchies in the professions and trades, the conflicting eth-
nic and linguistic loyalties, the length of time people have
lived in the city—all these create serious areas of friction.
Yet the general image of the worker remains almost immutable: the typical proletarian continues to be thought
of as a highly qualified French steelworker, or at least as
someone born in France whose rural ancestry is already
growing dim.

A highly qualified steelworker. The professional competence of militant workers is well known. Apparently this
is due not only to the moral qualities usually associated
with skilled workers but also to the actual historical circumstances that prevailed in France when trade unionism
first appeared. In effect, trade unionism was at first a
defensive reaction on the part of the best-educated jour-
neymen in the old building and steel trades.[53] The priority
and predominance of skilled workers represent a fact that
has obtained throughout our history. The reasons for this
are complex, indeed so much so that the whole subject of
the existence of a working-class aristocracy will require
considerable investigation. We merely note here that at
the Eighteenth Congress of the French Communist party
(1967), 349 delegates out of 409 were qualified professionals, compared to sixty unskilled and manual
workers.[54]

It would probably be just as profitable to ascertain the

53. For more ample information and especially a bibliography, see A. Kriegel, *Le Pain et les Roses* (Paris: PUF, 1968).
54. *Cahiers du communisme,* special no., February-March,
1967, p. 530.

extent to which the occupational composition of the party
(and of the trade unions) gives rise to the theoretical and
practical uncertainties which mark the attitude of communists on the question of wage hierarchies. Curiously
enough, the accusations of rigidity in regard to wage scales
—including both temporary and regular remuneration—
and the proposals for raising the wages of the most poorly
paid come from the CFDT (*Confédération française
démocratique du travail*, the Catholic trade unions).

This is a far cry from the egalitarian (utopian? of
anarchist origin?) preoccupations which in 1939, under
the aegis of the international trade-union federation of
teachers, the FISE (*Fédération internationale syndicale
de l'Enseignement*, an outgrowth of the *Profintern*),
pushed the communist minority of the teachers' federation
to insist publicly on uniform treatment for all teaching
personnel. Besides, the really poor, in the strictly economic sense, who, as we know, do not provide a high
proportion of communist electors, also do not furnish
many militants, despite periodic appeals to them to do so.

We have said "highly qualified," but why "steelworkers"? The pre-1914 Socialist party was a peoples'
party or, to put it better, a plebeian party. The little people
felt comfortable in it. The Communist party for its part
is made up of factory workers. This does not mean, of
course, that you never find in it any village artisans or
representatives of the city's little people, those who constituted the nucleus of Jaurès' following. But the *worker*
predominates; and his political development probably
coincided with the formation of the French Communist
party. Just as the workers' movement during the first
decade of the twentieth century was marked by the traditions of building trade employees, so the successful dissemination of communism in working-class circles during

the twenties was the particular accomplishment of two groups: railway workers and steelworkers.

In 1927 railway and steelworkers alone accounted for 430 of the 898 factory cells, or approximately 50 percent of the total. In the thirties, the increase in communist members coincided with the growing authority of steelworkers in the conflicts that arose at that time. Memory of the great days of the Popular Front, somewhat blurred by time, accounts for the persistence of the steelworkers' prestige in the present-day communist party. In any case, there can be no denying that steelworkers account for a fourth of all the delegates sent to successive national congresses.[55]

We must not, however, be misled by this to assume that all the steel plants are directed or controlled by militant communists. On the contrary, the steel mills as a whole are one of the most underorganized, underpoliticized branches of the country's industrial economy; they are completely dominated by the unorganized workers. And this has been the case for some time. In 1928, of the 250,000 steelworkers in the Paris region, only 3,000 were dues-paying members of the CGT. Approximately 1,500 constituted the stable nucleus of the trade unions.

The fact is that steel-making is a gigantic branch of industry, and as such it is complex. A distinction must be made, for example, between the automobile and aviation

55. On this basis of indications given by the official commissions, we can compile the following table:

CONGRESS	STEELWORKER DELEGATES	ALL DELEGATES	% STEELWORKERS
Twelfth	218	903	24.1
Fourteenth	186	787	23.6
Fifteenth	113	507	22.2
Sixteenth	119	496	23.9
Seventeenth	212	776	27.3
Eighteenth	209	788	26.5

sectors where different traditions and psychological traits prevail if only because of the difference in training patterns.

These are the reasons why we can at the same time regard the steelworker as the prototype of the militant communist and steel-making as a branch of industry where communist and CGT authority can be stopped in its tracks. It should be remembered that the strike in the Renault factories which split the cabinet in May, 1947, and precipitated the departure of the communist ministers from the government was inspired by militant Trotskyites despite the opposition of the CGT. The steel industry's trade union federation, imposing though it is because of the top levels of its apparatus, is in actual practice, a practice that has persisted for a hundred years, the one federation among many whose fluctuations in membership are the most extreme; its structures are at once the most sturdy and the most fragile, and its cadres have the greatest difficulty in imposing their authority. The explanation for this is perhaps to be found in the fact that people in the industry resemble very closely the stereotype of the French people: intelligent, clever, hot-headed, individualistic, capricious. Another possible reason is that the communist conception of trade unionism has had its most disastrous consequences in this industry: the loss of unionism's autonomy during the last thirty years; the take-over by the communist apparatus of all its chains of command; the about-face often imposed for strictly political and partisan objectives. All this has transformed the trade unions, which in earlier days had been imbued with libertarianism, into empty shells or cumbersome bureaucracies.

French or at Least Born in France? The incidence of linguistic affiliation is primarily a question that hinges on whether communism exists as an idea or party in the country of one's birth. It is obvious that Italian or Spanish workers furnish more party militants than do the blacks, the Algerians, or even the Portuguese. This is especially true in areas where they have remained a cohesive linguistic group and where specific forms of organization have been improved for their benefit through the cooperation of kindred parties.

Ever since April 9, 1964, when the Communist political bureau published a document reminding its readers of the necessity and prerequisites of action "on behalf of immigrants," and ever since the communist group in parliament drafted a bill granting "democratic and social status" to immigrants, a substantial effort has been made, especially in departments that contain large concentrations of foreign workers: in the Pyrénées Orientales where 37,000 Spanish workers constitute the majority of farm hands and a considerable minority of construction workers; in the Isère where in 1966 a conference was held on immigration, especially Italian immigration; in the Rhône, the Bouches-du-Rhône, the Doubs, Meurthe-et-Moselle, and of course the departments of the Paris region.

In constituting a federal MOI (*Main-d'oeuvre immigrée*, or immigrant labor) commission in appropriate federal bureaus, composed of militant immigrants of various nationalities and even, whenever humanly possible, federal MOI commissions organized according to nationality, the party's central committee attempts to estimate the number of foreign workers who are party members. Conforming to article 8 of the statutes,[56] a central work com-

56. "Members of foreign nationality will be organized into cells without reference to their nationality. They have the same rights and duties as any other members. Language groups, under

mission on immigration collaborates closely with the central committee. Immigrant workers are grouped according to their native language so that their members can deal with their particular concerns in their own tongue and thus play an active role among their compatriots.[57] Their tasks include the distribution of publications in their native language, such as *Verdad*, a monthly put out by the central committee, and the organization of propaganda meetings for one or another category of foreign workers.

The *recent rural worker* who "goes up" to Paris or to the chief town of a department is even more likely to be drawn into a political circle because he comes from a region where communism exerts a powerful influence. Sometimes the presence of a communist member of parliament from his district is enough to arouse his interest. As soon as the first demand is made of him, the young manual or unskilled worker turns to the person who has become part of his new world, the world of the factory. What is more, he now has a key to a better world, that of the big city.

Thereafter, membership in the party becomes the equivalent of an introduction to industrial society. This kind of rural worker is altogether different from the worker the communist parties attempt to politicize in third world countries. In France, the status that goes with being a communist is a sign of respectability, a form of

---

the direction of regular party agencies, have been instituted for the purpose of spreading propaganda among immigrants, who will be spoken to in their native tongue."

57. Polish language groups, which during the interwar period were very active, have now disappeared. In 1948 a resolution drawn up by "Polish language groups of the French Communist Party" was published in *Cahiers du communisme* (to express approval of the measures taken in Poland against Gomulka!), December 1948, p. 1435.

social advancement, a way of proving that one's social position has changed for the better, that personal as well as collective progress is now possible. But in a country like Brazil, for example, to be a worker is to belong to the closed group of the poor, to the closed world of those who have nothing, neither present nor future, who know nothing, have no influence on the present or the future. It's like being a black street-sweeper.

The French party, a fundamentally urban reality, serves to accelerate the integration of the rural masses into city life. Because the newly-arrived worker experiences no "lack," no void, having been welcomed to the city in a manner that is part of a nationwide plan, the communist severs his ties with rural society more quickly than does the noncommunist.

In the light of these facts, we can understand why so much emphasis is placed on "work among the peasantry." Such work is aimed not so much at outlining an agricultural policy, adding militants to the ranks, or acquiring peasant sympathizers, as at capturing the important resources that will bring fresh blood to working-class circles in the cities, especially at a time when a vast exodus is an annual occurrence—160,000 active workers abandon agriculture annually.[58]

From this perspective, the remarkably successful weekly, *La Terre*, has had a greater impact than the

58. It is curious that the only university research done on the subject of communism in rural areas is that of American scholars. See, especially, Henry W. Ehrman, "The French Peasant and Communism," *American Political Science Review*, March 1952, pp. 19–43; and above all, Gordon Wright, "Four Red Villages in France," *Yale Review*, 1952, pp. 361–72. By the same author, *Révolution rurale en France. Histoire de la paysannerie au XXe siècle*, Pref. by M. Debatisse (Paris: Editions de l'Épi, 1967), p. 352.

relatively weak network of the 5,776 rural cells. *La Terre* boasts 150,000 subscribers; 175,000 copies are distributed weekly, exceeding by about 50,000 the number sold by its principal rival. To some extent this compensates for the sizable decline in the percentage of farmers and agricultural workers who are party members (6.5 percent and 3.2 percent respectively in 1966 compared to 8.2 percent and 5 percent in 1959). This decline is becoming more pronounced—Italy is a good example—because young people who might have joined the party cadres are leaving for the city. In 1963 it was still possible to organize 453 cells; but by 1967 only 268 could be formed.

All in all, the Communist party's position is the very reverse of that of the Catholic church. Although the church has a firm hold on the rural youth, it has great difficulty maintaining the same kind of close contact with those who leave for the city because it has no deep roots in urban working-class neighborhoods.

Benefiting from the presence of peasants victimized by France's second agrarian revolution in ten years, the Communist party has actually succeeded in making capital of the passivity it had previously manifested in regard to a process of which it had not been sufficiently aware. Instead of bending all its efforts toward renovating and restructuring the agricultural sector, the Communist party concentrates on capturing the new city-dwellers. The departing peasants would have taken a dim view of such efforts anyway since they had not known how to profit from them while still on the farm. Communism, which in the country has remained the left wing of Jacobin radicalism, acquires in the city the loyalty of those elements that suffer socially and psychologically because of a decline in socioeconomic status.

It would be interesting to verify, through a differential analysis of the growth or decline of communist voting strength in the country, whether, as in Italy, the reverse is true; whether the migrants, who are well established in the cities, take procommunist theories back to their native villages and disseminate them.

We must examine one basic question to which we have not yet addressed ourselves: how much importance should be ascribed to the much-prized predominance within the party of its working-class members? Actually it is confusing to note that the party as well as its enemies justifies or congratulates itself about this. The explanation lies in the tendency of people to jumble together two extremely different entities: a *workers' party* and a *party of the working class*.

What matters most as regards doctrine and ultimate goals—the worldwide proletarian revolution—is the party's need to retain its identity as a *party of the working class*. A definition based on the premise of social passivity leaves virtually no room for the very essence of such a party. History affords many concrete illustrations of revolutions that have quite properly situated themselves in general movements of proletarian revolution—whether successful or not is of no consequence—even though they occurred in countries where proletarianism was either practically nonexistent or never played the role retrospectively assigned to it by theoretical pusillanimity.

Inversely, we know very well that there are political parties in which participation by workers has been remarkable, not only among the militant nucleus but also among the leaders. However, such parties have not been acknowledged to be working-class parties precisely because they did not conduct themselves as the agents

and representatives of the interests of a single group—
a workers' group, in this instance—within established society. And yet a "party of the working class" does not exist
until it is constituted as the anticipated embodiment of a
future society. To be sure, the advent of a new society
also requires the mediation of a group, but the latter must
possess social characteristics which, although initially
dormant, have been reactiviated and metamorphosed because it is invested with an historic mission.

The origin of the tendency to confuse a workers' party
with a party of the working class can easily be located: it
is to be found in the pre-1914 Social Democratic party of
Germany. At that time, through a particular conjunction
of circumstances, the establishment of socialism coincided
with the advent of an industrial society. An exceptionally
large number of workers joined the Social Democratic
party. And since, for many other reasons, the party served
as the model for all socialist parties of the period, the
fact that it was largely composed of workers was viewed
as the measure of its success. Although the passage of time
has dispelled this illusion, hasty conclusions, curiously
enough, continue to be accepted frequently and without
any apparent misgivings.[59]

Even today, the issue involved here has not been clari-
fied for many militant communists. They continue to think
that they are conforming to the essential theories laid
down by the Communist party when they say they can
guarantee the party a "good" social composition. This

59. For a fuller discussion of these fundamental theoretical
and historical problems, see, A. Kriegel, *Le Pain et les Roses,
Jalons pour une histoire des socialismes* (Paris: PUF, 1968),
in particular, the Introduction and the chapter entitled "Le
Parti modèle" (the Second International and German social
democracy).

represents one of the points on which they are out of step with Bolshevism; and consequently, it appears to be highly ominous. Can it be that the inclination to move toward social democracy materializes precisely at this juncture?

Are we saying that if the working-class composition of the party is devoid of doctrinaire significance, it possesses in itself no value whatsoever? No, that would be absurd. Its value is political in nature. It embodies a strategy. The French Communist party should be a workers' party, a party whose ties to the workers as a social group are close and trusting (even though such ties might be closer at given moments or in given regions, industries, and categories); the French Communist Party should hold out the hope that one day some form of socialism will be established which this time will make the workers the center of the laboring class and the urban proletariat the battalions of a proletarian elite. What are the chances? Did Lenin have an opportunity to accomplish this? Yes, he certainly did. But he also kept a strategy in reserve—"just in case!"

5 | Stratification

"Just in case"—that is, if circumstances should change, if they should appear to be favorable. But individual conversions are a little like revolutions—the circumstances, the occasion, must be propitious. That is why it is not enough to note the features (age, sex, social position) that *generally* characterize those individuals likely to be touched by communist grace. One must also examine *how*, in actual practice, the process occurs. And again, it is at this point that the notion of the "generation gap" appears to which I alluded earlier in my analyses of quantitative phenomena.[1]

The Generation Gap

This notion is not popular in the party's inner circle. Anything that might stir up controversy between the generations is immediately repudiated and held up to public obloquy, perhaps because such quarrels recall the "contradictions within capitalism" that socialism is supposed to resolve, or at least to restate in fresh terms. In the Soviet Union the problem of "fathers and sons" has long been considered, in spite of all the evidence to the contrary, as characteristic only of "Turgenev's period." Another reason, perhaps, is that whenever homogeneity is

1. See chapter 3 above.

the result of a deliberate, directed, and conscious process, it strikes us as being less enduring than if it developed spontaneously.

Official disapproval is all very well, but it cannot dispel the generation conflict, especially since this conflict is so apparent in the modalities of growth. The force of circumstantial variations affecting recruitment creates the divisions, auspicious moments, temporal gaps, ready-made situations in which such phenomena develop.

To divide the members of the party into five different categories, as the 1966 inquiry did, on the basis of the date when members joined the party, is one way of implicitly acknowledging the existence of internal stratification.

The following figures show what proportion of the party's members joined during these five periods:[2]

Before the war	12.9%
During the war	3.1%
The Liberation to 1947	19.4%
1948–1958	22.5%
1959–1966	42.1%

Motley Composition of the Party in the Initial Years
As early as 1920 the very heterogeneous groups that made up the newly formed Communist party met but did not always merge. To understand this, the reader must remember that the period had been marked by war and revolutions; that the party, far from having been founded ex-nihilo, was the result of a major split within the Socialist party (the so-called unified party, but its unification, having occurred in 1905, was fairly recent); that the Bolshevist phenomenon, in itself already quite complex, and in several respects as yet indeterminate in form, left

2. See Marchais, Report to the Eighteenth Congress, p. 271.

the way open for conflicting interpretations. The *Cahiers du Bolchevisme* humorously noted that the party at the time consisted of "20 percent Jaurésism, 10 percent Marxism, 20 percent Leninism, 20 percent Trotskyism, and 30 percent confusionism."[3]

The motley nature of the membership during the early 1920s, before Bolshevization, emerges even more plainly when we scan the biographical notes published by *l'Humanité* in April, 1924, in order to publicize the names of the forty-three candidates from the Seine who represented the workers' and peasants' bloc.[4]

If we compare and contrast these biographical sketches, we find that they reveal the coexistence then of four different ways of belonging to the party and of four different avenues that led to such affiliation.

First, there was the "generation under fire"—those who came to communism *from* the war or because they had been *against* it. To avoid ambiguity or error in interpretation, we must know how they became communists. Of the forty-three candidates in question, twenty-three were eager to broadcast the fact that they had "fought the war"; and they meant this quite literally. Only *one* of these said

3. No. 2, November 28, 1924. On this period, see Robert Wohl, *French Communism in the Making, 1914–1924* (Stanford University Press, 1964).

4. An amusing sidelight: Aware of the party's motley composition, and rightly concerned to avoid the kind of "combinations" that might result from it, the party decided to alphabetize the list of candidates (with the exception of the departing deputies). Since the electoral system functioned in such a way that only those candidates who headed the list could be elected, all the communist deputies' names began with either an A or a B. This is how it happened that Duclos, with his unlucky initial D, was defeated on Cachin's list. This was a method of selection that caused many a disappointment. The initial A does not necessarily fit a candidate for a parliamentary career.

that he "had been condemned to two years in prison for refusing to obey." Three others were Zimmerwaldists or Kienthalists. The majority, therefore, did not join the party because they opposed the war at the time it was being waged. They did not revolt against "the illusion of national defense." Even when there was still time, they did not choose to reject national solidarity in favor of class solidarity. The original mutineers of 1917 were not among these recruits. Yet for the twenty-three mentioned, who were "offspring of the war and opposed to it," the conflict itself was nevertheless the decisive factor. From it they derived their conception of what the political policy of the workers should be. They did so in two different ways.

First, the sufferings caused by the war belatedly awakened in them a sense of class consciousness. Of the twenty-three who fought in the war, seven had been severely wounded and two had been taken prisoner. Jacques Duclos' statement is important: "In 1917 he was taken prisoner. . . . The war he had waged turned him into an ardent internationalist." It was these workers, many bearing marks on their bodies and most of them scarred in their souls, who gathered to form the ARAC (*Association républicaine des anciens combattants,* or Republican Association of War Veterans). Through this association they found their way to the Communist party. The great humanist theme of peace and internationalism, of social-ism's special responsibility to protect the peace of the world, found a greater echo in these men than in anyone else.

Second—and this is no less important—many skilled workers returned from the front in 1916–17 to work in armament factories. The urgent requirements of national defense plus the individual activities of Thomas, the socialist member of the cabinet, created a situation that was particularly propitious for the action of the workers, even though the threat always hung over them that the "leaders" would be sent back to the front. The naming of "shop stewards" offered an especially favorable educational opportunity that enabled many militants to obtain the training they needed. Three of our candidates indicated that this was how they were initiated into the trade union movement.[5]

In short, a generation of communist militants was one of the direct results of the war. These men made their way either through the ARAC if they were veterans, or through the factory councils and workshop delegations if they were working at the time in munitions factories. The same men often used both channels.

But there is an older generation whose militant options go back to the prewar era, sometimes even to the turn of the century. These people have three distinctive traits. First: their members almost always came to the workers' movement through trade-unionism, and almost all of them were unionists. Many of them even took pride in the fact that they had helped to found the trade union in their plant. Second, a few months or years after joining the union, and while they continued to be active militants, they joined the party. It should be noted that these communists of 1924 alluded simply to the "party" when they meant the Socialist party of the years 1895 or 1905. For them there is no discontinuity, no gap between the socialist parties prior to unification, the unified Socialist party of 1905, and the Communist party after 1920. Only one person mentioned that he had joined "the old party." Third: these mili-

5. See M. Gallo, "Quelques aspects de la mentalité dans les usines de guerre, 1914–1918," *Le Mouvement social*, no. 56 (July-Sept. 1966).

tants continued to be active in cooperatives after they had joined the trade union and socialist movements. Of the thirteen candidates who were members of the prewar socialist party—the senior member had joined it as early as 1894—eleven indicated that they belonged to the cooperative movement. Among these last, four were members of a producers' cooperative formed for the purpose of coping with a lockout by the employers. The trinity—party, union, cooperative—was thus always present, in accordance with the great tradition of the Second International. The militants often continued to take an interest in the tenants' federation since at that time landlords, together with employers, occupied places of honor in the rogues' gallery. The housing crisis and the subsequent inauguration of public housing have helped to deprive the landlords of this special place. In some cases, for example in municipal elections, the militant worker would exercise a deciding vote.

Instead of citing innumerable examples, I will quote from a typical *biography*, that of Clotaire Baroux, born in 1881:

> One of the founders of the first teachers' union in France, established by him and a few friends in the department of the Somme in 1905. At that time he was a member of the party. Thereafter he never ceased to be active in politics and in the trade union movement of two departments: first the Somme, and then the Seine. Baroux extended his field of activity to embrace every domain: party, ARAC, cooperatives, tenants. He was elected to membership of the municipal council of Choisy-le-Roi. . . .

But, and here things become a little more complicated, the "prewar socialist generation" did not regroup within the Communist party of the twenties all those who belonged to the same age category, according to their civilian status. Former revolutionary syndicalists, whose anarchist or "pure syndicalist" convictions had kept them from joining the socialist movement during the first decade of the twentieth century, were not part of this group. They are easy to spot. In their biographies there is a hiatus between very early membership in the syndicalist movement and very recent adherence to the party. Take, for example, Martial Bichon, "born in the twentieth arrondissement into a worker's family with revolutionary antecedents. His father was one of the founders of the Bellevilloise" [a revolutionary group from the working class district known as Belleville]. As soon as Bichon returned from the army, "he joined the polishers' syndicate and devoted himself entirely to working-class activities." He did not join the party until 1922 although "he had participated in every workers' movement from 1915 to 1918." In other words, Bichon came to the party after the split in Tours seemed to indicate that the earlier reformist elements would no longer have a place in the new organization.

Finally, a fourth group is being formed, and here the word "generation" is once again altogether appropriate. It is made up of people who are not familiar with the socialist tradition, the pre-1914 syndicalist tradition, or the war. Lacking a doctrinaire past, these young people try to decipher the life of the workers with the aid of a Leninist code and within the context of both trade unionist and political action as defined by the Bolshevik Revolution.

Thus, the 1924 party embraced several traditions that coexisted more or less harmoniously. One objective of the Bolshevization campaign of 1924–25 was to merge all these traditions in order to reduce the heterogeneity— intolerable to good Leninists—of French communism. Once this had been accomplished, it was the fluctuating strategies and policies of the Third International that were thereafter to determine the crystallization of the distinctly different generations.

The Real First Generation

Doubtless successive generations do not have a common profile or a uniform individuality, but this is true of the history of human beings in general. The following three distinctive generations succeeded one another: those who joined the party between 1924 and 1934; the Popular Front generation; the generation of the Resistance.

Since the Liberation things have become terribly complicated because people belonging to different age groups are involved. The precise moment when French communism came into its own sprang from a precarious adjustment between the rapid ups and downs of France's experience—modernization in the '50s; decolonization and the war in Algeria (1954–61); Gaullism since 1958 —and the no less frenzied ups and downs of the international communist movement: the final metamorphoses of Stalinism (1945–52); destalinization (the Twentieth Congress and Budapest, 1956); desovietization, polycentrism, and schism (1960s). The generation of the 1950s saw faith in the major beliefs badly shaken. The generation of the 1960s is difficult to characterize even though the decade is nearing its end.

We still need to clarify the concept of "generations," of groups of men who, sharing a common history, also share the same psychological universe, a universe replete with images, songs, gestures, celebrations, words that for them are so many signs of recognition.

The communist generation of the years 1924 to 1934, and the generation of 1936, were in a sense shaped by their very different images of the main lines and relationships of power in the world.

For the first generation, the USSR was the focal point of interest. The Soviet Union was building socialism in a single country, but it would have been glad, if the occasion presented itself, to include the entire universe in the joyous bonfires of a gigantic worldwide revolution. On every side of it all-pervasive capitalism stood watch. Undifferentiated, monstrous, still dripping with the blood of the millions of proletarians it had sacrificed from 1914 to 1918, it battened on the sweat of the workers—those victims of the infernal fluctuations of new systems of rationalization imposed by people like Ford and Taylor. At times, however, capitalism grew thin as a consequence of the emaciation brought on by the agony of the Great Depression that ravaged and destroyed its organisms. Thereupon one great shout arose: "Class against class!" There was but one model to emulate, one country, the Soviet Union; one flag, the Red flag; one song, the International.

Although a time was bound to come when people would be more sophisticated, for the moment no one sensed this. Everywhere, around people, within them, there was nothing but filth, ignorance or worse, ideological stupidity, derision, the cops, impotence, the priests, and the army. It was urgently necessary, in view of the circumstances, to differentiate ruthlessly, so that revolutionaries would be able to recognize each other: the intellectuals (beginning with the teachers), the "pseudosocialists" (who, during the worst times, were counterbalanced by the "social-fascists"), the "yellows" (they first appeared among Jouhaux's CGT trade unionists); the "softies," who at times sold out because they were too closely tied to bourgeois society, with families to look after, small properties to keep up, careers, ambitions, dreams (to become a deputy!), plans, luxurious tastes, personal preferences. This was not true of the communists (either they forgot about such things or they instinctively sensed that these were now inappropriate). To the youth with empty hands who approached them, asking to join their movement, they responded by giving him a pile of pamphlets. "There you are, comrade." Shortly thereafter, hounded by the police, his name inscribed on employers' blacklists, the neophyte found himself unemployed. From then on he had plenty of time—time to be hungry but also time to spread the good word (when he was able to eat thanks to the money he collected selling the pamphlets). No one had bothered to teach him what to say in spreading the good word but he knew enough anyway. He knew with a certainty that there was one country in the world where the workers had waged a revolution and made themselves the masters of that state, the bosses of the factories, the generals of the Red Army.

Besides, since he had plenty of time, he read. What interminably nerve-racking days! Where could he go? He could only talk to his "pals" very early in the morning, at the entrance to the factory, at lunch time, or in the evening. Whether in jail or out of work, for him it was a time for learning, not from books (not yet) but from pamphlets, tracts, and newspapers.

The atmosphere was tough, circumscribed, harsh, marked by futility and naiveté, the atmosphere of a sect whose words were being obliterated in the sands of time, a sect that was perishing in a milieu dominated by outrageous curses, sordid excommunications, and oriental mirages.

And yet, let there be no mistake about it: this was a decisive period.[6] The sect, after all, was part of the International. Amid a great flurry that was more or less clandestine, amid lightning-like consultations, denunciations, and complaints,[7] the French delegates to the Komintern and the French members of the executive committee of the International patiently sorted out those men and women who had revealed a talent for class warfare. They were sent to a school for class warfare in Moscow, to the Leninist school. There were many failures to be recorded along the way.[8] But there were also successes, enough of them so that ultimately it was possible to

6. Three significant observations: (a) At the Eleventh Party Congress (Arles, December, 1937), which was held *after* the enormous influx of new members in 1936–37, *not a single* new member was added to the political bureau; its composition remained identical to that of the Eighth Congress at Villeurbanne (January, 1936), in other words, before the experience of the Popular Front. (b) Of the thirteen members elected or re-elected to the political bureau at the time of the Twelfth Congress (Gennevilliers, 1950), at least ten had been members before 1934. (c) Lastly, of the nineteen members of the political bureau formed at the Eighteenth Congress (Levallois, January, 1967), eight can be classified as being part of the "basic generation."

7. Jules Humbert-Droz, *"L'Oeil de Moscou" à Paris* (Paris: Julliard, 1964), faithfully depicts the atmosphere of the early twenties. Equally telling is the description of the atmosphere toward the close of the thirties in two unpublished manuscripts, *Souvenirs de militant et de dirigeant communiste*, by Henri Barbé, and *Journal* by Albert Vassart.

8. In reference to this, Henri Barbé wrote: "As for the French Communist party, I have noted that the number of students selected five or six times during the course of the period from 1927 to 1933 came to roughly 100. Of this 100 only 10 at the most are presently members of the party. . . . Of the 24 students who were classmates of Waldeck Rochet, only 5 are presently party members. The other 19 left the party years ago." Quoted by Branko Lazitch, "Les écoles de cadres du Komintern," in *Contributions à l'histoire du Komintern*, edited by J. Freymond (Geneva: Droz, 1965), p. 241.

fashion a nucleus of communists that tallied with what the Kremlin had had in mind all along.[9] The nucleus was so sturdy and durable that the history of the French Communist party from that time until the present is largely intertwined with the history of the Kremlin. Wasn't Waldeck Rochet himself a brilliant member of the group of pupils selected in 1929–30?[10]

The Generation of the Popular Front

1934. Perhaps not as rapidly as the history books maintain, but quickly enough, an entirely different generation came to occupy the stage.

9. The Bolshevization (see above, chapter 4) of the French Communist party after 1924 constituted not only a modification of organizational structures (the favorite form of organization being that of the company cell) but also and above all the creation of an apparatus consisting of a vast network of "professional revolutionaries" (see below, chapter 8). The old militants of the social democratic era could not be transformed into party functionaries for the sole purpose of establishing a network of "professional revolutionaries." New cadres, inculcated from the start with the Bolshevik point of view, had to be recruited. That is why the various agencies needed to create a network of "functionaries" date from this time. In November, 1924, the first Central School of the Communist Party was organized in France. The commission on cadres was instituted in 1932. (See below, chapters 10 and 11).

10. On Waldeck Rochet and the Leninist School, see a few interesting remarks in Henri Barbé, quoted by B. Lazitch, "Les écoles," p. 250: Students from the Leninist School had been sent to a Soviet factory for training. "Upon their return to the school a violent and passionate debate raged within the French group. No longer did discussions center on the differences between the capitalist and Soviet systems; rather, they focused on the disparity between theoretical courses on socialist production in the USSR and the living reality as observed by students in the factory they had just visited. . . . Only one student stubbornly held out, opposing the others. He was Waldeck Rochet, who went so far as to repudiate the facts the students had brought back with them."

What was there about these Popular Front communists that differentiated them so radically from their predecessors? The discovery of ambivalence within themselves and around them, an ambivalence plainly disclosed by the very recent plurality of their vision of the world, of the times in which they lived, of their own style of social action.

The plurality of their vision of the world. Upon earlier, classical capitalism-socialism dichotomy there was abruptly superimposed a new battleground where fascism and democracy were pitted against each other.

For years the truth was deliberately stretched in order to fuse the images of these two monsters. Consequently, the destruction of one automatically entailed the eradication of the other. Only the German catastrophe of 1933 could force the International and its sections to accept the notion that the two were not identical, and to plan thenceforward intermediate stages and objectives. Thus, two different conceptions of international politics were finally dissociated from each other.

Plurality of the times. Formerly, a revolutionary lived only for the future. But now the present was once again perceived as a reality, a reality no longer uniformly gray, contemptible, deplorable, but capable, on occasion, of bringing great joys, of inspiring great enthusiams. Because of inexperience, there was doubtless temptation at first to place the revolution directly on the agenda in the hope of bringing this unknown present closer to a familiar future. But weeks passed, and eventually the notion that the present existed in its own right and should be lived as such was accepted, even though it was merely the harbinger of "bright tomorrows."

Plurality of modes of social action. Hitherto, by virtue of a common though implicit accord, the relations of the communists with established society had remained entirely exclusionary. To be a communist was equivalent to being a pariah, an untouchable, an outcast. Now, suddenly, the communists began to have an existence of their own, although they had not in the process changed their spots. They were seen, counted, appraised, and discussed; alliances were formed with or against them—in short, their existence became an acknowledged fact. This transition from the status of total outsiders to that of an integral part of society brought with it a fantastic metamorphosis of their whole value system. Democracy, country, culture—even, strange as it may seem, war itself, the most hated of all evils, hitherto stigmatized as a vile trap set by the class enemy—became so many subjects of controversy within the party. The republic, the tricolor, the *Marseillaise*, Victor Hugo, the student-officer corps—all these were reinvested with their original ambiguity and thus gave the proletariat, by viewing them in a certain light, an opportunity to convert them into added attractions for use in their own camp.

The consequences flowing from the discovery of this ambiguity soon became apparent. A relative heterogeneity was disclosed in a party undergoing an extraordinary growth—and this growth, contrary to current opinion, was not the cause of the heterogeneity but was the product of the ambiguity.

Three kinds of reaction and behavior resulted from the discovery of this ambiguity. The left wing of the party comprised individuals unmoved by all these sophisticated maneuvers and fancy games. For them, the earlier way of looking at things was all that mattered; the only split that still counted, so far as they were concerned, was the schism between the communist world and the world of all the others. Suddenly they became distrustful, even disgusted;

they went off shouting "betrayal." Or else they fabricated some kind of personal rationalization: the new outlook was nothing but an amusing way to fool the enemy, justifiable because it was accomplishing its purpose; in reality it was a revolutionary trick, a wink of the eye, a gesture offered in bad faith, a Trojan horse.

The party's right wing comprised other kinds of militants. They had come to the party at a time when the gods of the new age were being worshipped every morning, and they had remained quite unaware of those other gods that had been the original foundation of the movement. These people said all they had to say when they described themselves as avant-garde republicans, pioneering antifascists, determined patriots. They reconciled their Jacobinism with Bolshevism, the teachings of Robespierre with those of Stalin, the Great Terror of the French Revolution with the Moscow trials.

The members of the petite bourgeoisie who joined the Communist party because they regarded it as a sort of updated radicalism were nevertheless not very numerous in 1936. At that time, in contrast to what was to occur ten years later, traditional radicalism had structures of its own with which to welcome members into the confines of the Popular Front. Looked at from this point of view, the distance between the National Liberation Front and the Popular Front is considerable. This gap does not spring from the difference (basically secondary) between the political lines of the two periods and the essential preoccupations which they reflect; rather, it stems from the degree of polarization and from the structure of the alliances within the French left. This explains why the communist generation of 1936 constituted a simple body from the social point of view. The workers then represented the overwhelming majority, whereas the communist generation of 1945 was the result of a merger.

Once this becomes clear, it should also be noted that the center, the bulk of those communists who belonged to the 1936 generation, took up the challenge they had addressed to themselves: that of living ambivalently on several levels.

Their elders were crude, simple, pure, irresponsible. They, on the other hand, were going to be subtle, complicated, calculating, and *responsible*. The idea that the communists have an eminent sense of responsibility is a theme which has been complacently exploited ever since (but preferably at the expense of unruly chance companions and allies, sanctimoniously reproached for being "impulsive"), and it accompanied this aggiornamento. In short, upon discovering the "real world," they immediately claimed that they alone were capable of running it. But in so doing, they showed a willingness to risk their own innocence; they discovered just how uncomfortable certain subtle positions could be. Anyone who thought he could quickly decide what was "good" or "bad" about the inevitable compromises that followed was indeed a fool. The communists proceeded to don ties and speak like books. They were received by mayors, or even became mayors themselves. Nothing that was respectable was alien to them. With closed lips they intoned the well-known refrain of *La Jeune Garde*, in which, without distinction, "the lancers, the bourgeois, the gluttons, the priests," are all roundly denounced.

Between the generation of the late 1930s and that of 1936 the distance is simply the gap that results from any great cultural revolution. Two symbols demonstrate this gap: holidays and verbal expressions.

From time to time the calendar of holidays was completely turned around; for the masses, this had a very potent educational value. Toward the end of the twenties, the demonstrations scheduled for certain prearranged dates and that saw a few tightly-knit, cantankerous communist battalions go into the streets, were restricted to a few uniquely "proletarian" occasions: the first of May (the anniversary of the Commune), the first of August (the day of international opposition to imperialist war). After 1935, the number of holidays celebrated by the entire left—February 12, for example[11]—or by the entire nation—the chief of these was, of course, July 14—increased substantially. The presence of crowds of women and children attested to the fact that proletarian violence, the clenched fist, was imposing the peaceful discipline of its theories.

Nor is the complete change in vocabulary any less significant. During the middle thirties, the transition from the "class against class strategy" to the "Popular Front strategy" was accompanied, so far as slogans were concerned, by a shift from the Russification of communist expressions to their "Jacobinization."

In 1924, the "Bolshevization" of the party resulted in the Bolshevization or Russification of the terms used to designate different levels of the party apparatus. The word *cell*, for example, which refers to the basic unit of organization, is a translation of the Russian word *ïatcheïka*. At that time, the early leaders of the French Communist Party did hesitate about which of the three different words they should choose: *alvéole*, the most literal translation of the Russian term; *cell*, which unfortunately was a reminder of prison (during the twenties the first communists in the factories were often derisively called *cellulards* or "jail birds"); *nucleus*, a term which was used earlier by the revolutionary syndicalist group clustered around

11. February 12, 1934, the day of the first joint Communist-Socialist antifascist demonstration in Paris; prelude to the formation of the *Front Populaire.*—TRANSL.

the *Vie ouvrière*, but whose meaning diverged somewhat from the Bolshevik connotation. After some vacillation, which is doubtless reflected in contemporaneous communist newspapers and periodicals, *cell* was finally adopted, in spite of its obvious drawbacks.

The most curious story is the one about the word *rayon*, or "spoke." In the Russian language, *raïon*, itself a Gallicism or at any rate a Latinism, denotes a district or a section. This being so, the word *rayon* or *section* came to signify during the mid-twenties a minor unit in the hierarchy of French communist organizations. But very soon a confusion arose in the minds of the militants. The problem was how to distinguish between the *rayon* meaning district and the *rayon* meaning the spoke of a wheel. The second of these implied the division of the Paris region into triangular-shaped districts like the space between two spokes of a wheel. Such a division would be politically advantageous because it entailed a merger of industrial, proletarian neighborhoods with petit bourgeois or peasant areas. But there was also a drawback: the militant who lived within the arc of the outside circle would find himself several kilometers away from the center!

The decade from 1924 to 1934 was characterized by this translation of Russian terms, usually in abbreviated form. Expressions such as *agit-prop* (agitation-propaganda), *org's office* (party headquarters), and others, were current. This remained so as long as the isolationist strategy of "class against class" continued to prevail, a strategy that plainly stressed the point that the USSR was the only country in the world where one could find revolutionary workers. Inversely, in 1935–36, when the strategy of the Popular Front (to be followed by that of the French Front) led the French Communist party to emphasize nationalism and patriotism, the Russification of the communist vocabulary was abandoned in favor of a traditional, national revolutionary vocabulary, that of 1789 and 1792.

At a national conference held on January 23, 1937, the French Communist party decided to resume the use of the word *section* to designate a district or *rayon*. It claimed that *section*, being a "simple" term, was "more in keeping with existing traditional forms of organization in our country." As a consequence, communist and socialist sections once again coexisted side by side. I cannot resist the temptation of adding one fine point: the communists referred to the "section of the fourteenth" (arrondissement), whereas the socialists called it the "fourteenth section"!

From then on, Russian words such as *Komintern*, meaning the Communist International, or *Inprekorr*, signifying *International Correspondence*, were used by the enemies of communism to underscore the foreign nature of the French Communist party. However, a few communists of the older generation continued, from sheer force of habit, to use the Russian terminology.

A Generation Sacrificed

Every generation did not contribute equally to the formation and enrichment of the patrimony. We may therefore speak of generations that were glorious and others that were sacrificed.

The generation of the decade from 1924 to 1934, actually the "first generation," proved to be basic in the sense that the entire edifice rested upon it. On the other hand, the generation of the Resistance must be called a "sacrificed" generation.

The statistics on the seniority of party members can not be ignored. These extraordinary figures show that only 3.1 percent of the Resistance generation belonged to the party during the years of the Second World War.[12]

One thing is certain: this is easy to explain.

First, the generation in question acquired its own special characteristics within a very short period—scarcely three years.

Almost all of the party's members at that time had come from the ranks of antifascists who for more than four years had been imbued with the idea that any war on the side of the democracies was a just war and that such a war was virtually inevitable. We should remember that the party would have collapsed completely in the autumn of 1939 if the official anticommunist repression had not forced many of its members to remain silent about their dismay, their despair. In behaving thus, they had been motivated by considerations of honor, or else by the desire to avoid being suspected of cowardice.

Then, once the short interval of the "phony war" was

12. 3.1 percent was the official figure given by Georges Marchais in *Cahiers du communisme*, February-March, 1967, p. 271. What does this percentage represent in absolute terms? It is impossible to calculate it with any degree of certainty because Marchais gave no detailed information about the actual figure on which the published percentages were based. We can, however, get some idea of what this basic figure must have been. At the most, if we bear in mind the 425,000 membership cards delivered (the official figure) by the party's central treasury, we readily see that a percentage of 3.1 represents 13,000 indivduals. At the least, if we base our reckoning on a total of 275,000 actual members, the percentage represents 8,525. But in January, 1945, Léon Mauvais announced that the party had 387,098 members, whereas "immediately before the war" it had had "scarcely 300,000" (organizational report presented on January 22, 1945, to the central committee, pamphlet published by the French Communist party, p. 16). In other words, it is difficult to see how the party could have had less than 100,000 members during the war: one out of every 10, approximately, would have been a party member.

over, the military and political debacle, the great exodus,
the flight of much of the nation's industry to the south,
the transfer of a million youthful prisoners to Germany,
the division of France into three zones—all these torren-
tial disasters finally swept the party away just as they
swept away all of the country's institutions.

Meanwhile, a specifically new element was added to
the general disarray within the party: The dual strategy
laid down by the dispersed, clandestine apparatus.

The core consisted of a handful of leaders who were
not subject to mobilization for reasons of age or other
circumstances, or who, like Thorez, had deserted on orders from the executive committee of the Komintern.
Complying with directives received from Moscow via
Belgium and Switzerland, this nucleus of leaders stubbornly defended the Nazi-Soviet Pact which held that the
war, far from pitting fascism against democracy, was
really a conflict between two capitalist, imperialist blocs.
From then on, the French communists, like Lenin in 1917,
began to vie for the forfeited power against the Vichyites,
the direct heirs of German or British imperialism, and
this at a time when all the social structures of the bourgeois state were collapsing. "Power to Thorez!" became
the principal order of the day. Had the French communists attained their avowed goal, they would doubtless
have had to accept German control, at least for a while.
In 1917–18 Lenin too had been obliged to accept a temporary arrangement with the Central Powers.[13]

13. The communist leaders continue to deny or to remain
silent about the sinister mistakes committed in 1939–40, as
attested by Germaine Willard's obstinately defensive attitude,
La drôle de guerre et la trahison de Vichy (Paris, Ed. sociales,
1960) and, for orientation, chapter 9 of the official *Histoire de
PCF, manuel* (Paris, Ed. sociales, 1964). No less official is *Le
Parti communiste français dans la Résistance* (Paris, Ed. so-

In any case, the first step was to recover the legality
which the bourgeois republic, using the war against Hitler
as a pretext, had wrested from the party, thereby preventing the seeds of disintegration from wreaking their full
havoc. This strategy explains the famous move to obtain
permission from the Occupation authorities to publish
l'Humanité openly once again.[14] It also explains the in-

---

ciales, 1967), which seems scarcely more concerned with maintaining even the slightest degree of objectivity, save for an
acknowledgment, the first ever made, of the episode involving
the republication of *l'Humanité*. Besides, one should not over-
estimate the role played by personal and group affairs in the
"party secrets" of that time. The association of Maurice Thorez
with Jacques Duclos was in large measure based upon their
solidarity in this matter, and "the spirit of the party" was for a
long time judged on the basis of the attitude assumed during
that period. All this turned out to be vain. Historical research
can do no less than to confirm the precise assertions, including
names, dates, and references, which A. Rossi (Angelo Tasca)
first set forth in several informative books. Among these are:
Deux ans d'alliance germano-soviétique, août 1939–juin 1941
(Paris: Fayard, 1949); *Les Communistes français pendant la
drôle de guerre* (Paris: Les Iles d'Or, 1951); *les Cahiers du
bolchevisme pendant la campagne 1939–1940* (Paris: D. Wapler,
1951); *La Guerre des papillons. Quatre ans de politique communiste (1940–1944)* (Paris: Les Iles d'Or, 1954). A little later,
Auguste Lecoeur was to contribute his direct testimony in *Le
Partisan* (Flammarion, 1963), 2: 105–208, and especially in
*Le Parti communiste français et la Résistance (août 1939–juin
1941)* (Plon, 1968). Lastly, it might be useful to consult
L'Histoire du PCF, (Ed. Unir, 1965), obviously edited by a
group of militants who personally experienced all the events
discussed. I quote, for instance, one example among a hundred
because it is completely unambiguous: "The July 4, 1940, issue
of the underground *l'Humanité* stated: 'The people of France
want peace. They are demanding energetic measures against
those who, on orders from imperialist England, want to drag
France into the war again'" (p. 33).

14. The most complete account of this affair is to be found
in *L'Histoire du PCF* (Ed. Unir), 2: 24–28. According to this text,

credible directive issued in the summer of 1940 urging
party members in the Paris area to return to their homes
and there make their presence felt, without bothering to
take any precautions.

Meanwhile and concurrently, more or less autonomous
groups in various regions throughout the country began
to lean in the opposite direction. Without pondering the
implications of the German-Soviet Pact—in the hurly-
burly of that first winter of war there had been no time to
assess its true significance—they reverted spontaneously
to the attitudes they had adopted before catastrophe overtook the party and the country. Affecting both the party
and France, this misfortune helped to clarify a position
whose roots had been buried deep within the history of
France.

It should also be noted that certain contradictions existed in the minds of people rather than in their acts. At
that time the party was a phantom, and the presence
within it of two different political attitudes amounted to

---

a letter signed by Maurice Tréand, who was responsible for the
"clandestine administration" of the party, was handed to the
German authorities by Robert Foissin. It ran as follows: "We ask
for authorization to publish *l'Humanité* in the form in which it
was presented to its readers before its interdiction by Daladier,
immediately following the signing of the Nazi-Soviet Pact.
L'Humanité, published by us, would undertake to act in the
service of the people and to denounce those responsible for the
present situation in France. *L'Humanité* published by us would
assume the task of denouncing the activities of the agents of
British imperialism who wish to drag the French colonies into
the war. It would also appeal to colonial peoples to fight for
independence against their imperialist oppressors. *L'Humanité*
published by us would assume the task of pursuing a policy of
European pacification and of furthering the conclusion of a
Franco-Soviet pact of friendship, which would complement the
Nazi-Soviet Pact and would thus create conditions for a lasting
peace." Cf. also Auguste Lecoeur's detailed account, *Le PCF
et la Résistance*, pp. 93–95.

no more than the coexistence of stray impulses whose vague contours could only be inferred from the party's indecisive gestures, abortive plans, and hesitant declarations.

In actual practice, the party was content—this in itself was no mean achievement—to localize the militants, to regroup them and reestablish links at every level of the apparatus, to cope with the urgent problem of safeguarding families and possessions.[15]

This frightfully thankless and disappointing task was still being pursued when the Nazi invasion of Russia put an end to the dilemma, thereby abruptly restoring harmony within the party as well as within the heart and soul of each communist. And it was only then, in an atmosphere of renewed vigor and certainty, that the recruitment of members was resumed and the party's manpower augmented.

The generation of the Resistance was constituted within the space of only three years—from 1941 to 1944 —a very short time indeed, especially since the pace was very slow until 1943, when the achievements of the Soviet army evoked universal admiration and put every French communist on his mettle. But the period of the Popular Front had been equally short; consequently, this line of argument in and of itself does not suffice.

15. It is here that we find the nub of the question, the ambiguity of the entire affair. When the French Communist party dates its acts of resistance back to 1940 it is playing with the fact that as early as 1940 its militants were trying to reconstitute a party which would later become a most dynamic element in the Resistance. The reconstitution of such a party represented a permanent anxiety about survival (something that is at the heart of any social organism threatened with destruction) that exceeded by far its concern about resisting the Nazi invader. On other aspects of this, see, Lecoeur, *Le PCF et la Résistance*.

There is, however, a second explanation. If today there are so few communists who had been party members during the Resistence, the reason for this is to be found in the fact that the generation in question had been decimated. At this point, unfortunately, we must once again cite figures and statistics; it is painful to have to make sordid computations when even a single death represented an irreparable calamity.

We know that the Communist party claims the honor of having lost no fewer than 75,000 of its members through executions. This figure is an integral part of the mystique that nourished the spirit of every militant and that no one in the party any longer calls into question. Time and again, on every conceivable occasion, members are very formally reminded of this martyrdom.[16]

We also know how the figure of 75,000 originated. On August 20, 1944, a joint proclamation was issued by the following groups: the unions of the Paris region; the communist leadership in the Paris area; the National Front; the Francs-tireurs and Partisans. The proclamation called for the formation of a united front for the purpose of making sure that the "75,000 Parisians shot in Châteaubriant, Mont-Valérien and elsewhere did not die in vain."[17] The real object of those who issued the proclamation was to nip in the bud the possibility of a truce. But in *l'Humanité* of November 2, 1944, Marcel Cachin alluded to "75,000 French communists who had been shot by the Germans and the Vichyites." In the same issue the newspaper noted that "General de Gaulle bowed

16. As they are today, the very day I am writing these lines—October 11, 1967—in *l'Humanité*.

17. The text of this proclamation is in the appendix of Adrien Dansette's book, *Histoire de la libération de Paris*, 38th ed. Fayard, 1946), pp. 497–98.

his head before 850 tombs, which included some of the 75,000 Parisians who had been shot" (no mention was made of their political affiliation). It is therefore quite likely that the locale was widened—the Paris cadre was changed to the French cadre—and that the political affiliations of the dead men were narrowed. Be that as it may, from that time on, the figure 75,000 was constantly reiterated to designate the number of communists who had been shot.

The figure itself is certainly incorrect. For one thing, the few verified lists that appeared in *l'Humanité* between 1944 and 1947 contain only 176 names[18] (including eight of the fifty members of the last prewar central committee, elected in 1937);[19] for another, an exhaustive list has not been published since 1947. France's legal representative at the Nuremberg trials presented a report on the number of Frenchmen shot during the German occupation, but without, of course, indicating their political affiliations. Based on an investigation of war crimes carried out by the Ministry of Justice, the report concluded that no more than 29,660 people had been shot.[20]

Even this figure, however, is excessive, or at any rate questionable. Henri Michel has explained why in all probability no definite figures will ever be forthcoming: "Scrutinizing the names of those who have been shot, it is diffi-

18. The lists were published on September 12, 14, 20, 24, October 18, 19, 1944; January 16 and 27, July 21, 1945; May 24, August 25, 1946; February 8, June 15, 1947. See Paul Viret, *Les 75,000 fusillés communistes* (MLS).

19. Pierre Sémard, Félix Cadras, Jean Catelas, Charles Nédelec, Gabriel Péri, Barthélémy Ramier, André Rebière, Georges Wodli. See *Décembre 1937–juin 1945. Du congrès d'Arles au congrès de Paris. Rapport du comité central pour le Xe congrès national du PCF.*

20. Document F 420. Vol. 6, p. 145 ff. and vol. 37, pp. 211–12.

cult to identify which of them were hostages or members of the Resistance; nor is it easy to identify corpses in a mass execution."[21]

A decimated generation it certainly was, and also one marked, deformed for life by the experience it had undergone. It was marked by the effect of two things which the force of circumstances had inescapably thrust upon it; clandestinity and partisan warfare.

Not until the war broke out had the French Communist party known total illegality. It is true, of course, that one of the twenty-one conditions to which a Communist party had to subscribe in order to join the Third International stipulated that an illegal apparatus must be maintained alongside the legal one. This clause applied, at least partially, to specific sectors. Included among them was the "struggle against militarism." The purpose here was to organize revolutionary propaganda and activities among conscripts and young soldiers inside the barracks. The need to preserve the continuity and security of every form of contact with the Komintern's executive committee operating in Moscow also demanded the establishment of complex and clandestine networks.

In 1926, when a government of National Union was formed, the new Minister of the Interior, Albert Sarraut, announced that communism was the real enemy of France. The aftermath of the war in Morocco, the demonstrations against the execution of Sacco and Vanzetti, the Crémet affair involving Russian espionage—all these were used by the French courts during the latter part of the twenties to hand out decisions that totalled thousands of months in

21. Henri Michel, *Bibliographie critique de la Résistance*, (SEVPEN, 1964), p. 135 (chapter 3, section 6, is devoted to the communist Resistance [pp. 88–96]).

prison. Most of the youth and party leaders had to work clandestinely, "illegally," because they were being sought for questioning. But this was merely a matter of avoiding the rigors of French justice, which, all things considered, were not too awesome, at least in the civil courts; the military courts were reputedly more severe. It did not matter too much whether the accused gave themselves up or yielded to arrest; they could still pursue their political activities in the Santé prison under relatively comfortable conditions. In the autumn of 1927 Pierre Sémard, together with members of the political bureau—all of them under sentence for having plotted against the security of the state—called a conference in his cell. Present too were Jules Humbert-Droz, a delegate of the Komintern, and his assistant, the Argentinian Codovilla, secretary of that Communist party and a member of its executive committee.

A few days later, in the Santé prison, the secretary of the Communist Youth Federation conferred for an entire weekend with seventy departmental and regional delegates of his organization.

After 1940 the situation changed. The entire organization had to go underground. A single imprudent act could cost the lives of many people. We know that in general, or at any rate from 1942 on, clandestinity proved to be successful. Experience in the international communist movement, the habit of discipline and isolation, the meticulousness and élan that were traditionally a part of the organization—all these were among the contributory factors.

Clandestinity is a complex psychological experience and probably a traumatizing one insofar as it leaves an almost indelible imprint on the individual's behavior.

One must, of course, make allowances for its more

romantic aspects. A reading of the Communist Manifesto generally turns out to be a rather interesting pastime; but it is even more exciting, using a copy that will be handed on the next week to some other group, to read it aloud to a circle of comrades seated around a fire in the woods. However, one soon wearies of the romantic element. What remains is the tedium of imperative orders concerning security measures that can be summed up in one sentence: never allow yourself to be so pressed that you do not give yourself ample time to plan each separate stage of the undertaking.

The boredom that results from such a measured pace is nonetheless tempered by an inventive, ingenious spirit. And it is just such a spirit that finds infinitely varied means of establishing contact, arranging meetings, coming to someone's rescue, organizing an impromptu conference, moving from place to place, or transmitting important messages.

Naturally, there are some who can live peacefully while remaining underground. For such people, clandestinity is a way of life that they have no urge to romanticize; they simply adjust themselves to it whenever necessary, and abandon it when the proper time comes to do so. The international Komintern functionaries have for so long been accustomed to remaining underground and then surfacing that they tend to take these alternating circumstances for granted; or perhaps their prosaic attitude may be attributed to the fact that their initiation occurred so long ago that they have ceased to be mindful of it.

In most cases, however, clandestinity is a fearsome experience, one that can easily lead to schizophrenia. Upon a person's real identity, which involves a certain kind of behavior and a whole set of social relationships (family, neighborhood, occupational, cultural), there is superimposed an imaginary identity no less concretely experienced and also involving a certain type of behavior and social relationships. The latter may be imaginary at first, but they become increasingly real if the undertaking is properly executed. Paradoxically, if clandestinity should suddenly impoverish an individual by stripping him of the social identity with which his earlier life had endowed him but which he himself had not chosen—his name, his place and date of birth, his nationality, the re-religion he was born into—then he finds himself mar-velously naked, a *tabula rasa*; he is free, incredibly free to choose his own identity, and his choice is, of course, a form of self-expression.

This freedom, which the underground communist often uses in a strangely polemical and accusatory manner toward his own person, is so intensely intoxicating that often he finds it impossible to resume his former identity and status. And so he retains, together with his "war alias," an artificial social status. Stated in more general terms, revolutionary onomastics is a very curious auxili-ary science, indispensable for a psychological understand-ing of the international communist movement; at the same time, however, it does come up against some indecipher-able enigmas.

Initiation into the techniques of partisan warfare was another characteristic feature of the life of an active com-munist during the period of the Resistance, and it too involved a recognizable kind of distortion somewhat simi-lar to the one experienced by the volunteers of the Inter-national Brigade during the Spanish Civil War. Such distortion explains in part the often tragic and more often unfortunate fate of this group of heroes.

Partisan warfare was an altogether new experience in France at that time. Some of the problems that came with

it were rather happily resolved, all things considered: the
separation of the civil and military apparatuses; the maintenance of civilian primacy over the military; the exchange of services between the two, with the civilians
providing recruits for the military, and the military fur-
nishing personnel to assist the civilians, thereby enabling
them to pursue interventionist and diversionary policies;[22]
and finally, the establishment of objectives, with the military goals determined by the political. (It was at this time
that the party, which until then had struck deep roots only
in certain regions, became truly national—at least in
terms of its size.)

But in spite of all the precautions taken to preserve the
primacy of the political over the military, it proved impossible to prevent the preferential recruitment (on an
individual basis) of the "athletes," the name which underground slang gave to the members of the FTP, and consequently a specific type of militant and communist cadre.
For them, the introduction of the military into politics
was not regarded in quite the same way as the "pure politicos" viewed it. Nothing was to be done that did not
affect at a given moment that solidarity and superiority
within the communist community that compel "the weapons of criticism to yield to the criticism of weapons."[23]

22. According to a communiqué from the political bureau,
l'Humanité, October 4, 1952, p. 6, from 1941 to 1944 the French
Communist party gave "10% of the party's troops and cadres"
to the Francs Tireurs and Partisans. (The Francs Tireurs
and Partisans—the FTP—were guerilla partisans.—TRANS.)

23. In Lecoeur, *Le Partisan*, pp. 197–205, one reads with great
interest the curious pages devoted to an exchange of reports
immediately after the liberation of Paris, between Duclos, who
then represented the highest body of the party, and Charles
Tillon, president of the National Military Committee of the
Francs Tireurs and Partisans. In 1952, at the time of the Marty-
Tillon affair, Léon Mauvais, charged with preparing the indict-

I must make one last and probably fundamental observation: short-lived, decimated, forever marked, the generation of the Resistance perhaps still remains first and foremost the victim of a misunderstanding. Was it a generation that had been duped?

The participation of French Communists in the national war of liberation was, in theory, the corollary of a global analysis based on the crucial fact that the Soviet Union, the heart and the bulwark of the international communist movement, found itself involved, owing to the German attack, on the side of the Allies. But this fundamental fact was counterbalanced by secondary justifications that stressed patriotic reasons for the antifascist struggle. The young men who had clambered aboard the communist train after it began to move were aware only of these secondary considerations. In their eyes, the national objectives of the communist resistance appeared to express quite naturally and faithfully the very essence of communism. From then on, so far as they were concerned, communism represented a modern version of traditional patriotism in its purest and most resolute form. Understandably, therefore, among the lower echelons of the party and in accordance with the explanations that had been given to them, the keen competition between communists and Gaullists within the Resistance was interpreted in terms of the national interest.[24] These lower echelons

ment, maintained that after August 10, 1944, Tillon deliberately "cut himself off from the leadership of the party" (*Cahiers du communisme*, October 1952, p. 1042). Tillon vigorously denied this but Lecoeur believes that he "was furious because he thought that the Francs Tireurs and Partisans, not the party, should issue the call for insurrection."

24. It is interesting to note that Lecoeur maintains that this was the only concern of the party leaders at the time, whereas Tillon claims that he himself was fundamentally anti-Gaullist

were told that the communists, because they were the most sincere of patriots, must counter the shilly-shallying of the more tepid, of those who were paralyzed by sordid calculations or concerns about class solidarity. This was the kind of reasoning that served morally to justify the otherwise surprising fact that "undercover" communists were willing to join or become part of the Gaullist Resistance, regardless of their own political affiliation; surprising, too, was the fact that men who were already in the Gaullist movement when they joined the party proved willing nonetheless to continue to fight in the Resistance.

Even more thoughtful men, who viewed patriotic objectives from the perspective dictated by circumstances and permanent class goals, managed to appease their consciences. In addition to the fact that France was traditionally "the country of the Revolution"—1792 and the Commune, that's us—it was inconceivable to them that there could be any conflict between the *true* interests of France and the aims of the socialist revolution.

The academic issue of the relations between class and nation is of no importance here. What is important is the fact that an entire generation was shaped by a process of thought in which national independence was assimilated and identified with, reduced or increased by, the magnitude of the class struggle.

Doubtless, in spite of everything, national values should have been properly weighed in order to equate them with class values. But the operation at best is a delicate one, and the conclusions reached are unreliable because they are based on uncertain principles. In practice, this weighing of values is rather arbitrary because the authorities

---

from the outset. Cf. Lecoeur, *Le Partisan*, p. 197 ff, and Tillon, *Les FTP* (Paris: Julliard, 1962), p. 588.

who in the last analysis sit in judgment confuse their judgments with their personal leanings. Any assessment of values also tends to generate "opportunistic" or "sectarian" excesses. Implicitly and secondarily, such an assessment is based on class criteria. But since class criteria had to become more flexible in order to respond to the tactical necessities of various patriotic alliances, they were unimaginatively interpreted in terms of humanistic and progressivist values. There are, of course, popular figures who are children of the people. Consequently, I'll accept them. But what about Joan of Arc? Yes or no? She was a shepherdess (well, maybe) but she was also a saint (a recent one, to be sure, but just the same, the church does have priority).

Be that as it may, once values have been weighed in this way, the national values that have been retained can be converted directly into class values. This process was bound to be pounced upon, and for good reason, when, circumstances having changed, one had to resort to the one reliable criterion that was based on the internal logic of the communist movement: the interests of the international socialist revolution as defined at the historic moment of October, 1917, and embodied in the Soviet Union.

This explains why people who, for patriotic reasons, embraced communism directly after the outbreak of World War II, experienced the same disappointment as those who came to communism at the beginning of World War I because of their love of peace.

Moreover, during the black interlude from 1941 to 1944, a misunderstanding of communist dogma was to have an adverse effect on the party's ability to find new converts. Here we touch on a sensitive point.

Everybody knows François Mauriac's famous remark: "The working-class masses alone remained faithful to a

desecrated France." Unquestionably, from the very outset, the Vichy regime seemed to be the most reactionary
regime France had had in a long time. This fact remained
incontrovertible despite the propaganda efforts of certain
trade unionists and socialists who thought they could, by
operating from the inside, exploit for their own purposes
the aspirations for change toward which the "national
revolution" appeared to incline. The workers, who at first
did not understand that this was a foreign government,
did realize that it was a government that was foreign to
them. This initial gulf could but widen during the four
years of occupation.

It is likewise incontrovertible that important groups,
such as the railway workers or postal employees, fur-
nished excellent fighters and performed magnificent acts
of resistance and sabotage. As for the premature strike of
the Pas-de-Calais miners in 1941, it was a very complex
and terribly ambiguous affair. But probably Auguste
Lecoeur was right in contending that even though the
strike was called because of urgent and material dissatis-
factions—excessive work loads, insufficient supplies, especially of butter, meat, and soap—it nonetheless could not
fail to express the deep hostility of the mining population
toward the new German boss.[25]

25. Nothing shows up the initial ambiguity of this strike
better than the following quotations cited by Auguste Lecoeur
(*Le Partisan*, p. 17). *L'Humanité*, no. 118, June 20, 1941, wrote:
"All of you miners who have fought side by side should remain
united and tell yourselves that our common salvation is not to
be found in the triumph of one sort of imperialism over another;
it is up to us, the people of France, to save ourselves by uniting
and waging a joint struggle. The battle of the miners of the Nord
and the Pas-de-Calais heralds fresh demands and struggles;
from now on, everywhere, the workers must not allow themselves
to be stymied by the Vichy government's scandalously inadequate
measures. They must unite in the trade unions and fight together

Having conceded all this, it is nonetheless true that by and large the factories were still operating, though more slowly and unevenly. But the requirements of the clandestine struggle necessitated the severance of all ties with the legal, economic, and social life of the country. For the former hierarchy of cells, sections, and federations— where, as we have seen, the network of factory cells helped to insure the recruitment of new personnel, mainly workers—a new type of organization, based on "groups of three," was substituted. Despite all the recommended precautions, many people were caught. This unfortunately meant that the young communist could continue the fight only by "disappearing completely in the fog." He ceased living a double life, one legal, the other illegal, and went underground where all his ties—family, social, occupational—were cut. This break created no additional problems for those who had already been deprived of these ties, or were threatened with the early loss of them because the Occupation authorities so willed it. These categories included people who already were partially cut off from the world of the living: Jews, political refugees from countries under Nazi domination. Here is to be found an explanation of the tremendous role played by the MOI in the communist Resistance.[26] Here too is to be found an

---

for higher wages and all their other demands." The tone of the *Avant-Garde*, an organ of the *Jeunesses communistes* (Ed. du Pas-de-Calais) was quite different: "The occupier can see what the young workers and the laboring masses of the 'Kollaboration' he would like to impose on us are thinking. Let it be understood once and for all: our youth will never accept national oppression, and, on the question of independence for our country, there is but a single sentiment in the ranks of the young people: to be rid of foreign domination as quickly as possible."

26. The MOI was a "parallel organization" controlled by the French Communist party. For reasons of political and police

explanation of why the communist generation of the Resistance was socially marginal, as was the whole of the
organized Resistance.[27] This was especially true of those

---

security, it was linked to the party only at the very top. In a
single city there might be several communist cells, some of
which were linked to the regular hierarchy and others to the
hierarchy of the MOI language groups. The Jewish, Spanish,
Polish, and Italian groups were particularly active. Cf. The
testimony of Arthur London, until his arrest a member of the
national administration of the MOI, in Henri Noguères, *Histoire de la Résistance en France, juin 1940, juin 1941* (Paris:
Laffont, 1967), pp. 87–91. See also, David Knout, *Contribution à
l'histoire de la résistance juive en France, 1940–1941* (Paris:
Ed. du Centre, 1947); David Diamant, *Héros juifs de la Résistance française* (Paris: Ed. Renouveau, 1962); Gaston
Laroche (Boris Matline), *On les nommait des étrangers* (Paris:
Ed. sociales, 1965).

27. This explains in particular the considerable and important place held by intellectuals in such movements as the communist Resistance. On the one hand the primacy of the national
theme caused the intellectuals to share all the motivations
(which was precisely what made them intellectuals), not only
the political and social motivations, but the cultural and ideological ones as well. On the other hand, the specific form of the
struggle, which was clandestine, spurred the intellectuals to
join, just as, for example, it spurred their predecessors onward
in the pre-1914 Russian social democratic workers' party. Nevertheless, their participation in the economic and social life of the
country was often negligible and spasmodic. See R. Josse, "La
naissance de la Résistance à Paris," *Revue d'histoire de la
Deuxième Guerre mondiale* (July 1962); David Caute, *Le Communisme et les Intellectuels français, 1914–1966* (Paris: Gallimard, 1967), pp. 174–90. On the other hand, the relative decrease
in the working-class component of the party at the time can be
verified by contrasting the organizational structures of 1937 and
1945. In 1937, the company cells—3,750 of them—constituted
30 percent of the total number of cells (12,495) whereas in
1945 they constituted no more than 20 percent (3,416 out of
16,925). In terms of absolute figures, the number of company
cells *decreased* from 1937 to 1945 whereas the number of local
cells *increased* by more than a third—from 8,759 to 13,509.

who came to the party in 1942–43 (during the weeks and even the months that preceded the Liberation, the entire scene changed).

Little wonder then that the communist generation of the Resistance was quite often bewildered when the party commenced to check the social makeup of its various organs after calm had been restored. It began to rid itself of the militants who had doubtless covered themselves with glory but were now considered socially nonrepresentative. Instead, the party chose the neophytes who had little to boast about as resisters but who had the advantage of a positive social indoctrination. At least, by justifying its action in this way, the party was able to persuade those involved to allow themselves—some even wished it —to be suppressed, pushed into the background, put on half-pay or turned out to pasture.

6 | The Plurality of Militant Party Practices

The analysis of communist society in terms of classical sociological criteria—age groups, sex, socio-occupational status—has already brought to light an initial network of relations embracing the party community which, viewed from the outside, has the enigmatic appearance of an entirely smooth surface. Once the notion of generations was introduced, the picture acquired a perspective of sorts, a dimension in depth. One had to note the coexistence of groups previously involved in different historic events and bearing the very different imprints left by these experiences. We must now define a third mode of structuralization based on the plurality of party practices.

Everybody is familiar with Picasso's famous saying: "I was drawn to communism as one is drawn to a fountain." To understand the diverse types of members that encounter one another in the party it is necessary to ascertain how they came to communism. It is even more necessary to find out why they stayed there.

A Small Sun
In principle, the notion that a communist is *responsible* not only for himself but for others means that he must conduct himself like a small sun. He must shed light, exude warmth, and even hold in his orbit a ring of satellites: his neighbors, his comrades in work and in play,

and, in a general way, his companions in misery and hope. Therefore, and in order to discharge these functions, each party member, under the supervision of the cell to which he belongs, must "fulfill a task" in an association, organization, or movement that obliges him to cooperate with noncommunists. In this way he becomes "responsible" in the eyes of the party, even though the task may be a modest one. Not only is he responsible for the performance of his own duties; he is also responsible for the entire association of which henceforward he will be a member. His membership in the association is due not to any initiative of his own but rather to the wishes of the party which orders him to join it.

But in actuality things are far more subtle.

The status of membership in the Communist party is not something into which one is born, like being a woman or a hunchback or a fish. One *becomes* a communist.

At least this is true in most cases. Then there is the second generation of sons born and raised in the closed world of the apparatus, of tradition. They are the heirs and they are often unhappy, as heirs are wont to be—to wit, the unfortunate Svetlana. A very interesting study would be one entitled: "The Sons of Communists. Respectful, Rebellious, Cynical, or Indifferent."

As for the others, the men who became communists as adults, they are often an embarrassment to the party as the purveyors of false ideas, of superannuated beliefs and twisted prejudices. On the other hand, they are not mere empty shells stuffed with Marxism. They come to this new life with complex social backgrounds and diversified interests. They are the athletes, photographers, fishermen, public school parents, apartment-dwellers in a housing complex, travelers, stamp collectors, music-lovers, nature-lovers; they are the people who each year buy season tickets for all the performances at the TNP (*Théâtre National Populaire*).

The party is not apt to regard their various hobbies or cultural leanings—the remains of a "former existence"— as private matters that do not concern them. It is careful, however, not to censure in advance each and every one of these activities as being inconsistent with the duties of a good militant.

Probably under the pressure of seemingly objective considerations, the most urgent of which is the time factor, a selection is made that is more or less spontaneous, more or less deliberate. Those who seem to be full of idle curiosity, or whose behavior appears futile or unworthy, are dropped. We will return to this question of "individual reform" and practical reorganization because of and by itself it represents one of the criteria for differentiation within the world of the militants.[1]

For the moment it is important to note that the party is less inclined to forbid a certain mode of existence, to prohibit or encourage a particular way of living, than to give a new dimension to whatever form an individual's life may take.

This has its consequences.

On an individual basis, activities that were once discontinuous and fragmented, that had no meaning save a literal one, now tend to acquire an overall purpose. The very fact of belonging to the communist movement confers additional justification, significance, and dignity upon the most prosaic acts, thus in a way sanctifying them, and gives an individual that sense of fulfillment and harmony that accompanies any life devoted to a cause.

At this point we can perhaps guess the next step: how

1. See chapter 7.

the religious spirit dons the cast-off clothing of the rationalist, the better to fool the latter's world; how communism (to use psychoanalytic terminology), relies on some of those sublimated passions that enable the neurotic to compensate and become adjusted—in short, on a form of therapy; and finally, how in a world distracted by the death of God, the twentieth century can quickly reconstitute other opiates and other prisons for people. This next step is an altogether sensible one. But no one is entitled to cast the first stone since this is a century dedicated to happiness, not to truth.

Can this be one of the reasons that explains in depth the curious consonance between the times in which we are living and communism? Communists believe in happiness. While their merit is to believe in it for others, their reward is to attain it for themselves. They look upon happiness as the first goal on their general agenda; it even takes precedence over liberty.

"The French Communist party was founded to enable the working class to create the [necessary] conditions for the happiness and liberty of all men."[2]

In their modest way the communists even cultivate the pursuit of future happiness, as we can see by reading an account of a festival at Vincennes in honor of *l'Humanité*:

> Each of us shares a certain conception of the future, a certain taste for freedom and a desire for peace—in fact, we all share a certain conception of happiness. . . . If the sound of laughter, of songs, dances, and music resounds in Vincennes, it is because we are all happy to be here, at this festival celebrating what we are

2. The preamble to the new statutes adopted at the Seventeenth Congress of the French Communist Party, Paris, May 14–17, 1964. For a complete text see the special number of *Cahiers du communisme*, June-July, 1964, pp. 484–97.

fighting for: here, amid the marvelous gaiety
of the people, a gaiety that is now mocking,
now tender, amid a joy that can also turn serious.[3]

Are we dismayed by this bathos? It is certainly hard
to take. But one would have to be very hardhearted indeed, or very sure of oneself, to frown upon this spectacle
of people enjoying themselves. That is, unless one has the
strength to tell them, at one's own risk, that the slogan of
happiness is the most nauseating, miserable, and sterile
of all the mottoes ever whispered into the ears of men.

A Party-Society

The party, then, is pleased when those who join it are already involved in many other activities. It knows it can
provide an additional element of self-fulfillment; but it is
even more pleased because of its conception of its own
nature, of the relationship between the political and the
social, and because it possesses various channels through
which its influence can flow.

The Communist party is not in fact a party like other
parties. This slogan, which pleases the party's stalwarts,
can be interpreted variously. In the last analysis, it con-
veys the overriding fact that the party's place is fixed
outside of established society. Given its nature, the party
tends to reach beyond the strictly political domain of
traditional majority or opposition groups. It keeps its
distance from other parties whose purely political theories
it challenges. It also keeps its distance from a society
whose very foundations it calls into question. In short, it is
of and by itself a party-society, a party that is also a social
model. The party, to make this model plausible and viable,

3. Martine Monod, *l'Humanité*, September 11, 1967.

is not content merely to describe it in speeches or to make promises about it. The party itself represents the first blueprint of the model, the initial version, thanks to its internal apparatus, its mechanisms and procedures. This explains why so many typical features of Soviet society are also to be found in the French party.

This kind of a party-society is not in keeping with the Leninist school of thought. Rather, it was elaborated and perfected by the German Social Democrats around the turn of the century.[4] Lenin took it up, thereby demonstrating that he himself was the product of that period, the offspring of the world of the Second International. He also, however, underscored all the things that made the German experience precarious. As a socio-political power, eluding as it did the very goals of its creators, German Social Democracy soon ceased to be a force working for the destruction of the Wilhelminian society. Instead, it contributed to the further structuralization of that society. By succeeding almost miraculously in swallowing up Social Democracy, by attaining an ever greater complexity and subtlety, bourgeois society was able to consolidate itself. This reversal of direction, this successful process of integration, must in the last analysis be ascribed to the capacity of capitalism to adapt itself to changes while they are taking place.

In an effort to avert this kind of backsliding, Lenin emended the concept of the party-society by refining it. He retained of course the idea of autonomy, maintaining

4. Cf. J. P. Nettl, *The German social democratic party (1890–1914) as a political model*, "Past and Present" (April 1965), pp. 65–95. See also, A. Kriegel, "La Social-démocratie allemande et la IIe Internationale; le Parti-modèle," in *Le Pain et les Roses* (Paris: PUF, 1968).

that the party must remain radically separate from all the other elements or organs of modern society. Its place must be fixed at a maximum distance from the center of society. In addition, Lenin stressed the offensive dynamism which the party-society must show, pointing out as he did so that those ties with global society which cannot in any case be severed must be utilized for the purpose of enhancing the party's capacity to infiltrate society rather than to remove itself altogether from it. Thus oriented, the party would be protected from the kind of degeneration that overtook German Social Democracy. The cohesiveness of the enemy, not that of the party, would then be threatened.

The party must breathe life into the organizations which it has created, which can take care of the material needs and cultural aspirations of its members and also provide them and their families with the necessary forms of diversion. The list of these organizations is long and comprises a wide variety of interests. The existence of such organizations gives the communists and their kin the comforting sense of being integrated into a virtual microsociety already endowed with all the mechanisms and advantages of a society on the move, yet one which prefigures the socialist society of the future.

A party-society designed to break up and tear down the establishment's institutions? Such a party cannot curl itself up into a ball and remain in elusive darkness forever, although it certainly knows how to do just that in moments of danger. The party has to be flexible, capable if need be of joining and entering established society. Hence the need to dispose freely of its members, to send its militants on "missions" or find missions for them within organizations that do not belong, at least for the time being, to the apparatus of the future society. Hence too the need to recruit from the outside, from "alien fields," fighters who can play at being boy scouts or snipers.

Here lies the root of the practice known as "infiltration," which has caused so much ink to flow.

In order to judge it, one must naturally call attention to a problem that springs from it but that is not organically linked to it. Not content to recruit members from the outside, the party also requires them not to reveal and even to deny their affiliation—they must go underground.[5]

Justifications for this practice abound. Its defenders claim that infiltration is resorted to when society forces clandestinity upon communists who are operating outside the law through no fault of their own. The practice is one way to counter repression. The defenders of infiltration likewise claim that it is employed—the terms they use in this connection are quite revealing—exclusively within the framework of class warfare. Thus, even if clandestinity is not a *political* necessity, it is a *social* one. During the thirties any worker who disclosed his communist affiliation would not have lasted long in a factory job. There is, therefore, something wrong when certain people, failing to take into account the real conditions of class warfare, feign indignation over the advice given by Lenin: "One must be willing to make any sacrifice, to use any strategy if need be, resort to ruse and clandestinity, to conceal the truth."

Actually, this Jesuitical attitude is a divided one. While it is true that the undercover agent at first tries to conceal the fact that he is a communist from the enemy—the bourgeois state, the employer—it is also true that eventually he must also conceal this fact from friends, allies, teammates associated with him in combat. As a result, many people feel they have been taken in and regard the

5. See above, chapter 4.

entire procedure as morally questionable, especially because in the end it enables the communist to take over the
controls, to the detriment of his partners.

It is a mistake to believe that the practice of infiltration
is part of the underground activity, or to attribute to the
latter the success of the former.

The practice of setting up "communist nuclei"—such is
the official term, used in Article 9 which defines the conditions for admission to membership in the Third International—is a thoroughly effective one. The general
object here is to prevent communists from becoming enclosed within their own small group and being swallowed
up by the society around it.

The capacity to acquire new positions is not the result
of the wiles communists use to deceive their partisans; it
stems from the nature of the relations that are inevitably
established within any organization where communists
and noncommunists coexist. These relations are not the
kind that one individual has with another, as man to man.
Instead, they are the relations that develop between a collective power and an isolated individual.

This type of relationship is not wholly advantageous to
the militant communist. A man alone represents only himself; this leaves him a useful margin of autonomy.

The strength of the militant communist lies in the
knowledge—and his interlocutor should have this knowledge, too—that he has at his command a formidable reserve of forces, the entire party, the working class, the
Soviet Union, the international communist movement—
a reserve of advice, men, and money.

The outcome of this kind of confrontation is never in
doubt. One even wonders why there are still men who
willingly lend themselves to such confrontation. The answer is simple: the situation is devoid of ambiguity. A
man wants this kind of relationship or none at all. The

dilemma could be solved only if it were possible to confront the communist party with another organization of the same ilk. But that is a pipe dream: such an organization cannot be artifically created; rather it springs into being in response to a specific situation and becomes a party which, although outside of and in conflict with established society, nevertheless extends its jurisdiction over the entire human sphere.

Two Types of Militant Practices

In practice, thanks to some sort of division of labor, we can ultimately distinguish two types of militants. The first category comprises those who devote themselves exclusively to the affairs of the party. In the second are all those who are active outside the party, who work in and through the "mass organizations"—associations of various kinds where communists are likely to meet noncommunists.

The distinction between the two types is meaningless from a doctrinaire point of view because in theory all communists participate equally in the life of the party. The members of the first group, although quite sophisticated about this, are nevertheless often reminded that they must go forth, breathe the air outside, and "assume duties" within the mass organizations. The members of the second group are from time to time commanded to breathe the maternal air by coming home and paying regular visits to their party organizations.

The difference between the two types is not hierarchical. The "party militant" does not necessarily have more political authority than his comrade in a mass organization if the levels of responsibility are similar. Both are closely associated at every level whenever and wherever decisions are made.

The difference is functional, but nevertheless enormous.

Whereas the "party man" is the personification of legality, permanence, principle, the communist assigned to a mass organization is always called upon to play the role of prophet, to take refuge in whatever circumstances happen to prevail, and to stress the realities. The party man tends to think in abstract terms. He is weighed down by his penchant for speculative thought; his major trait is his capacity for synthesis. His task obligates him to direct a complex apparatus whose various aspects he knows only by hearsay. His role may be likened to that of a chess player manipulating pawns, planning where and how to employ them. The communist assigned to a mass organization is riveted to concrete matters. He runs the risk of being suffocated by a mass of technical details. What saves him is his ability to analyze reality shrewdly. In effect, he lives in the midst of endless dialectics. As the party's representative to all those "others" with whom he is associated, he must make sure that the party takes due account of their interests, concerns, and aspirations.

In other words, the party man has a broader horizon, yet he can also be more rigid, violent, and abrupt. For him there is perhaps a greater opening to the external world, but he can also become lost in the clouds (or in files stuffed with resolutions). For want of any genuine contact with the everyday, concrete realities around him, he can easily become a dried up human being. In other words, the militant in a mass organization is often more flexible, more attentive and sensitive to his surroundings, less doctrinaire.

But we must not attach too much importance to relatively secondary psychological traits. For example, during the years that followed the Twentieth Congress of the Communist party of the Soviet Union, some people persuaded themselves that Benoît Frachon, together with

Thorez, might possibly penetrate the thick fog of French Stalinism and clear the way for a "return to Leninism"—to use the liberal formulation of the phrase. Frachon's silences, his prudence, were falsely interpreted as indications of his basic political position, whereas his outward behavior was really due to the constraints placed upon him as head of the trade union movement. This being so, his conduct was considered to be fully justified.

Setting aside these very tenuous psychological interpretations, the fact remains that communists who work in mass organizations must cope with the difficult problem of determining the proper propaganda dosage. The dialectical movement alluded to above, although in theory interminable, actually slowed down and became stabilized. The man at the center of any such movement will eventually have to decide on the kind of role he will play: he either elects to serve as the party's delegate "to the outside world," to be "on mission," or he sees himself as the representative of his organization and of the members who have placed their confidence in him, regardless of their political affiliation. The fact of being a communist may grow blurred, even in his own eyes. To avoid this, and also to prevent the emergence of vested interests or the creation of lobbies and strongholds, the party periodically gives new assignments to those of its militants who are operating in mass organizations.

Communists in the Unions

Our analysis would be overly abstract and psychological were we to equate, under the heading of "mass organizations," purely minor associations and a spearheading organization the size of the CGT.

The party naturally sees to it that its trade union members are organized. Although one might assume that such vigilance is superfluous, this is not at all true. "Out of 96,733 trade union comrades eligible for CGT membership, 23,177, or 24 percent, are not members."[6]

But the problem we must now tackle is altogether different. It concerns the uniqueness of the kind of militant who is active in a trade union, a uniqueness arising from the complex tradition that molded and motivated him.

In the beginning, two radically different traditions clashed.[7] One of these, the tradition of French revolutionary syndicalism, holds that syndicalism as such suffices in all matters. It propels the working class toward social revolution and the establishment of a classless society in which the syndicate would be the basic unit. The second of these is the tradition of Russian Bolshevism. Among all the Russian socialist currents, it is distinctive for its opposition to the development of an autonomous workers' movement, which it labels an "economist" deviation. The theory of the trade union's subordination to the party, with the latter serving as the sole focal point of the revolutionary movement's thrust and direction, is one of the constants of the Leninist ideology.

Nothing is more equivocal than the dogmatic view that both French syndicalists and Russian communists early took of the nature, significance, and purpose of syndicalism in relation to revolution and socialism.

This basic ambivalence in the domain of dogma was all the more unfortunate because only a fraction of the French trade union movement during the years immediately after the October Revolution turned toward Bolshevism. This fraction, however, provided a framework for the initiation of the communist movement in France.

6. M. Servin, Report to the Thirteenth Congress (1954).
7. For a more ample treatment, see, A. Kriegel, *Aux origines*, vol. 1, the conclusions in the second part, pp. 522–47; vol. 2, part 3, section II-B, pp. 725–54 (with bibliography).

At the same time, the members of the group remained entirely convinced of the rightness of their own ideas about syndicalist affairs. To be sure, they viewed the October Revolution as a purely *soviet* phenomenon, but they also saw in the soviet itself a Russian version of the French syndicate. In their eyes, the soviet, like the syndicate, was an organization representing the sole revolutionary front for the proletarian masses. In addition, it was to be the basic unit of production in any postrevolutionary society.[8]

In 1919, when a strong International Federation of Trade Unions was reconstituted at Amsterdam, the Bolsheviks decided that it would be impossible to destroy the high regard which the Western proletariat had for traditional trade unionism. They were therefore willing to seek a compromise which, while not contradicting the Bolshevik theory regarding the subordination of the trade unions, would preserve the special nature of European trade unionism sufficiently to permit left wingers to lend at least a measure of dynamism to the international communist movement.

The compromise resulted at the international level in the creation of a Red International Trade Union (better known as *Profintern*). Although affiliated with the Communist International, it nevertheless retained a separate identity, or, to use the Leninist terminology, it led an "independent" existence. Thus, any trade union that wished to be identified with the October Revolution had only to recognize officially one trade union organism.

In renouncing any direct affiliation with the revolutionary trade unions of the Communist International, the Bolsheviks hoped, however, that they were making a mere temporary and practical concession to what they

8. Ibid., vol. 1, part 1, section III, chapters 5 and 6, pp. 282–347.

called the prejudices and vestigial survivals of the French
workers' movement. They insisted in theory on such basic
theses as the priority and superiority of the party vis-à-
vis the trade union—the legitimacy of the party's recognized power to lead. They demanded that all orthodox communists devote themselves to making certain
that their ideas prevailed. That is why the ninth and
tenth conditions of the twenty-one laid down by Moscow
for membership in the Third International explicitly stipulated that, in addition to waging "a persistent and systematic propaganda campaign with the trade unions,"
each applying party set up "communist nuclei" which,
"entirely subordinate to the party as a whole," would have
the task of winning the trade unions over to communism.

From the very outset, the compromise appeared to lack
strength. Soon it was further weakened by a discussion
that took place within the Bolshevik party in the autumn
of 1920. The discussion ranged over a number of subjects.
These included ways and means of injecting the Russian
trade union movement into the new Soviet society; how
to halt the spread of a critical attitude toward the Soviet
system among those French trade unionists who were
most favorably disposed toward Bolshevism; and lastly,
the presence in the French Communist party of so many
former socialists (the syndicalists had never cared for
the old socialist party) that they constituted the single
largest group in the new party.

All this explains why the Bolsheviks had to wage an
uphill battle within the French party in order to convince
their own partisans that their syndicalist theories were
sound. At the young Communist party's first congress,
which took place at Marseille in December, 1921, the
French delegates protested regulations that would make
them subject to the authority of representatives from the

Communist International in matters of trade union activities:

> The theses on trade-unionist policy drafted by Amédée Dunois were severely criticized by the delegates because their acceptance would impose upon the French branch the key idea of the Komintern: suppression of trade union autonomy and subordination of the trade unions to the party. The majority retained the form but altered the substance of the Komintern's proposal, thus virtually repeating what it had done in regard to the problem of the presidium. The theses on trade unionism were modified in accordance with the criticisms voiced by the majority. Later, when the theses were approved by the congress, the French party's official line was exactly the reverse of what the Komintern had asked for. The Marseille congress proclaimed that the party intended "to respect the right of trade unions to govern and administer themselves without any injunction, tutelage or subordination.[9]

In 1924–25 it proved necessary to eliminate for all practical purposes the communist generation that had issued from revolutionary syndicalism. This had to be done in order to give free rein to the Bolshevik view of the trade unions. For the same reason, the CGTU, the outgrowth of the schism within the CGT, came to include communists as well as revolutionary syndicalists. The ideas of the latter, along with the men associated with them, were gradually eliminated.

From the very start of 1923 the communist tendency had methodically organized itself in the form of "trade union commissions" headed by the party's "central trade

9. *L'Action communiste et la Crise du Parti* (1922), p. 27.

union commission."[10] Very soon it became apparent that this was merely an attempt to adapt to the French climate of opinion the Bolshevik notions about the party's relations with the trade unions.

The attempt was made with great vigor. At its tenth plenary meeting in 1929, the executive committee of the Komintern decided, on the basis of the Manouilski report, that communist members of the trade unions would have to become more combative if they wished to succeed in persuading the entire trade union movement to acknowledge "the party's leadership." In Moscow a text was drafted which the communists were expected to support at the next CGTU congress:

> The Congress [of the CGTU] announces its determination to work in every field in close cooperation with the communist party, *the only proletarian party*, and the only revolutionary party in the class struggle that has, throughout all the battles of this past period, won a place for itself as *the sole avant-garde proletarian leader* of the workers' movement.

But when it came time to present the text to the CGTU congress, the French communists were not too convinced of the urgent need to force the small CGTU unions to capitulate publicly to the party, especially since the rival CGT would be the beneficiary. In addition, they were afraid that the large minority which continued to be loyal to the trade union tradition of independence, would simply refuse to vote for the Moscow text. They therefore decided to add a paragraph that would attenuate the bluntness of the text. It ran as follows:

> The proclamation regarding the leading and acknowledged role [of the party] should not be interpreted as implying a subordinate role

10. See below, chapter 12.

> for the trade union movement or as modifying
> in any way the organic and statutory relations
> between the communist party and the mass
> organizations of the CGTU.

This in no way coincided with the intentions of the
Communist International. It called upon the heads of
the French section of the Komintern to condemn the additional paragraph as a very serious political error.

> Ostensibly designed to dissipate the confu-
> sion that has prevailed within the confederal
> majority, this addendum actually attenuates
> and revises the definition of the party's lead-
> ing role as stated in the original text. In the
> last analysis, it constitutes a concession to the
> minority and to the vacillating members of the
> majority; it must therefore be categorically re-
> jected by the communists.[11]

The fact is that in 1929, during the famous "third
period," the leaders of the Communist International were
not subtle in matters of detail and did not attempt to
smooth the rough edges. Throughout the ensuing years,
without calling into question any of its own basic principles, the party indicated without necessarily announcing
this *urbi et orbi*, that it would be content to acquire the
administrative posts of the trade unions. Pursuing the task
of coordinating the activities of the communist cells in
the various trade unions, the central committee of the
international federation of trade unions succeeded in
doing just that.

In 1936 there was a reunification of the trade unions.[12]
Why was this accomplished so easily whereas all previous

11. *Cahiers du bolchevisme*, January 1930, p. 78.
12. See Antoine Prost, *La CGT à l'époque du Front populaire*
(Paris: Colin, 1964), especially chapter 3. See also, Georges
Lefranc, *Le Mouvement syndical sous la IIIe République* (Paris:
Payot, 1967), especially pp. 374–80.

attempts made during the same period to reunify French
socialism had failed utterly? The reason, it appears, is
to be sought in the fact that the communists themselves,
who were about to try to "colonize"—as their enemies put
it—the reunified trade unions looked upon trade unionism
more or less in a non-Bolshevik fashion.

How could this be?

The schism in the trade union movement, institutional-
ized by the CGT explosion of 1921, was not actually dis-
creditable if trade unionism were equated in the Bolshevik
manner, with a pedagogical course in the communist
education of the revolutionary proletariat. On the other
hand, from the point of view of traditional syndicalism as
defined and practiced in pre-1914 France, the split in the
trade union movement and the destruction of its unity
constituted a negation of its very purpose: the unification
and organization of *the* exploited class—the "producers"
—in opposition to *the* exploiting class.

The reunification of the trade unions definitely demonstrated that, after the unfortunate attempt to introduce
the Bolshevik conception of trade unionism, which was
alien to the French workers' movement, the traditional
and classical concept triumphed.

Doubtless this lesson was obscured and even masked
by a subsequent development. In 1936 the communists
launched an attack on the various levels of command in
the reunified trade union movement. From their earlier
theoretical defeat they were not able to extract extraordinary practical advantages. Actually, the assault was understandable from a purely trade union point of view, inas-
much as traditionally clashing tendencies already existed.
The conflict in any case should have materialized within
the union movement; furthermore, it should have given
expression to a clash that sprang from the soil of trade

unionism, from its very entrails. In reality, however, the battle between warring tendencies, as waged by the communists, was fought between two camps. One represented the vanguard of an army; although it pitched its camp on the battlefield, it actually fought on the outside. Furthermore, the battle was waged with communist techniques, which consisted of seizing power from within, a procedure that has wrought miracles.

The textile, leather, paper, and fur industries were soon added to the six federated trade-union organizations— agriculture, the building industry, chemical products, metals, railways, and glass employees, all of which were dominated by the communists after the reunification. To the seven departmental unions that had had a CGTU majority in 1936—the Alpes-Maritimes, the Gard, the Vaucluse, Isère, the Loire, the Lot, and the Yonne— another twenty-odd unions were added.

After Bolshevization, the Komintern had demanded the creation of a sizable network of permanent, professional revolutionaries. As a consequence, the communists now disposed of a very mobile, diversified reserve of cadres. I am inclined to believe that the party's exceptional technical success in the union battle described above should be ascribed to the existence of these cadres. All in all, the fundamental role played by the communist generation of 1924–34 is here confirmed from a fresh angle.

We must remember that the reunification of the CGT occurred at a time of enormous increase in trade union membership. In September, 1935, the two main trade union federations boasted a combined membership of 785,000. The remarkable new wave of registered members in the early months of 1936, then the "trade union rush" of June, which still continued during the subsequent months although at a slower pace, gave the CGT four million members by early 1937, probably the largest number it had ever had.

Even though this last figure may be called into question, the crucial point nonetheless holds.[13] The former framework was inevitably overwhelmed by the drastic change in the size of the reunified CGT. Under the circumstances, we can understand the ease with which the communists were able to place their men in strategic spots, especially at the level of horizontal trade-union structures (local and departmental trade unions). These men had the advantage over all those who might later emerge from the mass of new unions. They had been trained and hardened; in any case, they could rely on the resources made available to them by the party, resources upon which they drew to meet their new responsibilities.[14]

Because its apparatus had been centralized, and because it had the support of the group of cadres that was responsible for updating the files of all members and keeping track of their assignments, the party administration was able to place the militants wherever they were needed.[15] It could in all haste dispatch men to the most advantageous and essential points. Then it would be up

13. The membership of the CGT by federation, according to the table published in the newspaper *Gringoire* in 1939, came to 4,748,000 in 1936 and 4,988,626 in 1937. For a discussion of these figures, see A. Prost, *La CGT*, p. 196, and G. Lefranc, *Le Mouvement syndical*, pp. 415–16.

14. Georges Lefranc also points out the considerable role played by *La Vie ouvrière*, formerly an organ of the CGTU and thereafter expressing the tendencies of the ex-CGTU. At that time *La Vie ouvrière* printed 100,000 copies. In summarizing his analysis of the communist victory over the trade unions, Georges Lefranc finally wrote: "There was no need for a colonizing plan. All that was needed was the presence of habits of agitation and a discipline that was well assured."

15. See below, chapter 10.

to the organized splinter groups to find the means of imposing their authority. Of course, all this was possible only because of the imperfections of the democratic process in trade union elections—but imperfect democracy is the fate of any organization that experiences a sudden and unexpected spurt.

This is the reason why Pierre Sémard virtually ceased to take any interest in trade union affairs from 1922 to 1934. In the summer of 1921, at the Fourth Congress of French railway workers, he had been elected secretary-general. From 1922 to 1924, after the split in the trade union, he served as secretary-general of the CGTU federation of railway workers. A member of the political bureau and secretary-general of the French Communist party from 1924 to 1929, Sémard, in the wake of the Fourth Congress at St.-Denis, became a member of the central committee; he also directed *l'Humanité* and held the post of secretary-general of the Communist party's Paris region. In November, 1932, he left for Moscow, in compliance with a decision reached at the twelfth plenary meeting of the executive committee of the Komintern. That body wanted him to complete a course in reeducation.[16] Upon his return, the leadership of the French Communist party took further action. He was replaced in the railway workers' trade union federation in order that he might be free to buttress a communist cell. In 1935, as a consequence of the previous year's merger of the two railway workers' federations, Sémard became one of the secretaries of the unified federation.

Another example is the career of Charles Tillon, steel worker and secretary-general of the regional federation of trade unions in Nantes. He was named in quick suc-

16. See below, chapter 12.

cession to head two very distinct trade union federations, one comprising chemical products and the other docks and ports.

But the strangest case is that of Ambroise Croizat, who after the Liberation became Minister of Labor and Social Security. It seems that before becoming a permanent member of the communist youth organization in Lyon, the young Ambroise had done very little work in the steel industry or anywhere else for that matter. He was a very rare person. His natural cordial reserve; his thoughtful simplicity and patient, somewhat melancholy seriousness; the conscientiousness and unselfishness with which he devoted himself to the task at hand—all these have remained vivid memories in the recollections of those who knew him. He was called to Paris in 1926 to assume nationwide responsibility for the social program of the communist youth federation. From this post he was suddenly transferred to the apparatus of the trade unions: in 1928 he replaced Rabaté as head of the steel federation of the CGTU because Rabaté, it seems, had become involved in a sinister bit of espionage and was forced to flee to Moscow to avoid arrest.

However enormous the return on the communist investment in the CGT, whatever the reasons for the profitability of the venture, this is not the most important point I want to make. What matters most is that the communists put everything they had into an effort to win practical advantages rather than to score an ideological victory over the enemy.

One of the clearest illustrations of how the communists conducted themselves is afforded by the way they manipulated the statutes that the Villeurbanne Congress had ratified in January, 1936. Chapter 14 of the statutes adopted in 1925 was entitled Party Cells. Consisting of six very detailed articles, it stipulated:

> In all workers' and peasants' organizations
> and in organs outside the party (trade unions,
> cooperatives, cultural and educational groups,
> athletic and other clubs, veterans' associa-
> tions, factory councils, unemployment organ-
> izations), in congresses and conferences, in
> municipal governments and local councils, in
> parliament, etc., whenever at least two com-
> munists are present, communist cells must be
> organized for the purpose of increasing the in-
> fluence of the party (Art. 49).

Furthermore, Articles 50 and 51 defined the various
ways of tying the cells to the appropriate committees of the
party. Article 52 stated: "The cells, in cooperation with
the appropriate committee of the party, will present candidates for all the important posts within the organization
for which it works."

This crucial chapter implemented the concept of the
party's "leading role" in a practical and concrete way and
stated with precision the various techniques that should
be employed. However, it disappeared altogether when
new statutes were drafted in 1936. This drastic deletion
speaks for itself. It shows that the party had no intention
of altering its basic position in this matter but that to
say so would merely complicate matters by placing a concrete obstacle in the way of the strategy of unification.
What was being done would continue to be done, but there
was no need to announce it.

Should the members of the federation demand, as a
condition for reunification of the trade unions, the acceptance of the principle of trade union independence, then
the CGTU, where the communists made the rules, would
subscribe to it. But such a demand would hit hard at the
thesis that unions must be subordinate to the party, as
well as at the practice of setting up "communist nuclei"
or some other outside organized opposition. The famous

accord of July 24, 1935, proposed to deal that blow. The CGT and CGTU delegations adopted a text that was subsequently inserted into the preamble of the reunified CGT's statutes:

> At every level the trade union movement governs itself and determines its program of activities wholly independently of employers, governments, political parties, philosophical sects, or any other outside groups.

To insure the concrete implementation of this independence, which was acknowledged in theory, the two confederations demanded that the holders of certain trade union posts be forbidden to hold political posts at the same time. The communists did their best to restrict the scope of this inconvenient stipulation. They deliberately interpreted the phrase "political post" to mean solely an *elective* post. This would exclude the holding of seats in parliament or in elective municipal offices, but it would not affect the purely political posts that existed within the internal hierarchy of the French Communist party. This being so, the communists at their Villeurbanne congress in January, 1936, did not object to the election of sixteen trade union leaders as members of the forty-five-strong central committee of the party. But when, a few weeks later, the congress of the reunified CGT at Toulouse explicitly decided that members of the confederal bureau could not belong to "the leading organisms of a political party," the communists acquiesced. With great fanfare, Frachon and Racamond resigned from the political bureau.

The French communists were extremely reluctant to make these concessions. Prior discussions in Moscow designed to obtain the green light had been heated. But now, much to their surprise, the French communists discovered that they could easily dispense with the service of cells. All the defenses dreamed up by the trade union confederations to foil communist penetration proved illusory. The militants in the trade unions were subjected to a more flexible control. This had the effect of interesting the entire party, not just the specialists, in the concerns of the trade unions.

Matters continued in this way. To be sure, the clause prohibiting the simultaneous holding of trade union and political posts was allowed to lapse. Benoît Frachon was reinstalled in the party's political bureau at the Fourteenth Congress in 1956. He probably had never missed a single session since 1936. As for the rest, thanks to the trained cadres at his disposal, the party could take pride in the various administrative techniques with which it had experimented in 1935–36. Members of the party's bureaus and committees were called upon to sit in the union secretariats—openly but discreetly—since the communist secretaries of the departmental trade union federations were members of more important bodies. Trade union affairs were discussed at every level of the party. These included not only general problems of administration but also such concrete matters as the goals, techniques, and tactics of the workers' struggle.

Finally and most important, it was up to the party's organizations to name the candidates for the various trade union posts. Whenever the delegates to union congresses elected militant unionists who were also party members to important positions, those so chosen had to have the party's prior permission. Inversely, communist officials of trade unions were quite often removed from their posts for reasons that had nothing whatsoever to do with their union activities. Thereafter, it was generally understood that whenever the party intervened, the militant's career within the party and his career in the CGT would both be equally respected. Even better, whenever the strength of both groups was roughly equal, the party's organizations would name those noncommunists whom the communists could vote for in union elections. This would eliminate the most resolute adversaries of the party, so that indirectly, as the communist hold grew stronger, the noncommunists named to positions of responsibility in the unions were as completely controlled by the party as were the communists themselves.

The CGT Today

As it exists today, the CGT (and the union movement in general, thanks to the power of the CGT) is the product and center of incredible confusion. It is torn between a desire to maintain the principles inherited from the earlier era of French syndicalism and a yearning to adhere to the rules that govern communist action.

It is this confusion that explains why militant communists in the trade unions are imbued with ideas that are entirely foreign to the purely communist patrimony. This distinguishes them unmistakably from their militant colleagues in the party's apparatus.

It is also this confusion which doubtless is responsible for the curious lag in the adaptation of the trade union movement to the tempo of modern times. The atmosphere of chaos in which it operates and its own rigidity are severe handicaps.

Yet many observers believe that the upheaval the communists have experienced during the last ten years, their increasing uncertainties, can be expected to have special repercussions in a domain as sensitive as trade unionism. The changes in economic structures, in industrial relations, in the social composition of the workers' world—

all these should have made communist militants in the unions more eager than ever (and more so in this field than in any other) to revise outmoded practices and to see to it that the party was persuaded to adopt fresh and untried attitudes. They could have done this by continually raising new questions and by asking them in a manner so technical that they could have been answered only by specialists.

It cannot be said that the latest developments in the trade union confederation confirm these expectations.

The Thirty-Seventh National Congress of the CGT that met at Nanterre from June 12 to 16, 1967, was disappointing. Save for a few superficial details—for example, the delegates' decision to refrain from following the communist custom of throwing confetti on the members of the CGT's new bureau—its actions were entirely patterned after those of preceding congresses. There was the usual interminable report when the meeting opened. It was approved, developed, and vividly illustrated (but not discussed) by first-rate orators, most of whom had been selected in advance. They were chosen either because of the important regional or occupational organization they represented, or because of the repercussions resulting from recent battles waged under their auspices. In addition, certain men were asked to speak because they were slated for promotion to positions of great responsibility; this was a convenient opportunity for them to be heard and seen by all the trade union cadres.

The only surprise was a speech delivered by Benoît Frachon which was mostly devoted to the affairs of the Middle East. It was the last speech he was to give as secretary-general.[17] Was he making his final appeal when he

17. The following is an excerpt from this very curious speech: "They [war correspondents] have shown us—replete with the details that go with a great demonstration of faith—a ceremony

urged not only that the CGT should have no *other* political policy than that of the Communist party but also that it should subscribe to *all* of the party's political policies? Or was he seeking to circumvent any questions or misgivings about the man chosen by the party to succeed him as secretary-general? The party had chosen Georges Séguy. For a while some trade unionists had had other candidates in mind, men who had participated in a broader range of activities but who had the misfortune of being Jews. Whatever Frachon's purpose, his listeners realized with some discomfort that the highest authority in the workers' world had committed himself to an archetypal, virulent brand of antisemitism. Frachon did not even bother to resort to the well known technique of dressing up remarks

---

at the Wailing Wall. Because of the time and the place at which it occurred, amid the dead, in the midst of a struggle that has just ended, it was, to say the least, inappropriate. The presence of certain high financiers conferred upon it a significance that had nothing to do with the religious fervor which the true believers who participated thought to find in it. The spectacle makes us think that, as in *Faust*, it was Satan who led the dance. Nor was the golden calf missing; there it was, just as in the Gounod opera, standing up contemplating its feet, amid the blood and the filth, the results of these diabolical machinations. And indeed, we are told that two representatives of a cosmopolitan tribe of bankers attended this saturnalia, people well known throughout the world: Alain and Edmond de Rothschild. At their feet lay the dead, still bleeding. Among them were Jewish workers, who died for them; Jordanian workers and peasants, who also died for them. In this orgy of turpitude in which the instincts of the primates manifested themselves—a resurgence of the days when, still struggling in darkness, man was at the dawn of consciousness—it is comforting to find men who dare to speak the truth and to stand up courageously to the clamor of unleashed passions" (*l'Humanité*, June 17, 1967). Everything is there, the devil, gold, blood, sex (saturnalia, turpitude), the suspicious solidarity (tribe, primates).

about the current political scene with some expression of interest in the trade union movement.

All in all, the designation of Georges Séguy as secretary-general of the CGT created something of a problem: how and why was this rather commonplace man chosen to occupy a key position? Was Frachon planning, from the shelter of a lesser position, to retain control of the CGT's operations? Or should the appointment be attributed to the manner in which candidates were selected—that is to say, to a form of nepotism? The most striking thing about the new secretary-general was his unbelievable lack of *real experience* inside or outside the party. This indeed was a poor example of what was meant when the relative inexperience of militant communists within the trade union was stressed—communists whose basic loyalty to the party was never in doubt. But when such men became immersed in the world of trade unionism and had to face socioeconomic realities, they tended either to return to their home base or, on the contrary, to become innovators in some field of their own.

Outside the Party? Benoît Frachon, the son of a miner, was eleven years old when he went to work in a factory located in his native town, Chambon-Feugerolles, near Saint-Etienne.[18] At the age of sixteen he participated in a strike for the first time, joined the local trade union, and became a member of a libertarian group.

"When I look at my old books that date from those days," he said, "I find a little of everything except works on scientific socialism."

18. See the memoirs of Benoît Frachon, "Premiers pas d'un militant ouvrier. De l'anarcho-syndicalisme au communisme," *Cahiers de l'Institut Maurice-Thorez*, 5 (April-June, 1967) : 63.

A soldier when war was declared, he was assigned from November, 1914, to January, 1918, to the armaments factory at Guérigny in the Nièvre. This was a navy arsenal where hundreds of specialists were concentrated, among them many trade unionists. Called to active service in January, 1918, he was transferred to the air force and served in it as a mechanic. Whether at the camp at Avord in the Cher or in camps located at Bron, in the Vosges, in Alsace, in the regions of the occupied Rhineland, the various aviation depots where Frachon was stationed proved to be particularly active centers of revolutionary agitation—the term is used here in the broadest sense. Demobilized in August, 1919, the young steelworker settled in Marseille. There he assiduously frequented a group of libertarian trade unionists employed in the building industry. In 1922 he returned to Chambon-Feugerolles where he worked in the steel mills of Firminy. It was not until 1924, after a period of unemployment (he was censured for his refusal to participate in the production of a torpedo), that he became a "functionary" of the Communist party.

By this time, Frachon had almost twenty years of diversified experience behind him—human, occupational, trade-unionist, and political—when, together with the Communist party, he came to the decisive turning point represented by Bolshevization.

There was nothing comparable to this in the life of Georges Séguy. The son of a well-regarded communist railway worker, he belongs to the category of "respectful sons" who embraced the faith of their fathers. To be sure, because of this, he experienced the terrible ordeal of deportation, when he was only seventeen (he was born in Toulouse in 1927). But on the other hand, he has had virtually no occupational experience. He was a typographer who, for reasons of health, had been forced to give up his trade. His father got him into the SCNF (*Société Nationale des Chemins de Fer*, France's national railways). He was not quite twenty-four and had been in the party less than five years when he became a functionary.

Within the Party. Frachon was so devoted to and identified with the trade union movement that we tend to forget that he did not become secretary-general of the CGTU until January, 1933, when he was forty. Furthermore, his devotion to trade unionism was interrupted during the period of the Resistance. At that time, together with Jacques Duclos, he headed the clandestine forces of the French Communist party. Frachon's duties were primarily political in nature. He was the assistant to the mayor of Chambon in 1922. After serving as secretary of the departmental trade union federation from 1924 to 1926, he became the party secretary for the Lyon region. In the spring of 1926 he went as delegate to the plenary meeting of the Komintern's executive committee (this was his first trip to Moscow). In the course of the same year, he was elected to the central committee of the French Communist party. In 1928, as an alternate member of the Komintern's executive committee, he was asked to head the central trade union committee and to join the party's secretariat. These responsibilities were laid aside in 1929 when he spent a stretch in the Santé prison. Vassart replaced him temporarily. Released in May, 1930, Frachon resumed his duties. In the parliamentary elections of March, 1932, he presented himself as a candidate in Aulnay-sous-Bois but was unsuccessful. In the wake of a decision reached at the twelfth plenary meeting of the Komintern's executive committee in September, 1932, he was replaced by Gitton, whereupon he himself replaced Monmousseau as secretary of the CGTU.

These biographical details merely serve as points of comparison. As we shall see, matters were much simpler for Georges Séguy. After being admitted to the secretariat of the railway workers' federation where aging, all-powerful Tournemaine ran things in the manner of his ancestors, Séguy merely attended the party's central school. Thereafter, he advanced without hitch or incident to all the higher echelons of the hierarchy: member of his federation's secretariat in 1949; assistant secretary-general in 1956; secretary-general in 1961 when his immediate superior reached retirement age. Thereupon, like all the secretaries of large federations, he took his place in the CGT's administrative committee. At the same time—this is customary for all communists in charge of important trade union posts—he became a party dignitary: member of the central committee in 1954; alternate member of the political bureau in 1956; reelected as alternate member in 1959 and 1961; titular member of the political bureau since 1964.

This biographical profile raises a serious question. Séguy has always been a communist, but one whose experience was limited to the party apparatus and to a single area. He has all the earmarks of a tranquil functionary operating in a family-type political party in which he spent his childhood and adolescence and finally reached manhood. This being so, is he susceptible, or open, to new ideas?

Moreover, Séguy's experience in the trade union movement has been a very special one. The railway workers' federation is a remarkably structured organization and, like the electrical workers' federation, one of the most prosperous. It is quite capable of teaching the art of administration to potential new leaders. Its basic choices, however, go back to the time following World War I. After the dramatic failure of their 1920 strike, the railway workers have been content to continue a policy laid down somewhat fortuitously during the First World War, save for some very brief, violent, and revolutionary episodes. Thereafter, this traditional policy has been followed by trade unions in all the large plants regulated by statute. It is characterized by a functionalism that has played a definite role in the mechanisms of social relations within each factory. The primary concerns have been such things as the application, protection, improvement, and extension of the regulating statute and its corollaries.

This type of trade unionism, although it does have some merit, cannot facilitate a better understanding of the problems raised in sectors where social relations are formulated in quite a different way. More important, it cannot assist us in understanding how economic life functions, which is something altogether different from the workings of the SCNF.

This is doubtless the reason why Georges Séguy, unless a miracle occurs or he has a revelation, is less likely than any other member of the younger generation of communists active in the CGT to set a new course or to find an answer to the distressing, complicated problems involved in applying the methods of trade unionism to the mechanisms of contemporary society.

Here perhaps is an additional reason for believing that the evolution of communism, presupposing that it does evolve, begins at the center of the system rather than in its peripheral zones. In contrast to what happened in 1936, the unity of the trade union movement runs the risk of encountering the same fate that befell socialist unity. Is this a way of saying that we cannot expect to see communism triumph in the near future?

These pages were written before the events of May, 1968. I do not feel that I should alter them or bring them up to date. In the very complex situation that prevailed during the spring of 1968, Séguy showed that he had correctly assimilated the teachings of traditional communism, of which he is a product. He went through this baptism of fire more than honorably—if judged in terms of the party's criteria. But there still remains the question of his capacity to depart from well-trodden paths in order to meet the unexpected challenges now confronting the world of labor; in these I do not include such things as strikes and the occupation of factories, even on a national scale, because they have become commonplace occurrences.

7 | Degrees of Allegiance

The sociology of religion lists indicators that make it possible to measure the degree of loyalty of the faithful. Similarly, political sociology measures loyalty by participation in various kinds of cultic ceremonies. For communists, attendance at cell meetings corresponds, roughly, to attendance at Mass for Catholics. The average number of evenings devoted each week to militant activity probably constitutes a valid criterion that enables us to distinguish between the "active militant" and the ordinary member. The latter, like the "Easter Catholic," can be distinguished by his participation in two major ceremonies: renewal of his membership card in January of each year and attendance at the annual "Fête de l'Humanité" in September.

This procedure, however, has one drawback: distinctions between members are made solely on the basis of their outward behavior, which is not the most important issue. The real question is how much change for the better each person undergoes as a result of belonging to the communist movement.

Political Allegiance

There is, to be sure, one initial way of being a communist, a way we might call "Cartesian." This applies to every militant who fulfills his political duties rigorously.

To conceive of one's allegiance to communism as an allegiance to a political party, as the choice of one political policy among many, is in no way proof of intellectual honesty or clarity of vision. It merely signifies that certain communists are to be found at the plebeian levels of society, people who have joined the Communist party because it was the most "radical" of the leftist parties, the most "republican" of groups within the republican camp, the legitimate heir of Jacobin radicalism, of Guesdist socialism. Communists south of the Loire, of the red Midi, and especially those who live in the southwest, often belong to this category. This explains why the communist peasants of Corrèze and the Dordogne never felt guilty because they failed to give fervent support to any program for the collectivization of farms, even in the most modest and modern form of agricultural cooperatives. Communists of this kind would be extremely astonished if one deduced from the mere fact of membership that the party had anything to say or even an opinion about all those things in life that have nothing to do with politics. On the other hand, they like "politics" and they are active in it. But, as we shall see, orthodox communists "do not like politics" and are not active in it—I am using the word *politics* here, not in a strict electoral and parliamentary sense but in a far broader one: public affairs, world affairs.

Speculations at the café; political discussions among friends; the concrete "political dimensions" of local or national life, more rarely those of international affairs: these are some of the things that communists of this stripe like to indulge in. They are the sons of an open-air civilization where attendance at the forum is proof of the dignity of free men. Isn't it to such communists that we owe the widespread idea—one that is well founded—that communists have a feeling for the State? Or, to be more precise, a feeling for the City? To be sure, they have substituted the grimmer, more somber word, "comrade," for the plain one, "citizen," with its consciously intended juridical and "political" resonance. But at the very first appeal from a leftist union, full-bodied republican conceptions of discipline and public welfare spring up in their minds.

Existential Allegiance

There is another, broader, less selective, but no less relaxed way of being a communist: an existential way. This applies to those who equate membership in the Communist party with a state of nature—who belong to the party "from birth." Their attitude is not necessarily attributable to the fact that they were born into communist families. Rather, for them the communist option is of a piece with their national, social, occupational, cultural inclinations. Less a political party than a milieu in which one lives, the Communist party is for them the hospitable structure that is in harmony with and attuned to their initial potentialities; allegiance to it is felt to be something logical, rational, *normal*. This explains why, for such persons, membership in the party rarely takes place in the youthful years. Indeed, unless something exceptional should come along to hasten his evolution—a strike, a period of political agitation, occasionally a political campaign—the young worker is in no hurry. To become a militant is somewhat like becoming a father. It means the assumption of new responsibilities, the kind that are natural enough but that also imply that one is growing older. Unlike the student, who often becomes a party member quite young because membership for him means a break with his family, or at least an attempt to break with it, the worker who joins the party because he is seeking a means of self-expression is usually around twenty-four or twenty-five—when he returns from military service. Often he joins the party after a rather long interval during which he acquires the habits of his trade and a measure of occupational competence. The decision to join the party often stems from an internal debate that centers on whether a person should engage in the political struggle or improve his professional skills. He asks himself: should I become a militant or a technician, maybe an engineer?

One cannot ignore the fact that this pattern, while it indicates choices and implies sacrifices, is nonetheless dominated by the idea of conformity. This explains why such militants—the favorite protagonists of proletarian novelists as well as the leaders of cadres—are solid individuals, entirely mature, having totally internalized their options: serene, convinced, deep-rooted, representative. But they are also men threatened with sclerosis; their consciences tend to wane and they feel too much at home in their environments.

Here we touch upon one of the elements that have caused the party to slip away bit by bit from its revolutionary sphere. Many of its militants are extremely "well adjusted," by which we do not mean that they have become bourgeois, an accusation too readily made, but rather that they have accustomed themselves to a party that has become for them a way of life, part of the air they breathe.

Ideological Allegiance

Finally, there is a third way of being a communist, one that might be called ideological. As a general rule, this is the road traveled by students and intellectuals.

It is quite true that we find many intellectuals who

can be classified as belonging to the first of our three categories. These men continue the tradition of the pre-1914 university, of these "flesh and blood socialists": Jacobins, patriots, Freemasons, Cartesians (because they were mechanistic), Kantians (if they had the nerve for it). They scorned a dialectic that a rigorous mind could only condemn; their vision was somewhat narrow; on occasion they were petty, childishly ashamed of human weaknesses whose mysteries offended them, discreetly ambitious but timorous, and ultimately indifferent; not always as naive as they wished to appear, they loved mystification if its object was our Greco-Latin past. All in all, they were scrupulous, erudite, affable; they believed in goodness, progress, justice, work, and truth.

Actually, such intellectuals—professors, physicians, scientists—are quite numerous in the Communist party, and they are highly prized. Care is taken not to trouble them with matters unrelated to their clear conception of the world and to their delicate sensitivity—this last, needless to say, being somewhat arid and devoid of imagination. The party does not bother them, for example, with problems that concern the intelligentsia in the socialist countries. Their penchant for abstraction, their capacity to reduce the complexities of the real and the concrete to notions, essences, blueprints, principles, makes them skeptical and consequently rather easy to handle. In short, never having had to make themselves over in the image of the party, they are quite willing to accept the fact that the party is not necessarily fashioned according to their image. This imperceptible distance between them and the party constitutes that mixture of a little contempt and a good deal of mutual indulgence that makes for good relations.

One even wonders if this type of communist intellectual

may not represent the majority. Discreet, they constitute
the ironic, detached, obliging backbone of the university cells. Yet, no matter how numerous they may be, they
are not really significant; they are interesting relics of a
period that is receding in memory, of the pre-Leninist
period—the "classical" period, all things considered. Besides, they came to the party quite late. Many of them had
for long accommodated themselves to the "old house,"
the SFIO (*Section Française de l'Internationale Ouvrière,*
the French section of the Second International). It wasn't
until the years of the Popular Front, the Resistance, and
the Liberation that they gradually and unobtrusively
adopted the kindred allegiance, not because they had
changed their former rationalist, positivist opinions but,
on the contrary, because they had remained true to themselves.

The communist intellectuals who matter are part of an
entirely different heritage; they are motivated by very
different dynamics, the dynamics of a *spiritual conversion.*

As we have noted, those French intellectuals who were
among the first to be won over to communism during the
twenties came from anarchist and syndicalist-revolution-
ary backgrounds dominated by the influence of Sorel, and
to a lesser extent, by that of Bergson. The small world
of the Romain Rolland intellectuals, united in Switzerland as early as 1914, lent vigor to pacifism by lacing it
with Bolshevism.

Tired of the arguments and the excessive logic of our
scientists, the French intelligentsia of the 1890s was cap-
tivated by anarchism. It was a fire that spread, scorching
the edges and cracks of organized society. Having smol-
dered for a while, it blazed high and clear, with all the
suddenness and gratuitousness of cosmic catastrophes. By

intelligentsia I don't mean intellectuals or professors, those who regard life as a long career in which truth is captured gradually, one point at a time. Nor do I mean the many solid writers and artists who have all the self-assurance that talent bestows. I mean the very young, the marginal people, the lazy, the foolish, the geniuses, the down-and-outers, the dreamers, the restless, those who are incurably ill with an unknown malady, the doctors, the tired heroes, the "outsiders," the "refractory ones," the "black sheep"—these are the sobriquets bestowed upon them by anarchist newspapers—in short, all those who for professional, social, intellectual, or personal reasons are a headache to computer programmers because they are unpredictable, unclassifiable.

What is anarchism? A schism. A negation. A refusal. A radical externalization of the world, of society, of civilization and all established values; the identical stupefying stubbornness that cut libertarian intellectuals off from the trial of the Thirty (1894), from the survivors of the Bonnot gang (1913), the dadaists, the surrealists who appeared after the bloodiest of wars. In the light of this chronology, how is it possible to regard May, 1968, as an incomprehensible aberration?

But to be an anarchist means something more than breaking with established society. It is a more intimate, more demanding kind of rupture: a break with the established self in an established society. The biography of any anarchist contains evidence of such a split, of such a death and resurrection. This kind of conversion represents an alteration of one's entire person. To change life, one must first change one's own life.

To be a communist, according to a certain interpretation of the phrase, involves this same internal wrench, entails this same process of condemnation, expiation, and rebirth. In accordance with German Social Democracy's orthodox interpretation of Marxism, Bolshevism and its offshoots have assumed the absurd and pathetic task of establishing the theoretical foundations of the party, invoking the socialism of the future, declaring right now what is true and promulgating this truth. Hence the perpetually recurring crises that take place in the relations between the Communist party and its intellectuals. By their very existence, and in any case by the nature of their specific activity, the intellectuals belie the contention that the party—the sole precursor of the world to come—is the source of all science. Herein lies the true originality of the communist intellectuals—and the challenge they address to themselves. A communist intellectual is not only a man who "honors" his party, a militant who contributes to the political life of the organization of which he is a member. He is also a man who dares to initiate within himself a complicated experiment. Or at least he could be such a man; everybody does not move at an identical pace along the path, and sometimes people do not move at all. Membership in the party marks the beginning of a long and hazardous process at the end of which, the individual having "placed himself in the position of the working class," according to the traditional formula, a "new type of intellectual" must appear.

It is a fascinating experiment. Whether at the end of the twenties, the thirties, or after World War II, a considerable number of men who were neither completely stupid, completely naive, nor completely perverse (taken as a whole they were for the most part ordinary people, men of good will, professionally qualified), tended to accept a general interpretation of the world which subsequent events proved to be largely fallacious. Fallacious too were the notions they had about the society they were opposing, about the era in which they lived, about the men they trusted. It matters little in this connection that their error bordered in some respect on criminal complicity. The chronicle is a chilling one: the Nizan affair; the Markos affair; the Tito affair; the Rajk, Kostov, and Slanski trials; the David Rousset-Daix trial where the issue was whether or not deportation camps existed in the USSR; the Lysenko affair; Stalin's seventieth birthday celebration, at which he was honored as a linguist and economist: the affair of the White Shirts; and closer to us in time—in fact, very close—the Solzhenitsyn affair, and the Siniavski-Daniel affairs, and the great silence in Warsaw.

Nonetheless, and this is the nodal point we cannot disregard, all these perturbances stimulated the creative energies of talented men—nothing, of course, not even perturbances, can have any effect where there is an absence of talent.

We probably ought to be more precise about the phenomenon. For eminent communists like Picasso, Eluard, or Joliot-Curie, the relationship between their art or science and their political convictions was not nonexistent; it was, however, episodic, relaxed, loose. In this connection, one must make allowances for the parochial boastfulness that is endemic in the Communist party. Daix and Stil were not great writers; their closed world, to which classical standards were foreign, was naively ignorant of currents of noncommunist thought and works of noncommunist literature. It is therefore extremely difficult to make an overall assessment on an individual or on a collective basis. In the last analysis, it all comes down to a matter of private conscience.

But the innovative nature of the act of joining the party was such that to take the step did not absolutely or in every instance spell defeat. Although it was very unlikely that a biologist could find in the predatory nature of the party any promising field of research, poets, artists, philosophers, and theoreticians could generally find in it the inspiration and vitality that a fresh bit of beauty or truth always offers wherever there exists a world of human beings that is at once real and mythical. Even in the darkest moments of Zdanovism there were periods of faith and enthusiasm, moments of illuminating discovery, invigorating insight, new avenues one had first to pursue before discovering that they led only to ruins. And, among the perishable multitude, there were works that survived— the political order's eternal flowers of evil.

Finally, it perhaps would not be too venturesome to suggest that it is here we discover the narrow passageway that connects French communism to a more ancient phenomenon: the centuries-old phenomenon which in religion is represented by the Reformation.

In a country like Italy where even communism is not placed clearly outside the confines of the church—communists there continue to be baptized, married, and buried in the church—the fact of belonging to the communist movement is less an expression of religious aspiration in the midst of an atheistic environment than a sort of symbolic typification of the Protestant Reformation. The communist leader, Pajetta, shrewdly observed: "The section is what the Protestant parishes were in the early days of the Reformation."

In France, things are more complicated.

During the first years of its development, the French communist movement also appeared to be a kind of Reformation. One is struck by the number of individuals born to Protestantism who pictured the transition from anarchism to communism as the secular expression of man's basic desire to put an end to all compromise. Exemplary in this connection is the tumultuous and tragic personality of the writer Raymond Lefèbvre.

It is equally probable that the amazing fascination that Marxism and communism continue to exert even now on left-wing Catholics in France can be attributed less to a clear understanding of what Marxism and communism actually represent than to a veiled search for the spiritual values and the religious cults of the Reformation.

Generally speaking, however, the communist movement in France has taken shape completely outside the church. The communist militants as well as most communist voters, are completely dechristianized. This being so, the party is free to act as a substitute, an ersatz, for the church. For those who have no religion of their own, it can be a real church, with its own saints—the great precursors—its hero-martyrs, its ceremonial gatherings, its processions and parades, its full-time priests, its more or less practicing faithful militants, its rites and its language.

Besides, we cannot forget that neither occultist nor clerical allurements have ceased to highlight the history of socialist and revolutionary movements among French workers. The guilds and secret societies of the 1830s and 1840s; the phalansteries where, at Godin's for example, tables were made to move; surrealism—all these were phenomena that occultism bewitched. Robespierre's religion of the Supreme Being, the Saint-Simonian church, Guesdism—"Guesde is a priest," Jaurès used to say—these were so many examples that attest the power of clerical allurements.

The French communist microsociety tends to secrete a new kind of clericalism. In this respect, it resembles all other civil societies—the Soviet, the American, the societies of the Third World. The decline in popularity of the conventional church is paralleled by the growing popularity of this new church as a caste, by the attempt to crystallize an order that one hopes but does not believe will be an agent of the future, giving significance to life.

The communist intellectuals, in an effort to protest the role that is thrust upon them, and more generally, to protest a global evolution that alters the deeper significance of the communist phenomenon by drastically clericalizing it, tend to move in two more or less contrary directions. When, like Althusser, they seek to follow both of these partially opposed directions, they end up by being fragmented. On the one hand, they wish to destroy the party as a pseudo-church, to return to rationalism and find the road back to the positivism of the great men of the early socialist movement. On the other hand, they want to destroy the party solely in its functional capacity as a Catholic church. This they hope to accomplish by reincarnating it as a church of the Reformation. The two directions, however, are incompatible. Hence the following strange appeal:

> To become "ideologues of the working class" (Lenin), "organic intellectuals" of the proletariat (Gramsci), intellectuals must drastically revolutionize their ideas. They must undergo a lengthy, painful and difficult process of reeducation: an endless struggle, within and without (Althusser).

What reason have we to believe that Marx, Lenin—especially Lenin—Mao subjected themselves to this lengthy, painful and difficult process of reeducation"? And if they did not, who gave them permission to dispense with it? Wasn't it precisely such thinking about the need for an initiatory asceticism that destroyed all dignity, honor, and the simple capacity to think, precisely in the field of "reeducation"?

Conclusion

What, exactly, have I tried to demonstrate? That most militant communists, the communist people, are not a mass of interchangeable individuals. They constitute a population with age pyramids, male-female relationships, socioprofessional groups, culture conflicts on both the theoretical and practical levels.

This statement as it stands calls for several observations.

An analysis of the kind I have attempted enables us to understand why allegiance to the party is felt to be something good. The party gives its militants a chance to become integrated into a subsociety so complex and heterogeneous as to seem to be in nowise artificial; narrow enough not to subject members of the elite group to a loss of prestige; large enough not to be weakened by the limitations of a unidimensional and unifunctional sect.

The party can evolve and change precisely because it is a structured society, endowed with its own internal mechanisms. But we can already see how nonanarchical are the processes of renewal and stability, at least as long as the organism remains healthy. An institution so complex cannot expand or contract in directions foreign to its nature; to overlook this point leads only to fanciful speculation.

Last and most important, the initial, relative homogeneity of the party as a community contributes to a global

balance of the whole to the extent that it is opposed, reduced, conquered, and finally transformed into a unity
won by the effort of the dedicated corps in the permanent
apparatus. In one rather extreme sense, the party needs
members, militants, the help of the many who constitute
its outer circles, circles which become increasingly indefinite and fluid as one moves away from the center. Only
thus is it able to exercise *in vivo* that subtle alchemy designed to transform the multitudes into a single whole.

Now it is time to become acquainted with the alche-
mists themselves.

III | The Apparatus

8 | A Dedicated Body: The Functionaries

Apparatus is a word the communists don't like and never use. It has crept into the vocabulary of political science not so much to designate a network of organs whose armor, though well concealed, constitutes the framework of an institution, but to identify a dedicated body, the functionaries. To put it briefly, the apparatus is to militant communists what the clergy are to the Christian people.

Cadres and Permanent Members

Actually, the very notion of functionaries is no more acknowledged than is the apparatus. At no level, in no public document, are those referred to in the peoples' democracies as "party functionaries" distinguished as such or classified separately. At times they are even considered to be merely a kind of indispensable machinery, devoid of any distinctive character, possessing no special rights, and performing no additional functions. The party prefers to stress a kindred, supplementary notion but one that is quite distinct: the notion of responsibility.

All this explains why the party so carefully computes the exact size of its cadres, whose members in the lower echelons are called the responsible ones. In the office of a cell or a section, the "member responsible for literature" is the man who tries to convince his comrades to buy the

periodicals, pamphlets, and books published by the party.
It is he who is in charge of the literature tables placed at
the entrance of halls where local or public meetings are
held. The word *literature*, so dear to the clandestine revolutionary movements of tsarist Russia, is used to designate
all the various writings employed in propaganda campaigns.

The careful inventory of cadres which the party draws
up does not of course tally with the list of permanent members. ("Thirty thousand members responsible for cells,
25,000 section leaders, 3,300 federal leaders. With our
1,400 mayors, 21,000 municipal councillors, and 150 departmental councillors . . . with our tens of thousands of
communists responsible for mass organizations and movements, we have cadres totalling far more than 100,000").[1]
Above all, in the lower echelons, there are many "responsible" members who continue to work "in production."
Inversely, many "permanent" members exercising important functions—by no means exclusively technical
ones—are not included in the official count of the cadres.

Every social institution contains a recognizable and
more or less developed framework. The French Communist party is definitely no exception. To be sure, it devotes
particular attention to recruitment and to the organization
of its cadres. But it does so because the existence of a very
rigidly defined hierarchy insures the carrying out of an
essential process: the transformation of the party into a
"countersociety." Here, the possibility of advancement

1. See G. Marchais, Report to the Sixteenth Congress,
Cahiers du communisme, no. 6 (June 1961), p. 235. The figure
of 100,00 cadres is an arbitrary one. It is the result of an addition
in which the same militants are counted twice (or even more
often) because they had different functions at different levels.
But it gives an idea of the size.

plays the same role as does the upward movement of the elite in a mobile society. In everyday life there are many forms of social etiquette that are invaluable from a pedagogical point of view: speeches, ceremonies, the press, very minutely regulated laws governing the granting of titles; priority in the order of processions and in seating arrangements at public functions; material and intellectual privileges affecting every level and category, including the amount of monthly wages paid various individuals. And there are other kinds of rewards for service: the make of an administrator's car; the right to have or dispense with a bodyguard; the right to dine in such or such a canteen or refectory; the privilage of obtaining a particular kind of lodging or of going to a particular Soviet or Bulgarian resort for a vacation. All these things are the insignia of *power* in an ordered society. The order in question is socialist, not bourgeois, but it is an order, or, to use a favorite term of the communists, a legality—the legality of the party, and therefore distinct from that of the state, a legality that is specific yet restraining.

Here again we find, in a socialized form, the role played by order in communist strategy. We can see how mistaken it is to connect this very ancient penchant for order with the recent trend toward social democratization. The fact that the Communist party is a hierarchical microsociety foreshadowing an equally hierarchical future society is not the result of a belated distortion but of an option made at the very outset. One of the fundamental features of the party's ideology is the condemnation of the anarchist plan to destroy order, hierarchy, authority. Let us recall that the Bakuninian adversaries of Marx invoked an "anti-authoritarian" slogan when they assembled for battle. Even Marx himself was not free of a certain anarchist fever in 1848 and in 1871. Lenin, too, especially in 1917,

saw with admirable revolutionary intuition that it was
best to allow the rage of iconoclasts and egalitarians to
run its course for a while in order to insure the birth of a
new socialist society.

Bolshevization and the Professional Revolutionaries

It is necessary to indicate the connection between the
existence of a network of "permanent" members and preoccupations of an entirely different order. We are not
dealing here with the kind of organization or institution
that sets itself up as the model for a certain kind of society.
Instead, we are concerned with a radical distinction between a Bolshevist-type party and all other parties that
are classified as socialist, especially social democratic
parties.

Indeed, it was Lenin who developed and obstinately
implemented the thesis that a truly revolutionary party
must of necessity be composed of essentially "professional
revolutionaries." This was invoked in 1924 when the Bolshevization of the French Communist party was effectu-
ated.

I have repeatedly alluded to this crucial episode in the
history of the French and international communist movement,[2] but at this point it may be helpful to situate it
within a broader context.

We know that the French section of the Communist
International (PC—SFIC), founded at the Congress of
Tours in December, 1920, was the result of a moderate
compromise. The majority within the unified socialist
party that had left to join the Third International was in
effect a combination: besides the "leftist" current—a
small minority group that endeavored to take up a posi-

2. See chapters 4 and 5 above.

tion favorable to Bolshevism—there were the numerically preponderant "centrists" who hoped to revive French socialism, which had been severely weakened by the war and the postwar setbacks.[3] They yearned to preserve their own traditions while capturing some of the dynamism of the Russian Revolution.

The Leninist nature of this compromise was plain: for the Russian Bolsheviks there was no question of making any permanent concessions to the traditions, remnants, and prejudices of the French workers' movement. When the chips are down, the revolutionary movement needs a steadfast political party. Such a party is defined in the twenty-one conditions laid down for admission to the Komintern. But the amount of time it takes to constitute a party of this kind depends upon circumstances. In a situation like the one that existed in the twenties, when it clearly seemed necessary to assume the possibility of a prolonged world revolution, it was thought that there would be enough time to set up a Bolshevik-type party in France. The idea that a considerable interval of time must separate the founding of such a party and its ultimate completion was acceptable. This being so, there was no reason to disdain the advantages to be gained from belonging to a party like the Communist party of 1920, which already was deep-rooted and had, in addition, a relatively large membership. But it was understood that this party, whose Bolshevik indoctrination was inadequate, would have to be destroyed from within and pa-

3. I will take the liberty of referring the reader to my doctoral thesis for further developments on this subject, *Aux origines du communisme français (1914–1920)* 2 vols (Paris: Mouton). More condensed analyses are in the volume in the series "Archives": *1920. Le congrès de Tours. Naissance du PCF* (Paris: Julliard, 1964).

tiently reconstituted on a basis that conformed to Leninist doctrine.

And this is precisely what was done. In January, 1923, the exclusion of the first secretary-general, L. O. Frossard, and of his like-minded colleagues completed the destruction of the centrist majority.[4] From June to December, 1924, the expulsion of Souvarine, Monatte, Rosmer, and their friends doomed the leftist minority.

In 1924–25, Bolshevization was the turning point which marked the transition from the first stage of the international communist movement to the second. We are not speaking of France alone in this connection but of all Europe. The first stage consisted in the destruction from within of all the communist parties created during the twenties that were not oriented strongly toward Bolshevism. During the second stage, these same communist parties were reconstituted along Bolshevik lines and became mere national sections of a worldwide party directed exclusively by Moscow.

Bolshevization, although coinciding with Stalin's takeover of the Bolshevik apparatus and the decisive phase of the Soviet Revolution, does not seem to be connected with the global phenomenon of stalinization. It was a stage whose logic was spelled out by the terms of the compromise reached in Moscow under the guidance of Lenin himself at the time of the second world congress of the Communist International in July, 1920.

What exactly was this much talked-about process of Bolshevization? In a literal sense, the Bolshevization of the French Communist party meant the application of the Bolshevik party's principles of organization as proclaimed by the fifth world congress of the Communist Interna-

4. On this episode, see J. Humbert-Droz, *"L'oeil de Moscou" à Paris* (Paris: Juillard, 1964).

tional held in Moscow in June, 1924.[5] Concretely, Bolshevization entailed a threefold revolution in the domain of organization.

The first step was to alter the foundations upon which the pyramid of organizations rests. In this connection, the decision to substitute a new unity, the factory, for the traditional district, the commune, helped to preserve the party's working-class makeup.

The second step was to scrap the traditional autonomy of the lower organisms in relation to the higher ones. In the French socialist movement, every echelon of the traditional pyramidal hierarchy had enjoyed great autonomy. Such had been the status of the section, at the level of the commune; of the federation, at the departmental level; of the permanent administrative committee, the CAP, at the national level. Power and authority had been very diffuse. As a consequence, the pre-1914 unified socialist party needed its periodic national congresses to make sure that some minimum concensus of opinion existed among all these members, groups, cells, currents of thought, and

5. On the works of the Fifth World Congress of the Communist International, see Communist International, *Les Questions d'organisation du V*e *congrès de l'IC. Cellules d'entreprise, statuts de l'I.C., directives pour l'organisation* (Paris: *l'Humanité*, 1925), 104pp. During the Fifth World Congress the executive committee of the International also convoked in Moscow two organizational conferences: one from March 16 to 21, 1925; the second in March, 1926. The substance of the work done by these two conferences will be found in two large brochures. The first: Communist International, *La Réorganisation des PC. Rapports et décisions de la conférence d'organisation de l'IC* (Paris, *l'Humanité*, 1925), 192pp. The second: Communist International, *La Seconde Conférence d'organisation. Décisions et résolutions adoptées par la II*e *conférence du comité exécutif de l'IC et ratifiées par le bureau d'organisation du comité exécutif de l'IC le 26 Mars 1926* (Preface by Piatnitsky) (Paris, *l'Humanité*, 1926), 98pp.

varying tendencies to warrant the application of the socialist label to each of them. On the other hand, socialism probably had penetrated and colored French national life to a remarkable extent. If, as Jaurès had hoped, "socialist life" was thoroughly enmeshed in "the life of the country," this could be ascribed to the fact that socialist policy had been elaborated and determined on the basis of the concrete realities of a nation that was still largely rural and provincial in character.

The new communist organizational hierarchy, as determined by the central committee in November, 1924—cell, district, region, central committee—presumably stemmed from the Leninist conception of democratic centralism. Spontaneity, initiative, power, authority—the entire decision-making process—were to be mobilized by the center, which formed the highest level of the hierarchy. Although the intermediary organs (section/district, federation/region) could roughly correspond to one another, the same is not true of the CAP (which, in the interval between the two socialist congresses, was exclusively a coordinating and executive body) and the central committee. The latter monopolized the power to make political decisions and to plan for all of France during the interval between the two communist congresses. We will return to this point and examine it more closely. For the moment we must study the mechanism associated with decision-making and consider the meaning, scope, and bounds of the relationship that has sprung up between the concept of the communist militant and that of party discipline.

What matters most in this connection is the third and by far the most important element in the organizational revolution: the creation of a nucleus of leaders and the establishment of an apparatus of functionaries.

The French Socialist party, in its classical form, ascribed complete primacy to initiative emanating from members on the lowest rungs of the organization. Moreover, it had no central apparatus. During the years that preceded the First World War, it took pride in its capacity to maintain four or five "propaganda delegates" who were selected for their eloquence. Serving as "pilgrims" of socialism in their journey from town to town, they accepted all invitations to preach their rather personal gospel. But such activities left the ordinary militant little additional time for his duties as a member of mass organizations. As a consequence, two categories emerged: socialist journalists and socialist members of parliament. Both categories, behaving like professional politicians, came to dominate the party. This being so, it is not difficult to understand why the socialist party inevitably became a plebeian rather than a workers' party. Ultimately, those who counted within its ranks were the writers.

The same was true of the French Communist party prior to 1924. Moreover, the workers, especially the minority still influenced by anarchist ideas, had little confidence in the leaders of trade union organizations and in political appointees of any kind. Such individuals were suspected of seeking soft berths for themselves.

The decision to create a "real organizational apparatus" was arrived at in Moscow. In September, 1924, Guralsky, the Komintern's delegate in France, addressed the secretaries of the department federations (the latter, originally organized by the unified Socialist party of the pre-1914 period, have been retained by the French communists): "The armor of a revolutionary party must comprise a vast network of professional revolutionaries." Ten years were required to bring such a network into being but, once formed, it proved a lasting success.

A Solid, Stable, Protected Nucleus

The consequences of this accomplishment were considerable. The Communist party acquired a nucleus that was
solid, stable, and impervious to repression. Around it was
a protective, more or less impenetrable (the degree de-
pended on circumstances) wall of militants, members,
and sympathizers. The change, in effect, amounted to
nothing less than the replacement of amateurs by professionals. At a deeper level, it represented the triumph of a
certain conception of the revolutionary act.

The dividing line between party functionaries and nonfunctionary members did not consist solely in the material
and objective frontier that separates those who give a
good deal of time to the party from those who do not. Of
course there are nonfunctionary members at all levels
who are scarcely distinguishable from functionaries save
for one very concrete dissimilarity: the functionaries
think of themselves as communists "twenty-four hours a
day" even though a part of the time is "sacrificed" to a
wage-paying job, and they conduct themselves accordingly. The status of such men is, all things considered, exceptional. It is also temporary and provisional. Sooner or
later, however, it is "regularized" by the anticipated promotion from one stage to the other.

In reality, the dividing line between the two kind of
members is more spiritual than material. It separates the
men who have burned their bridges behind them from
those who have not.

Even communists of high rank are vaguely aware of
this difference and express it in the way they conduct
themselves and in the options they make.

Some enthusiastic militants decline the "honor" of becoming functionaries, either because they are modest and
fear they will not be worthy or because they are loath to

be "separated," however imperceptibly, from their families, friends and colleagues. To be a functionary is equivalent to joining the "elect"; not to be one is to retain a small measure of privacy, to be free to make one's own decisions. Many communists consider the party important —enormously important, as a matter of fact. At the same time, however, they regard the party as something that cannot give life its full meaning or significance. Even in the higher echelons, there are men who feel this way and who consequently refuse to give their all to the party. As a result, they are considered "different," although their comrades would be at a loss to say just why this is so.

On the other hand, for most militants who become functionaries, the change is quite far-reaching—indeed, the most drastic one imaginable. The material sacrifices involved are usually emphasized, but this is mere party propaganda. It is true that functionaries earn less money than they would if they remained in their jobs or worked overtime. At least this is so of those who are appointed by the managers of the party's exchequer. There are union functionaries who are legally entitled to collect their monthly pay from the firms that employ them, minus, of course, certain fringe benefits. But the real difference in earnings between permanent and nonpermanent members is not very great. The party leaders were forced to grant substantial increases in wages because in many areas they needed the services of good technicians. And the increase in the wages paid to technicians inevitably entailed an increase in the salaries of communist politicians. All in all, the needs growing out of the kind of life a functionary leads are primarily social in nature; he isn't really deprived. He has the companionship of other permanent members and doesn't actually suffer, unless his wife and children become dissatisfied with his lot. His more modest earnings are the visible signs of the dignity of his position—they are the other side of the coin—to say nothing of the slight symbolic privileges accorded his status.

Far more decisive than any material sacrifices are the sociocultural consequences of the acquisition of the status of a functionary. "To quit production"—a phrase that still flourishes because of the persistence of the Proudhonian worker-production tradition—is to forsake a life governed by working hours, characterized by physical labor and nurtured by the individual's contribution to a specific socio-occupational milieu. It means leading a life in which there are no hours, in which one is always available—a life dedicated to intellectual pursuits: reading, writing, discussion. It is a life enriched and stimulated by contact with people, things, and problems whose common denominator is that they transcend the individual's former, more restricted environment.

The personal together with the collective benefits and hazards that this kind of conversion entails tally exactly with those that accompany the attainment of priestly status in a different sociopolitical and cultural context.

The Benefits. On an individual basis, the change represents something of an adventure. In many respects it is a way of achieving social advancement on the basis of criteria other than the usual ones of technical proficiency or scholarly attainment. Collectively, the functionaries serve as a regulatory agency. During defensive periods, the party falls back on itself and forms a closed society, offering no breach through which the enemy can penetrate. When the party is on the offensive, the permanent members constitute a sizable reserve from which support is drawn for the advance of the masses. Serving as a sort of welcoming committee, the functionaries also provide continuity, stimulate solidarity, and generate loyalty to communism in its original form. In a party where remembrance of the past is often concealed for the sake of the cause, they are the repository of tradition. The main vehicle for the transmission of wisdom, they represent stability at the center of the movement—we have seen how unstable is the community of ordinary party members.

The truth is that misunderstandings about the role of this hard core, this shielded nucleus, have given rise to many fanciful prophecies about the imminent demise of the French Communist party. The severest acts of repression, the most serious blunders committed by the International, by Stalin, by the worldwide communist movement, the most catastrophic predicaments, all have been surmounted, resolved, or absorbed. This was true in 1925–30, in 1939, 1956, and 1958. During each crisis the party lost a fair share of its members. Like a sponge abandoned by the ebbing tide, it became dry, shrank, and hardened, but it was always capable of swelling up again when the tide returned. The mechanism that makes this possible should not be underestimated. It explains the resiliency of a party three times put to death and three times reanimated, the blasé endurance of its leaders and probably, too, their somewhat automatic confidence in renewal through the lifesaving processes.

The Hazards. On the individual level, many fervent, generous, unselfish "professional revolutionaries" found that they had been transformed into bureaucrats, briefcase-toting high priests, and this throughout long years, as they waited for something to happen that never did. Pitiful figures, their sole and ultimate refuge was to become inured to their condition. "To return to production," to be excluded from the sacred circle, was not only to smash all the social frameworks of a life conceived in a single dimension, measured by a single reality, the dimension and reality of the party; it was also to have the sword of Damocles hanging over them. Formerly skilled professionals, the functionaries had long since forgotten the tricks of their trades, which at all events had changed quite often in the course of time. Having grown rusty, these men contemplated with some anxiety the prospect of being forced to adjust themselves to a new and different life. Generally speaking, they were probably no longer of much use in the factory or shipyard.

On the collective level, the hazard consisted of a form of integration into a global society that became more and more structured, more and more compartmentalized, owing to the coexistence of subsocieties that had their own languages, habits, internal hierarchies, and a mobility of their own. All of this of course was based on the assumption that these subsocieties would settle down peacefully in the areas set aside for them. If worse came to worse, the Communist party, like so many other philosophical, social, or religious groups that lost their influence, would be abandoned by history. This closed society, which went underground and disappeared from the political arena whenever it suffered its worst setbacks, could become a dead planet and yet not die completely. It could vegetate and survive in much the same way that a comatose invalid deprived of real life survives. This is not idle speculation. The communist apparatus has the defects of all such systems: a tendency to become too gigantic. It proliferates. One apparatus is bound to nurture another and all of them grow inexorably.

Financing the Apparatus

At this point, in view of the various implications of the Communist party's transformation into an organization with a sizable permanent apparatus, we must examine an essential problem: the *financing* of the apparatus.[6]

The pre-1914 unified Socialist party, which had virtually no apparatus, likewise had no financial structure—or hardly any. The small amount of money in its coffers was handled publicly. A complete financial report was periodically submitted for approval to the national congress, the party's highest tribunal.

Showing an amazing attention to detail, Lenin, that implacable realist, had concerned himself personally with the question of party funds. He realized that money was needed to give body to his conception of a new type of party. Not that Lenin was in the slightest degree cynical. It never occurred to him that the revolution could be corrupted. He believed that the idea of revolution could be imposed as a guiding principle only if the party's adherents and newspapers assumed the responsibility of preaching the gospel to the masses. But adherents and newspapers are expensive to support. Lenin therefore always insisted that the question of finances would have to be dealt with openly and that it would have to be resolved. But how? Without fanfare but also without self-consciousness. After 1919 the proceedings of the Third International's congresses contained only the briefest of financial reports.[7] In Lenin's view, the source of funds was impor-

6. See a few additional elements in connection with this study, "Les Finances du Parti," supplement to no. 134 of BEIPI (July 1–15, 1955).

7. See in particular the two following documents: "Les documents de l'Internationale. Thèses, décisions et résolutions de

tant because money itself was merely a means in the revolutionary struggle. If any attempt should be made to corrupt the party, the revolutionary would have to use the money against the corrupters, at his own risk and peril, of course. If the revolution had failed in 1917 wouldn't Lenin have gone down in history as a "German agent"?

The young French Communist party was imbued with the traditional suspicion in regard to money matters inherited from both French socialism and France's Catholic society. Consequently, it found it difficult to adopt Lenin's attitude on the subject, as the following passage from one of Leon Trotsky's letters, dated July 26, 1921, shows. The letter was addressed to the leading committee of the French Communist party:

> The C.E. [executive committee] attributes much importance to the fact that the French party was able in difficult circumstances to overcome financial problems through its own efforts. This is proof of its vitality. At the same time the C.E. notes that the party is about to make many heavy financial sacrifices because of the need to develop the communist press, expand the publication of brochures, lower the cost of *l'Humanité* with an eye to increasing its circulation, etc. The C.E. is quite willing to give a certain amount of financial assistance to the French Communist party. It is absolutely impossible, in our opinion, for sections of the Communist International to have any reluctance or doubt about accepting help from a fra-

la XIIe assemblée plénière du comité exécutif de l'Internationale communiste (septembre 1932)" (Paris: Bureau d'éditions, 1932). "Rapport de la commission internationale de contrôle," in *La Correspondance internationale*, no. 60 (August 19, 1935), a special number devoted to the Seventh Communist International Congress.

ternal party, be it in opposition to the bourgeois state, as in most countries, or in power,
as in Russia. International solidarity would be
nothing more than a wretched hypocrisy, a
mere mask for concealing a vulgar chauvinism
like that of the Second International, if the sections that can provide help were to refuse to
do so; or if, conversely, those that need financial aid were to refuse to accept it out of fear
of bourgeois public opinion.[8]

To do justice to the French party, we must admit that
its initial experiences during the early twenties had been
unfortunate. Abramovich-Zalewski, one of the International's first delegates in Paris, realized that he was being
followed by the police. He entrusted the checkbook, with
checks dated and signed in advance, to Amédée Dunois,
a member of the administrative committee (it wasn't as
yet called the central committee) of the French Communist party and one of the editors of *l'Humanité*. Thereupon Dunois commissioned several comrades, including
A. Ker, another member of the administrative committee,
to go to the bank and cash a certain number of these
checks. In January, 1921, the arrest of Zalewski, Ker,
and Dunois precipitated an all-out press campaign that
focused on "Moscow's gold." Revelations purported made
by Zalewski to his prison companion, Pierre Meunier, the
former director of the pacifist newspaper, *La Vérité*, were
reproduced in detail. The party's secret funds were said
to reach the fantastic figure of fourteen million francs.

8. This part of Trotsky's letter to the committee head of the
French Communist party was not made public at the time. B.
Lazitch reconstructed it on the basis of an original document
he had in his possession. The letter appears in his very important article, which is about to be published: "Internationale
communiste sous Lénine (1919–24)." See below, chapter 12,
n. 13.

The truth is that "the maximum amount of money at Zalewski's disposal was 600,000 francs, of which two-thirds was earmarked for other countries."[9] This scandal in the French party produced violent reactions. Even before this occurred, the entire rightist minority, accustomed to the flexible federalism of the Second International, had begun to complain about Moscow's "interventionism."

In this domain as in so many others, Bolshevization represented the turning point. Under the rigid and meticulous direction of Piatnitsky, the Komintern's outstanding budget director and the only man in the secretariat of the Communist International who knew the exact state of the party's exchequer, the French section's finances were reorganized. The amount set aside for this reorganization was based on the needs of the newly established French apparatus.

The following statement was made, with maximum discretion, by Albert Vassart, who as Lozeray's successor managed the party's finances from November, 1931, to March, 1934:

> *Never* were financial matters or precise figures discussed either in the political bureau or even in the secretariat. Apart, of course, from the person at the top who administered the funds, only one of the secretaries [Thorez] was informed about such things.[10]

9. Excerpt from a letter dated December 21, 1921, in which B. Souvarine transmitted to the French committee head the conclusions reached by the commission investigating the Zalewski affair. At the instigation of the French, the affair was investigated in Moscow by the executive committee of the Communist International. Quoted by B. Lazitch, "Internationale communiste."

10. All the data concerning the financial structure of the Communist party during the early thirties are excerpted from

During this same period, expenses for the party's apparatuses—I am omitting certain subsidiary organizations such as youth groups, the Red Aid, and the many specialized agencies in this or that domain—were classified under four different headings: (a) The cost of administering the regular budget; (b) the monthly expenses in support of various special apparatuses (the apparatus attached to the International; the "antimilitarist" apparatus, the colonial section, and so on); (c) the cost of subsidizing the press and other party publications; (d) special expenses (an electoral campaign, for instance).

Four categories of revenue matched the four expense categories.

First: membership dues. In the early 1930s the party had only 30,000 to 35,000 members, and of these scarcely more than 20,000 to 25,000 paid their dues.

Second: contributions. The party not only called on its members to make sacrifices, it also appealed to sympathizers, voters, and readers of the communist press. These contributions, besides proving the self-confidence and success of the communists in such matters, added up to relatively sizable sums. They enabled the party—this was not the least important consideration—to include in the official list of receipts donations that did not necessarily come from modest contributors.[11]

Third: money paid or promised by the party's "enter-

Mémoires by Albert Vassart, member of the French Communist party's secretariat at the time. This document, which is exceptionally interesting, will be published shortly with an introduction and notes, by Gallimard publishers.

11. This should make us cautious about the conclusions to be drawn both in regard to the overall annual sums collected and to the "geography of the permanent subscribers" reported in each region to the communist electorate for an evaluation of the revenues, as Ranger suggests in *L'Electorat communiste*, p. 14.

prises." This was an old idea. It consisted in setting up small industrial or commercial firms whose profits would go into the party's exchequer. The idea proved difficult to implement because of a lack of experts. In 1932 the party boasted a "Purchasing Office for Municipalities"; a "Research and Documentation Society"; a "Technicians' Guild" created within the framework of the USTICA (*Union syndicale des techniciens, ingénieurs et cadres*); a "Study Bureau," whose mission it was to coordinate everything that required adjudication in the domain of municipal finance. None of these enterprises brought in much cash and some even cost the party money.

Fourth: the single largest item was "International aid" —the subsidy given by the Communist International to its French section. This "aid" was divided into two parts. One consisted of the regular monthly payment which took care of four-fifths of the monthly budget.[12] In 1931, for example, it amounted to a little less than 200,000 out of a total monthly expenditure of 250,000 francs. Since all arrangements were on a trimestrial basis, a sum of about 550,000 to 600,000 francs in foreign currency was deposited every three months by the communist functionary in charge of the OMS. (This was the International's technical service. It took care of everything connected with liaison between the national sections, whether legal or illegal, and Moscow. The transport of men, money, and "literature" was especially important here.) The second part of the subsidy, earmarked for unusual contingencies, was used to cover press deficits such as that of *l'Humanité*, which was in dire straits after the affair of the Workers' and Peasants' Bank; or the deficits of publications like the

12. In Albert Vassart's *Mémoires* we will find a precise analysis, with the figures, of the various categories in the ordinary monthly budget at the close of 1931.

Marxist Library, Lenin's *Complete Works*, and the International's various periodicals. This part of the subsidy also paid for trips made by militants outside the country (they were often summoned to Moscow for consultation) and helped to maintain the families of students who attended the Leninist School in Moscow.

What is happening today? Things have changed drastically. The Communist International died in 1943. As a consequence, international aid could no longer be as direct as it once was. Besides, such aid, under the form previously used in squandering it, became practically useless. During the period of the Resistance and the Liberation, the French Communist party developed its own roots among the nation's middle class. This enabled it to obtain the collaboration of many technicians and specialists who helped in a variety of businesses—especially import-export trade—during the last two decades, when industry was expanding.

The various ways in which the party benefits from the general prosperity of the nation can be detailed only in a very subtle study. Besides, in a country like France, where businessmen tend to be extremely discreet about their financial affairs, one can hardly reproach the Communist party for its secrecy in such matters. All I can say is this: although the party is not a "financial power," it is nonetheless an institution with a solid fortune behind it. This doesn't mean its functionaries or cells are rich. Rather, they resemble the poor priests and parishes of the still sumptuous Catholic church. Similarly, the party as such has considerable means at its disposal. These of course vary, depending upon the success of annual campaigns for public contributions, the number of contributors, and the size of the communist deputation in parliament. All deputies deposit their monthly emoluments in the party's central treasury; in exchange they receive whatever happens to be the going wage for party functionaries. In any case, most of the party's income is derived from outside ventures. These give the party sufficient financial security to run its apparatus regardless of circumstances—at any rate, regardless of political circumstances. Paradoxically enough, however, economic conditions are the cause of a far greater degree of anxiety.

The Power of the Managers

The other side of the coin is this: the world of the functionaries increased considerably in size, but it became a world ruled by administrators.

Today, subtle distinctions have to be made in defining the functionary. In theory, a functionary is a militant appointed by the heads of the party's exchequer. But this is too narrow a definition. Although militants who have been elected mayors or deputies do not, as we have seen, retain the full sum of their wages, others named to communal, occupational, or state administrative posts receive public funds, even though they have been designated for these posts by the party. Nor must we overlook all the parallel hierarchies that make up the party. Alongside the hierarchy of organizations that constitute the party directly and explicitly, there is a very large and diversified network of political, social, or cultural organizations. As a consequence of affiliation with all these bodies, many militants are functionaries in the fullest sense of the term. Nevertheless, both in theory and practice, they are employees paid by particular associations (newspapers, periodicals, publishing houses controlled by the party); by "mass organizations" (trade unions, cooperatives, child welfare organizations, youth groups, women's unions, athletic, cultural, tourist or leisure organizations, intellectual societies); or by workers' welfare organizations (dispensaries, infant care centers, canteens, vacation colonies, homes for the aged). In addition, there are the masses of employees who work in enterprises in which the party has an interest. Not all of these employees are communists, but a great number of them who work in political, administrative, or technical capacities are.

Lastly, there is one common denominator that links individuals of widely divergent status: a functionary is a militant who expends all his efforts in the position selected for him by the party. No matter what the nature of his work, no matter how he is paid for it, he is subject to the control and discipline of the cadre's directors. They have full authority over the way in which the party's human resources are utilized.

This world has thus become so complex that to make it intelligible one must divide it into subgroups. The most influential of these are the federal secretaries, whose status and functions are strikingly similar to those of prefects in the hierarchy of the state. Within certain limits, they outrank all other militants, including deputies. Communist journalists, communist members of parliament, communist trade unionists, communist administrators—all these represent different categories whose common and particular features must be delineated in relation to one another as well as to their "bourgeois" counterparts.

The definition of a functionary illustrates the difficulty of estimating how many such members there are. It explains the fact that the party has at its disposal a considerable reserve of energy during periods of tension and can thus concentrate its full force on this or that aspect of a problem, according to the needs of the moment or situation. It also explains why one is justified in speaking of a communist microsociety, especially in reference to the Paris region where several tens of thousands of individuals are directly involved.

The definition likewise underscores the fact that far fewer members are assigned to posts of political responsibility than to purely administrative jobs. I am speaking of the "politicos," as they are called, the *elected* individuals in a hierarchy that has priority—the party hierarchy, in the strict sense of the term. I am comparing them to the "technicos," those *chosen* for their competence (whether the position is a humble one, such as a porter or watchman, or a very important one, such as a bank director).

This being so, it is altogether understandable that the functionaries' world, whose ramifications are becoming increasingly tenuous and remote from the center of political action, should gradually tend more and more to become integrated into established society. In ordinary daily life, a manager is more preoccupied with the prosperity of the enterprise for which he has responsibility than he is absorbed by the anticapitalist revolution. He is more interested in new techniques, in marketing and management, than he is in the theoretical problems posed in connection with the determination of a worldwide antiimperialist strategy.

Weighed down in this way, the party machine, although operating smoothly enough, tends to function more and more for its own sake.

9 | Ordinary Men

Nothing is more exciting to a young American political scientist than the prospect of being introduced to a member of the communist political bureau. The species to which the latter belong is, to be sure, quite a rare one in the New World. Yet nothing is actually less exciting. You can recognize a communist leader by his very ordinariness.

Normality and Conformity

Let's be more precise. If he is an ordinary man, this is because he wants to be. What I am saying may seem paradoxical because the cult of personality, in the literal sense of the phrase, was a party "must" and it applied to every level. The following anecdote is a case in point. Complying with the party's traditional practice of singling out some individual to serve as an example of communist self-criticism, Thorez made fun of a twenty-five-year-old federal secretary who used his birthday as the occasion for a general celebration. (An order had gone out to denounce excesses of the personality cult in France.) Because the communist hero symbolizes the people, he must be the epitome of ordinary working-class virtues: warmth and simplicity, modesty, reliability. The party fell heir to a twofold tradition of distrust: of demagogues who in the past used the workers' movement as a stepping stone; and of the valiant veterans whom the post-World War I communist movement censured, pitting the proletarian revolution against imperialist war and national defense.

Anything that smacked of pretentiousness, anything that stood out because it was unique or exceptional, anything that attracted notice because it was unusual or distinctive, was suspect. This is hypocritical, of course, but it is a specific kind of hypocrisy. No effort was made to conceal run-of-the-mill vices or commonplace blunders. The party had only one end in view: to establish a model whose primary characteristic was normality.

Now normality, although it is a complex phenomenon, presents an unquestionable social element. Hence this paradox: a revolutionary party's proclaimed goal is to change established society, yet the Communist party requires its militants to conform to the norms of such a society. And in this it has been successful. The many eccentrics who peopled the anarchist movement—bastards, hunchbacks, pederasts, butterfly collectors, drug addicts, fetichists; members of cultural, sexual, or philosophical minorities; people who cared too much about such things as music, movies, open-air camping—all these simply did not feel comfortable in communist organizations.

The party's attitude was not based on moral objections. Communist rules of conduct were not founded on ethical principles but on the Leninist notion of the proper relationship between the militant and his party. The party constituted the unifying element that merged and engulfed all other elements. Every militant was expected to identify himself completely with the party, to look to it for everything, including the very meaning of life. "The party has given me everything"—this traditional expression of gratitude may sound like a simple statement of fact, but actually it represents a course of conduct the party attempts to instill in each of its members.

The communist leader does not look for men who are commonplace in appearance only. Most party members are ordinary through and through, and it is precisely this mediocrity that makes for problems.

Naturally it would be unfair to criticize the party without taking into account the fact that French politicians generally are prodigiously mediocre, regardless of party affiliation. One is taken aback by the poor quality of the country's top deputies. There is no reason to expect that communists as a whole will be different.

It would be equally unfair not to acknowledge that there have been, and are, unusual personalities in the French party. One cannot help feeling a certain embarrassment at the thought that these unusual individuals are treated like celebrities. They are known to be outstanding, yet they are expected not to take advantage of this, to stay where they are and not interfere with the serious affairs of the party. Such has been the particular lot of a few journalists and members of parliament whose gifts have been praised by the bourgeois public. Outside the party they are in the limelight, but that is not enough to give them a say in the party's inner circles, in the councils where important decisions are made.

Having put forward these reservations, I can't refrain from wondering why it is that the central committee and the political bureau are packed with men who are admittedly serious, competent, and hard-working, but whose only obvious asset is their enormous experience.

It is difficult to know whether this is a recent development. With the passage of time, historical personalities, even those who are still living, tend to acquire a certain aura. There is something more pronounced, more singular about them than ordinary people, although perhaps certain aspects of their personality are less likeable.

Are we to attribute to coincidence the fact that a generation of sacred monsters—Stalin, Khrushchev, Togliatti, Thorez—were succeeded by men like Brezhnev, Longo, and Waldeck Rochet?

Maurice Thorez

I will limit my remarks to Frenchmen. The personality of Thorez calls for an unbiased biography but one devoid of complacency. For the man was far more perplexing and difficult to understand than one would think from the descriptions of him that might have been lifted out of a *Lives of the Saints* or from a Trotskyite manual on the bureaucratic degeneration of stalinists.

First of all, it is plain that, contrary to the clichés about Thorez, and despite his burly physique and working-class origins, he had little inclination for either manual labor or physical exertion. To be more precise, Thorez, unlike Frachon who grew up in the steel industry, had no particular occupation. Although he came from a family of miners, he never acquired any special expertise.[1] To put it in more general terms, Thorez was not an active man. He

---

1. From 1912 to 1914 Maurice Thorez sorted stones in the number 4 pit at Noyelles-Godault, his native village. In September, 1914 (he was fourteen), he was evacuated, as he himself recounts in his book, *Fils du peuple*. On January 3, 1919, he returned to Noyelles-Godault. At first he was "hired to reconstruct the railroad from Lens to Douai." Then he worked again in pit number 4. But in March, 1920, he left for military service and when he was demobilized he was not rehired at his old job. He became a manual worker, then a house painter, and in 1923 (when he was 23), he became a party functionary.

liked long solitary walks, and, although not an athlete himself, enjoyed watching games.

Above all, he was averse to the rough-and-tumble. There is some reason to wonder whether he was really physically courageous. Even during the early days, when the party was too small to forbid its leaders to fight with the police, Thorez was never involved in a fracas. In June, 1929, he was taken prisoner at the Château d'Achères, but the circumstances were hardly glamorous: he was caught because his feet protruded from the closet in which he was hiding. On February 9, 1934, between the Gare de l'Est and the Place de la République, Doriot and a detachment of frenzied proletarians fought a street battle that resulted in six deaths. Thorez had somehow managed to get orders from the political bureau to stay away, in order to insure the safety of at least one party leader!

Actually, his aversion for physical combat apparently coincided with a deeper, earlier terror of death. Was this the result of some personal experience? That is quite possible. The catastrophe of Courrières in 1906 had impressed and disturbed him when he was a very small child. But also, he belonged to that race of working-class northerners who might be called sorrowful mystics— men who are regularly overcome with great gusts of boisterous joy at village fairs and saint's-day festivals.

Nothing, then, about Thorez was reminiscent of the type of proletarian who is master of his body if not of his fate. This perhaps explains the fact, which at first seems surprising, that Thorez was probably the only working-class militant of that first generation of communists who never expended any effort in working with the trade unions. From the very start he thought of his career and his activities as evolving within the framework of the party, as resting on a more abstract, less physical basis. In short, he regarded himself as a political theorist.

Actually, Thorez was endowed with many traits that tended to make him a rather unusual type of intellectual.

He had an endless desire to learn, to begin with. A brilliant pupil at the communal school, he never ceased to regret that he did not continue his education. But he was careful not to imitate certain self-educated people who frantically collected odd bits of knowledge but whose efforts were doomed to failure because they lacked the necessary background. Methodically and tenaciously he explored every area, acquiring a knowledge of Latin, Russian, and German in his efforts to become a cultivated human being.

In his studies he followed the example of the present-day worker who, far from condemning the "consumer society," is egged on by his desire to become a part of it. Excluded by birth from the cultivated world, Thorez took no pride in this fact. He did not tell himself, as many communists do, that he wanted no part of "bourgeois" culture. On the contrary, patiently making his acquaintance with the world of culture and taking it as it was, he refused to pick and choose, since he did not yet trust his own judgment in such matters. I think his cautious attitude, stamped with the seal of sincerity, subsequently served to inspire his conception of the "heritage" which the communists were later to praise, especially the cultural heritage. In 1936, in a speech now famous, he talked about "reconciling the tricolor of our fathers with the red flag of our aspirations." One sensed, beyond the mere words, his recollection of the hours when, as an adolescent in the family mining village, he first discovered the enchanted universe of French literature.

His native love of books probably saved Thorez from

falling prey to sectarianism and ideological leftism, even
during the time of Jdanovist obscurantism. He was careful, of course, not to place himself in open opposition to
Soviet cultural policy.

His love of books led him to read works that were
far removed from communist orthodoxy. I should like at
this point to relate a personal anecdote.

I sent Thorez a book I had written on the Congress of
Tours. Here and there my interpretations deviated somewhat from the official communist version. Thorez sent me
the following note, which I thought showed a certain sense
of humor: "Thank you . . . just the same!"

Two weeks before his death on July 1, 1964, he wrote
to me as follows about my book, *Les origines du communisme français*:

> Thanks and congratulations, although I am
> of a different opinion on more than one point,
> particularly in regard to the responsibility of
> the opportunistic leaders and the "bitter-end-
> ers" in connection with the bankruptcy of the
> Second International and the P.S.U. [*Parti
> socialiste unifié*]. I am also of a different opin-
> ion about the conclusions to be drawn from
> the history of the revolutionary movement.

These remarks are obviously quite different in tone
from the nasty and stupid article on the same subject that
appeared in the *Cahiers Maurice-Thorez*.

Again, it was his love of learning that enabled Thorez
to spend eight years—from 1932 to 1940—in harmonious
and almost daily collaboration with Fried, better known
as Clément, the delegate of the Third International in
France. The Thorezian legend attributes the miraculous
recovery of the French Communist party from 1932 on
solely to its hero. In so doing it overlooks the fact that

Thorez was backed up, aided, advised, directed, and in-
structed by the large team of international militants the
executive committee of the Komintern had hurriedly
despatched to Paris toward the latter part of 1931.[2] In the
circumstances, and unlike his predecessors, Thorez was
wise enough to use the presence of this team to give himself time to acquire experience and to accumulate enough
"know-how" to succeed eventually in dispensing with his
mentors. Viewed from a somewhat different angle, to be
sure, his behavior might be described as docile. In this
connection, André Ferrat has written:

> The major quality of Maurice Thorez was
> the docility with which he reacted to directives
> from the secretariat and representatives of the
> Third International. He would execute orders
> most painstakingly, continuing to do so until
> fresh orders were issued. If these were re-
> versed, he quickly complied.

Wasn't such docility characteristic of the "good pupil"
—of Thorez as a young man? Ferrat, at any rate, makes
this point:

> An industrious worker, eager to learn and to
> move ahead, he was the epitome of a good
> pupil, studious and respectful of his teachers.
> He felt a constant need to inform his superiors
> of his activities, even when they asked nothing
> of him, and he was always soliciting their ad-
> vice and criticism.[3]

2. For a fuller account, see below, chapter 12.
3. A. Ferrat, "Contributions à l'histoire du PCF. M. Fauvet
saisi par la légende," *Preuves* (February 1965), pp. 53–61.
Ferrat's account is particularly valuable for reasons he himself
gives: "I knew Maurice Thorez well and was familiar with his
political activities during the period that concerns us because
he and I were simultaneously members of the political bureau

Thorez was genuinely modest, and he did have a definite propensity for learning, but his basic motivation stemmed from the urge to satisfy a deeper need, the need for power.

He wanted power not only in the party but also in the state. Albert Vassart, who shared with him the vicissitudes of the 1932 parliamentary contest in which Thorez was elected deputy for Ivry, has this to say:

> I accompanied him on the day he made his first appearance in the Chamber as a newly-elected member. His broad smile conveyed a great deal more than any speech could have done. . . . Within a few days he had learned all there was to know about the advantages of occupying a seat in parliament. When, for example, we took a bus together (at that time secretaries did not yet have automobiles at their disposal), he took a childish pleasure in getting on last in order to exhibit his card, which entitled him to travel free of charge.

Vincent Auriol, for his part, described the curious, acute distress that gripped Thorez when it became plain that he would have to quit the government.

He had a taste for power that was based on innate skill. One cannot refrain from drawing a parallel here between his skill and that of General de Gaulle: an inclination to

---

for more than eight years, from July, 1929, to January, 1936. What's more, in 1928, when we were both 'illegal,' I lived with him for months in Brussels where we shared an apartment and worked together. . . . I have never had any personal differences with Thorez. When I broke with the party in June, 1935, I did so solely because of deeply felt dissenting views that I had been harboring for some time." Also, tradition has it that during the thirteenth meeting of the executive committee in December, 1933, Manouilski, in a moment of annoyance, went so far as to tell Thorez that he was "too servile to be a genuine leader."

resort to ruse, a tendency to be ungrateful, a predilection
for secretiveness, a penchant for granting unusual privileges—all this justified in the end by identifying oneself
with a mission that transcends the individual.

A predilection for secretiveness. Thorez, like de Gaulle,
used this as a means of exercising control. But here we
touch upon the major element in any revolutionary vocation. We shall return to this later and discuss it at length.

An inclination to resort to ruse. Very quickly Thorez
learned to maneuver, managing to be present whenever
necessary and absent when it was best to avoid taking
sides. It must be admitted that this technique was especially appropriate during the twenties and thirties. Here
is one example. At a time when the Third International
was uncertain whether Thorez or Doriot should be the
leader of the French Communist party, Thorez became
acquainted with the kind of penalty one could incur by
leaving the place where decisions are reached too soon.
In September 1932, Doriot left the twelfth plenary session
of the Communist International believing that he had
come out on top. He had explained why it was that in the
terrible defeat the party had suffered in the parliamentary
elections of that year, Saint-Denis was the only municipal-
ity where a triumph had been scored. But Thorez, staying
on in Moscow ten days longer, obtained permission to
"decentralize" the communist organization in the Paris
region and thereby regained some of the ground he had
lost. The purpose of his maneuver was to free the Paris
region from Doriot's influence. Eighteen months later, in
the spring of 1934, Thorez won a definitive victory. In
compliance with orders from the executive committee, he
went to Moscow and stayed there for a long time, whereas
Doriot refused to submit to the urgent and repeated
telegraphic summons to come to the communist capital
for consultation.

A tendency to be ungrateful. Friendship is not of course a prime feature of communist emotional life. Camaraderie is the rule; it can give way to a more familiar type of chumminess, but only rarely does it lead to the establishment of close relationships. There is a tenacious mistrust of "groupism," of "fractionalism." This, however, is not something peculiar to the communist nucleus. One should read the bittersweet remarks of Léon Blum, made in connection with Salengro's suicide, on the loneliness that power engenders.

Be that as it may, Thorez, like de Gaulle, did not seem to have a talent for friendship. In his lengthy autobiography, for example, the secretary-general of the French party failed to write a single word of appreciation or praise for Fried. Perhaps he refrained from emphasizing the personal role played by an emissary of the International—a Czech, to boot—for purely political reasons; probably, too, it was best not to be too specific about the kind of ties that link the French section to the Komintern. But all the same!

Moreover, it is altogether possible that Thorez never felt a genuine friendliness toward anyone except one man: Laurent Casanova. Nevertheless, in 1961, when it seemed that Casanova might be cashiered because he supported a more deliberate pro-Khrushchev policy, even friendship for this man did not deter Thorez from waging a relentless battle against Casanova. The latter, he charged, was a right-wing deviationist. But once Thorez had reestablished his full authority, he appropriated the ideas of his excommunicated friend and made them his own.

A lack of self-consciousness. Very early on, Maurice Thorez managed to persuade party members that he deserved special treatment. Already in the early thirties, he spent his mornings working at home, never putting in an appearance at party headquarters until the afternoon. His colleagues, the other functionaries, were expected to work at the headquarters all day long. It certainly gave Thorez time for privacy and reflection; from this point of view, his routine made sense. It also implied that visitors who wished to see him would have to come to his home. Auguste Lecoeur has pointed out that this inclination to prefer private talks to open discussion within the framework of the organization's regular collective agencies was part of his style, his way of running the party.[4]

Actually, this lack of self-consciousness was, in the last analysis, his way of expressing a very keen sense of his mission and of his responsibilities. We have striking evidence of this. In April, 1930, when Thorez was imprisoned in Nancy on charges of conspiracy, he decided on his own to pay the fine that would release him from jail, even though this was contrary to party regulations.[5] The letter he wrote to explain his action speaks for itself:

> After a day and night of reflection, I have decided to pay the 500 francs. I have weighed all the consequences of so doing. In my soul and my conscience, I believe that to pay the fine is consonant with the best interests of the party. I will account for my action to the B.P., to the I.C., and to the party. I think it is wrong to hand hostages over so easily without trying to get them out.[6]

4. A. Lecoeur, *Le Partisan*, p. 269.

5. The purpose of the rule against paying fines, as Thorez himself tells us in his book, *Fils du peuple*, was to "make a sharp break with certain 'legalistic' and opportunistic customs that were then current among party leaders." In particular, this "legalism" consisted in a willingness to pay fines. On this question see the political bureau's communiqué printed in *l'Humanité* of October 7, 1930.

6. Letter written by Maurice Thorez to Guy Jerram, quoted in A. Vassart, *Mémoires*.

Thus, when he was only thirty and not yet in possession of the authority and power he was to acquire after the Second World War—he was indeed very far from this—Maurice Thorez settled a matter that did not affect him alone. Nor did he bother to consult the political bureau first.

This portrait of Thorez is merely a rough sketch that probably needs a good deal of touching up. But as it stands, it at least suggests that, even during the Stalin era, the leader of one branch of the worldwide communist movement would never be content to serve as a mere errand boy. It shows, I believe, how intent he was, even within his own party, on learning his way around; on establishing criteria of his own for the regulation of his conduct and the formulation of his decisions; on acquiring the kind of autonomy that would enable him to show his skill in innovative and imaginative action.

Too Good a Memory?

What is changed today? What is it that makes Waldeck Rochet appear to be a man as incapable of committing gross blunders as of doing anything really original or new? The man is so perplexing that I must confess to some uncertainty about him. The present secretary-general of the French party is at once amazing—because you have to be very good to do what he does—and quite conformist—because you have to be a very limited person to do only what needs to be done.

How can one account for the fact that orthodox communist leaders—except for a few individuals here and there—are not prone to institute considerable changes either for better or for worse? They resemble certain scientific researchers who seem more advanced than their elders because of their unquestionable skill, but who nonetheless never "discover" anything. Can this possibly be because they have skill but absolutely no imagination, no inspiration, no creative talent? They know perfectly well *what needs to be done* in every instance, and they know how to proceed because they are enormously experienced. Almost never are they caught off guard. But if, momentarily, they should find themselves at a loss, they right themselves by gradually reducing the unforeseen to the foreseeable, the new to the dejà-vu or commonplace, even at the risk of destroying what is real. This is a curious paradox: in a party whose history has been so greatly blurred, so manipulated and falsified, a tradition has nonetheless developed whose substance, transmitted from generation to generation, tends, like the severity of a schoolmaster, to stifle all observation, all awareness of reality.

Is this due to an excessively good memory? If my hypothesis is correct, the origins of this excess should not be sought solely within the internal workings of the party. The entire structure of the worldwide revolutionary movement should be called into question. Of course, the internal workings of the party do contribute to the situation. This is what I hope to illustrate by analyzing successively the mechanisms of selection, training, and decision-making that govern the small world of the communist leaders.

10 | The Mechanisms of Selection

Who Chooses?

Theory is one thing and practice another.

Theory: in the hierarchy of the Communist party, as in all such bodies, leaders on every level are *elected* at conferences and congresses. The members of the bureau and the secretary of the cell are elected by the general assembly of the cell; the members of the sectional committee, who elect the sectional bureau and secretariat, are chosen by the sectional conference, usually held annually; the members of the federal section who elect the federal bureau and secretariat are chosen at the federal conference; finally, the members of the central committee who elect the political bureau and the secretariat, are chosen by the national congress which meets approximately every two years, although this varies considerably.

In theory, then, the procedure is entirely democratic.

But in practice things are quite different except at the level of the cell. There, the democratic process is thoroughly respected because the real problem is to find volunteers willing to take on the exasperating jobs of secretary and treasurer.

There's nothing that a "good" secretary of a cell doesn't do! He has to set up an agenda for the general assembly. Formerly the assembly met once a week; today it convenes twice a month, sometimes only once a month. Prior to

each meeting sectional planning sessions often take place.
Here directives and information have to be followed. In
addition, the secretary has the following responsibilities:
he studies various time-consuming practical problems and
tries to get others to take an interest in them; he must
not only edit the cell newspaper but also supervise its
publication and distribution; he posts notices on the bulletin board; supervises the sale of newspapers, especially
at mass meetings; backs up the CDH; distributes pamphlets; convokes occasional public meetings; sets up an
annual assembly for the "renewal of membership cards";
attends mass demonstrations, parades, commemorative
services, educational conferences; supervises the signing
of petitions; makes the preparations for major celebrations, especially the annual *l'Humanité* day; compiles lists
of contributors; lends a hand when needed to women's
organizations, youth groups, old people's clubs, the
Franco-Russian Society, veterans' associations. Partisans
of Peace, Friends of the Secular School. All this is merely
part of a routine and does not include the handling of
more urgent situations or emergencies.

Periodically, all this enormous activity, all these pressures, all this "performance"—that is the word usually
used in complaint by those in responsible positions—are
deplored. From time to time the communist hierarchy
tries to slow the pace. Every organization in the world has
exactly the same problems. The communist victims of all
this frenzied activity are subject to the same kind of non-
sense that plagues the victims of similar calamities in the
world at large. They take it or leave it, but mostly they
take it—unless, out of sheer exhaustion, they throw in the
sponge. If the work to be done in a cell is really taken
seriously by the militant, the pace will prove so exhausting

that, more often than not, the job will have to be rotated.[1] But there is also something reassuring about all this. When a person who is badly hurt thrashes around, you know he is still alive; when a communist performs his duties as a militant, you know that the revolution is on the move.

As for the mechanism of selection, practice is not at all consonant with theory, with the single exception of the cell. To be sure, in the plenary sessions of regular congresses, the leaders of communist bodies are elected. This is the official version. But actually the congress confers its approval automatically, even though at present the voting is secret. Prior to 1956 it voted by acclamation and by throwing confetti about.

The jurisdiction of higher agencies over lower ones is exercised through three converging channels: control of the list of candidates for membership in the bodies that direct the lower echelons; control of the list of delegates chosen by the lower echelons to represent them at congresses of the higher echelons; control of the list of candidates that lower echelons are called upon to put forward for posts involving the exercise of certain functions within the bodies that direct the higher echelons.

This tripartite jurisdiction of higher agencies over lower ones is designed to help the leaders make sure not only of the makeup of the managing and decision-making bodies during the intervals between congresses and conferences, but also of the membership of the congresses and conferences; for it is these gatherings that are officially invested with the power to choose the management and decision-making bodies.

1. See above, chapter 3. This reminds one of Lenin's famous saying in an article in 1923 on worker and peasant inspection: "Let's do less but let's do better."

This triple control takes place *before* and *during* conferences and statutory congresses.

During the weeks preceding a conference of the lower echelon, the upper echelon carefully studies the three lists that are submitted by the heads of the lower echelon.

This study is made initially by one particular organ, the "section of the cadres." What is it all about?

In the pre-1914 unified Socialist party there was a committee on conflicts whose task it was to adjudicate the unavoidable personal clashes that took place. Similarly, during the initial years of the Communist party, there was a central control committee (*Commission centrale de contrôle politique*) whose members were elected by the national congress. Its sole function was to hand down instructions on matters laid before it by the party's secretariat at the suggestion of the federations. At first the meetings of this central political control committee were presided over in debonair fashion by an old militant and former professor known as "Papa Dupont." Around 1931, the task was entrusted to Henri Gourdeaux, a militant trade unionist of the PTT (*Postes, Téléphone et Télégrammes*). His assistant was Lucien Midol, whose role in the 1919–20 railway workers' strike had made him famous.

To some extent the role of the CCCP was similar to that of the public prosecutor in society as a whole. But since the CCCP was elected directly by the congress, it enjoyed a certain independence and its members had a measure of personal authority—a hangover from the early days when autonomy outranked centralism.

It was therefore inevitable that Bolshevization should make itself felt. But this did not happen immediately. Not until 1932 was the CCCP replaced; on orders from Moscow, which were transmitted by Fried, a central committee for cadres was set up. The new body was wholly dependent on the central committee as regards the organization of sections. This meant that it was under the control of the organization's secretary.[2]

At the outset, however, the committee was expected to work for negative rather than positive ends. After the troubled years the party had lived through, years that can be summed up by recounting the history of the Barbé-Célor affair, it became urgently necessary to give proof of "revolutionary vigilance" by unmasking "suspects, undesirables, and agents provocateurs."

The technique employed at that time was therefore patterned after the one that had been fashioned by the Russian Communist party—the technique of "biographies," more familiarly known as "the bios." This worked as follows. The members of the central committee, regional heads, trade union minorities, individuals responsible for the party's organizations, members of local cadres—all these people had to fill out autobiographical questionnaires. The forms, duplicates of the one used by the Russians, stipulated that the answers must be "precise, complete, detailed, and verifiable."

The form of the 1938 questionnaire is well known because it was made public as a consequence of the Chalmette affair. In his capacity as communist mayor of a locality in the Alpes-Maritimes, Chalmette refused to fill out the questionnaire, claiming it violated his privacy.

2. The "central committee for political control" nonetheless has not disappeared. In theory, it is elected by the central committee. At the party's congress in January, 1967, a practice that had been shelved was once again resumed: to state precisely to the congress the composition of the central committee for political control (CCCP) after its members are elected at the first meeting of the central committee. Presently it has nine members of the C.C and its president is Etienne Fajon.

He resigned as a member of the party.[3] The following data had to be supplied by everyone filling out the questionnaire.

Identity: (1) Last name, first name, address, and pseudonym. (2) Date and place of birth. (3) Occupation. (4) All positions held and all places of work, listed chronologically from the time of the war to the present. (5) Present wage and, if possible, all prior wages. (6) Other financial resources and the date on which wage-earning began.

Parents: (7) Occupation of father and mother. (8) Parents' resources. (9) Their contacts and political opinions.

Marriage: (10) Name of wife or companion. (11) Her occupation. (12) Her wage. (13) Member of the party? (14) Her activities. (15) Her political opinions. (16) Her contacts. (17) Name of her mother and father. (18) Their occupations and wages. (19) Their contacts. (20) Any children? If so, how many?

Under the heading of "General Relationships" there followed a series of questions that reveals the measure of revolutionary vigilance. For example:

"Among your relatives and friends, are there any individuals who belong to the forces that oppress or repress the working class? Are they enemies or adversaries of the party? If the answer is yes for the relatives, state the degree of kinship. For friends, answer the following questions: How long have you known them? How did you make their acquaintance? Exactly why do you see them?"

Or again:

"Have you belonged to political groups other than the Communist party? For how long? Why and when did you leave them?"

3. *La Petite Illustration* no. 897, (1938).

One final question remained. Its purpose was to check wherever necessary the accuracy of the member's statement: "Do you know any members of the Communist party personally? Give the names of at least three of them and list their current responsibilities."

The technique of the "biographies" remained in use even after the war.[4] Headings that seemed excessively conjectural in nature were altered and a few leading questions were replaced by others. For example, at the time of Liberation, the following query was added: "What was your position at the time of the Nazi-Soviet Pact?"

If, despite all its deficiencies, this technique was used, the explanation is to be found in the belief that it would serve to eliminate the spies and informers who notoriously infested the pre-1914 workers' movement in France. Even the members of the executive committee admitted this was so, and in December, 1933, they credited the French section for getting rid of spies and informers. The task of safeguarding these "archives," even temporarily, was a very difficult one, especially during the pre-1939 period, for at that time they had to be shipped across several frontiers to reach the Communist International's headquarters in Moscow. The historian will be able to verify all this once the state archives have been opened. To do this he will of course have to take the time to check what the police "knew" and what they "didn't know" about the organization of the Communist party. In accordance with the stipulations of current legislation, it will be necessary to wait some ten or twenty years.

But all this is not important. It did not take long to

4. See J. Chaumeil, *le Problème des cadres*, report presented to an assembly of those responsible to the cadres of the Paris region and of the ex-Nord zone, organized by the central cadres committee of the French Communist party on October 7, 1944 (Lyon: Imprimerie commerciale), 31pp.

realize that the enormous file could be used for purposes other than the negative ones originally intended. Why not use it to establish a reserve of potential cadres made up of militants whose "bios" were in every way satisfactory?

Thus, the central cadres committee, together with its counterparts on the lower echelons—the "federal cadres committees" and the "agents of the cadres" in sectional committees—has been gradually equipped to "register" militants. This involves getting them to fill out their "bios." It will then be possible to pick them out without loss of time whenever they show signs of being able to assume responsible positions. The primary mission of the central cadres committee, possessing as it does all available information on the general disposition of forces in every communist organization, is to suggest the possible use of existing or potential cadres before the regular conferences or congresses convened.

Upon some careful prior examination, the secretariat of a given federation—to use the departmental echelon as illustration—can assess the composition of a committee in the section where the conference is scheduled to meet and determine which members should be retired and which promoted.

Naturally, the section involved must be convinced that the secretariat's decisions are wise. This brings into play the functions of the "federal" delegate at the sectional conference. It is customary for a delegate from a higher echelon to attend the conferences and congresses of every lower echelon. The delegate is no mere spectator. Not only does he participate actively in the discussions that take place in the plenary session; he also delivers the "closing speech" in which "conclusions are drawn." He may praise the section's activities or criticize the way things are being done. He discusses the current political picture, reminds his audience of the party's political objectives, and comments on various political doctrines. What is far more important, the delegate from the federation joins in the discussions and actually directs the "political committee" of the conference.[5]

This political committee is a small body elected in plenary session, and it attends all regular conferences and congresses at every level. It consists of one or several representatives from each "delegation"—from each cell in a sectional conference, from each section in a federal conference, and so on. Its function, in theory, is to supervise in a general way the manner in which the debates are conducted. It may deem it necessary to draw the plenary assembly's attention to the advisability of orienting the discussion in one direction or another. But its main task is to examine the candidatures to the administrative bodies. And so it is here, within a small group, that discussions take place regarding the personal qualities of individuals. The activities of those who are being replaced as well as the personality traits of the new men are weighed. At this point the representative of the federation (to the sectional conference) or of the central committee (to the federal conference) intervenes to influence decisions that have been predetermined. It is here that the list of candidates for administrative positions is drawn up and submitted for approval to the plenary assembly, as well as the list of conference delegates to the higher

5. "Political committee" or "Candidatures Commission." This commission may or may not be distinct from the "bureau" of the congress, and is also elected at the opening of the plenary assembly (but its composition is determined before the opening). The composition of this "bureau," moreover gives the first concrete indications of the candidates that will be proposed.

echelon congress; and finally, the candidates that the lower echelon has chosen to exercise functions in administrative bodies to be elected by the congress of the higher echelon.

A detailed analysis of these mechanisms of selection should enable us to understand why it is that centralism has always been assured. On one side we have militants, carefully screened by the political committee, who hardly know each other and have only a limited understanding of current problems; on the other, we have a delegate from a higher echelon armed with information gleaned from carefully kept files, someone whose perspective is broad and who comes equipped with already-made decisions.[6]

This does not mean that "spontaneity" is entirely lacking. First of all, the lower echelon, as we have seen, assumes the initiative. In the beginning the cadres committee of the higher echelon is guided by its suggestions. Then, in the conferences themselves, or at least at the level of the sectional conference where militants know each other well, new suggestions of genuine merit are often made and accepted, if only on an experimental basis. Moreover, to understand current practice, one must remember that there are frequent consultations, including those among high-ranking militants, in which the cadres

6. Cf. the testimony of Auguste Lecoeur, an expert on the subject since as secretary of the organization from 1950 to 1954 he had charge of the section of cadres: "According to the statutes the central committee is elected by the congress. In actuality the members are selected by the cadres committee, presented to the secretariat, and then the list of names retained is given to the political committee of the congress. At the plenary session, this list is ratified by acclamation, not by vote. No one may suggest the slightest modification" (*Le Partisan*, [Flammarion, 1963], p. 249).

participate when they prepare their suggestions. As in every authoritarian structure, it is naturally much easier to obtain approval for this or that leader if his nomination "from above" is preceded by discreet feelers among his future subordinates. Lastly, one must also remember that the theoretical pattern is often more flexible than it may seem, especially at the sectional level, because of the conditions that prevail in the provinces. The continuity of the communist social fabric in the Paris region is such that custom is rather strictly observed. But many provincial sections—where the local militants have to be treated with kid gloves because there are not too many to choose from—have attained a certain degree of autonomy. Each of them uses its militants as it sees fit, pleading its own special situation when called upon to deal with federal directives and emissaries of the central committee.

But the higher one goes in the hierarchy, the less chance there is for any initiative from below to make itself felt. There are two reasons for this. First, almost all the members of political committees in the federal and central echelons belong to the world of the cadres; they therefore know that prior study has already resulted in fairly firm decisions. Second, serious candidates cannot suddenly be imposed ex nihilo.

An understanding of the general situation makes it clear why the suggestions for reform that were made immediately following the Twentieth Congress of the PCUS (*Parti communiste de l'Union Soviétique*) were doomed to failure. The reforms envisaged a "return to Leninist democracy." Introduction of the secret ballot and listing a larger number of candidates than the number of posts to be filled are among the steps that might eventually be taken to put a little life into rusty mechanisms, but such measures would not put the mechanisms completely out of order.[7] If the mechanisms were really to be made inoperative, there would have to be a complete reversal of the current, a radical rejection of the open, discreet or camouflaged interference of the higher echelons in the affairs of the lower. This is a process with which other institutions in this centralized Jacobin country are familiar. It involves the pros and cons of "autonomy": all its advantages as well as its risks (the constitution of small, local, feudal systems, like those in the former Socialist party; the tendency to develop an inflexibility that makes it impossible for an organization with ample resources to come to the aid of another, poorer one; and so on).

Who Is Chosen?

Our study of the mechanisms of selection enables us to answer the first question: "Who chooses?" The answer may be somewhat less black and white than the one usually given, but it is nevertheless clear: the relationship between democracy and centralism remains overwhelmingly in favor of centralism.

But we still need to know the criteria of selection in order to answer the second question: "Who is chosen?"

7. The secret ballot, suggested in 1956 by the liberal "opponents," was resisted for a long time by the party administration. However, in the new statutes adopted in 1964, there was a provision for the secret ballot. See G. Marchais, "Intervention au XVII⁰ congrès," *Cahiers du communisme*, June-July, 1964, pp. 286–330. Even in secret ballot, it is hardly probable that 50 percent would vote against a candidate. On the other hand, the 1964 statutes continue to disregard another method: it would consist in presenting more candidates than there are positions and thus give the plenary assembly of the congresses genuine freedom of choice.

But we should first ask ourselves: Is there a choice? In other words, does the amount of competition that exists tend to eliminate along the way a large proportion of the individuals who aspire to head the communist apparatus?

This is a delicate question. Has anyone ever attempted to measure how much competition there is among French politicians?

Although the facts at our disposal do not provide a basis for definitive conclusions, we can at least begin with three working hypotheses. (1) At the level of the cadres as well as in terms of the total membership, the candidates are certainly numerous enough to warrant the criticism that a good deal of talent is wasted. (2) Nonetheless, what emerges from the whole picture is a nucleus so solid that the natural methods of elimination cannot, it seems, break down its stability. (3) All in all, the competition is uneven. Varying according to categories, it is in great part distorted by the fact that the collective notion of representation, rather than that of individual capability, prevails.

Substantial Waste of Cadres. From 1921 to 1924 the size of the administrative committee of the French Communist party was fixed. There were twenty-four members and eight substitutes. Then, in 1924, when the party was "Bolshevized," the composition of the administrative committee was made more flexible. To the twenty-four members and eight substitutes the following were added: five representatives from the province; four representatives of special communist organizations (Youth, Students, the Latin Bureau);[8] two representatives of foreign communist

8. "Latin bureau" was the name of the bureau whose mission it was to "follow" the activities of the communist parties in Latin

groups in France. In 1925 the administrative committee was renamed the central committee to emphasize its position as the supreme administrative organ in the intervals between congresses. It was also enlarged. Thereafter, its size varied. Until 1939 it had a minimum of forty-three members (in 1925) and a maximum of seventy-nine (in 1926). During the interwar period, the central committee averaged about forty members and ten substitutes.

After the war, from 1945 to the present, the size of the central committee increased from sixty-nine members in 1945 to ninety by the end of the Eighteenth Congress (January, 1967)—an average of eighty-six members. Recently an effort appears to have been made to limit the membership to no more than one hundred.

From 1920 to 1939, for the average of fifty positions that were available on the central committee, there were, at one time or another, 210 persons who were either members or substitutes. From 1945 until 1968 there were 214 persons for 90 positions.

Formation of a Stable Nucleus. During "Bolshevization," when the central committee was enlarged, its structure became more complex. At the first three congresses the militants were listed in alphabetical order, but in 1925 this was changed; thereafter they were listed in the order of merit. Later, the alphabetical order was resumed, but in 1936 Cachin and Thorez were singled out in order of merit. Another change occurred in 1937: it was then that a definite distinction was made between the former candidates and the new ones.

---

countries (France, Italy, South America, the Iberian Peninsula) and to report back to the executive committee of the International.

This internal hierarchization of the central committee, which led to the establishment of a pattern, culminated in 1945 in further innovations. At the Tenth Congress (June, 1945) the following categories were placed at the top of the hierarchy: central committee members who were also members of the political bureau (in the order of merit); central committee members who were also substitute members of the political bureau (in the order of merit); new central committee members (in alphabetical order); substitute members of the central committee (in alphabetical order).

A reaction against all this sophisticated ordering set in at the Sixteenth Congress (1961) and during deliberations at the Twentieth Congress of the PCUS. Thereafter, all the central committee members were listed in strict alphabetical order and substitutes were listed separately, also in alphabetical order. But this kind of dichotomy probably did not satisfy the need for an internal hierarchy. The Seventeenth and Eighteenth Congresses reestablished an additional echelon: both the former substitutes, whose status had not changed, and the new substitutes were listed after the names of the members.

The existence of this hierarchy within the central committee furthered the establishment of a stable nucleus at the central committee level, a fact which the simplest statistics demonstrate very clearly.

In effect, from 1920 to 1939, ten regular congresses proceeded to elect administrative or central committees. At the Saint-Denis Congress of 1929, however, the composition of the central committee was not made public. Many members of the central committee were then being threatened with arrest. As a consequence, only nine official lists are available for the interwar period.

It must be emphasized that we are referring here to

official lists. As such, they present no major problems because the Communist party itself was entirely legal despite individual cases of severe repression. Only a few pseudonyms need to be deciphered. Nonetheless, I must make one basic reservation. After 1925 the official composition of the central committee should not be confused with its actual composition. There are two reasons why such a distinction must be made. First, various individuals whose names appeared on the agenda were invited to attend meetings of the central committee. These included members of related central committees and services. Some of them were better informed than the de jure committee members, especially those who lived in the provinces, and actually had more influence. Second, clandestine members with full voting rights sat on the central committee. They were responsible for special sectors whose activities it would not have been prudent to mention. The responsibility of the clandestine members extended to the following: the activities of foreign communist groups residing in France; communist groups residing in the colonies; the antimilitarist apparatus; communist functionaries who held positions in the state apparatus; international communist organizations that had a branch in France, principally delegates of the Communist International to the French Communist party.

The *mobility* of the central committee is shown by the following figures for 210 individuals who, from 1920 to 1939, were at one time or another elected members of the central committee.[9]

9. The reasoning that follows is based on calculations concerning the *official* and *substitute* members. The hierarchical distinction is interesting in following the career of a militant. It is also interesting from the standpoint of the role it plays in the structuralization of the administrative bodies. But it is of

NO. OF MILITANTS	NUMBER OF TIMES ELECTED
115	1
44	2
29	3
10	4
5	5
4	6
1	7
1	8
1	9

As a consequence, one member out of two (104 out of 210)[10] from any one of the central committees elected between 1920 and 1939 was definitely eliminated as soon as the next election took place. The average rate of elimination amounted therefore to 50 percent.

But if we consider separately the composition of each of the central committees elected between 1920 and 1939, we find that the percentage of members eliminated at each of the ensuing congresses varies considerably. The table on page 242 makes this clear.

The variations are obviously due to special circumstances. The period from 1920 to 1924 was an agitated one. French communism was in the process of self-discovery. These years coincided with a period that saw a very rapid revamping of administrative organizations. The composition of the latter was intermittently and drastically altered by basic changes that affected the movement

---

no significance in terms of stability or instability. In fact, the alternates have the right to be present at central committee meetings and have the same prerogatives as official members. At least, that is the actual practice today.

10. Not 115 militants, but 104. Eleven militants were elected in 1937. But we are not counting them, since for the moment we are not taking the study beyond 1939.

as a whole. From 1924 to 1936 "Bolshevized" communism also experienced the process of self-discovery. Throughout these years the establishment of a stable administrative apparatus gradually took place.

YEAR	NO. OF MEMBERS	NO. ELIMINATED	%
1920	32	17	53
1921	31	19	61
1922	32	26	81
1924	40	19	47
1925	43	16	32
1926	79	56	70[11]
1932	54	15	28
1936	46	7	15[12]

This does not mean that the ephemeral cadres active only in the interval between congresses were completely eliminated. They comprised roughly a fourth of the members of each central committee.

On the other hand, the number of functionaries increased rapidly. If we figure (quite arbitrarily) that a militant who has been elected to the central committee at least four times achieves such a status, then it would apparently follow that out of 210 militants who at one time or another were members of the central committee between 1920 and 1939, twenty-one, or 10 percent, were elected anywhere from four to nine times.

11. The reader must have no illusions about the high percentage, 70 percent, of members eliminated from the central committee that was elected in 1926. Since we do not have the list of central committee members elected in 1929, this percentage actually covers the period of *three* congresses, not two.

12. This percentage, although low, is actually lower in fact. Some of the militants whose names appear on the 1936 list are no longer listed in 1937, not because they were actually eliminated but because, in view of the 1936 agreement against the accumulation of political and trade union functions, they officially gave up their political functions in order to retain their union functions. This was merely a game, on paper, of course.

Actually, only one member was elected nine times out of nine (Marcel Cachin); another was elected eight times (Henri Gourdeaux); another seven times (Renaud Jean); six were elected six times (Gabriel Péri, Henri Raynaud, Louis Sellier, Pierre Sémard, Maurice Thorez, Paul Vaillant-Couturier); three were elected five times (Johanny Berlioz, Lucien Midol, André Marty); nine were elected four times (François Billoux, Florimond Bonte, Gaston Cornavin, Alfred Costes, Jacques Doriot, Jacques Duclos, Georges Maranne, Gaston Monmousseau, Albert Vassart).

Each name recalls the special fate of the individual cited. The men were not all members of the same generation and they were certainly not all the same type of militant. Moreover, not all of those who played a major role in the development of the communist movement in France are in this list. Nevertheless, the list represents a valid sample of what we mean when we speak of the "permanent elements."

How large a proportion of the membership of each central committee does this stable nucleus represent? It amounts to approximately a third of the membership, as the following table shows.

CENTRAL COMMITTEE ELECTED IN	NO. OF CENTRAL COM. MEMBERS	PERMANENT ELEMENTS	%
1924	40	14	35
1925	43	15	34
1926	79	22	27
1932	51	18	35
1936	46	17	36
1937	50	14	28

After a first quick estimate, one might conclude that during the interwar period, about one-fourth of the members of each central committee were bound to be temporary and about one-third permanent. Isn't the above an answer, at least in part, to the ambiguities forever alluded to by commentators when they speak or write about the communist cadres? Occasionally they say, "They're always the same ones"; at other times they say, "They're always changing."

Postwar developments have confirmed a trend that began during the 1930s: the continuing and marked increase in the proportion of permanent members. From 1945 to 1967, nine congresses elected nine successive central committees. The following figures apply to the 214 militants who were elected to these committees at one time or another.

NO. OF MILITANTS	NO. OF TIMES ELECTED
40	1
53	2
33	3
17	4
26	5
17	6
12	7
5	8
11	9

Whereas from 1920 to 1939 one out of every two elected central committee members was definitively eliminated at the ensuing election, only one out of every six has been eliminated in all the years since 1945.

Furthermore, if we study the composition of the central committees between 1945 and 1968, we will see that the number of members eliminated at ensuing elections fluctuated between 4 percent and 34 percent of the total.

It therefore would seem that the number of ephemeral cadres fell to less than a fifth of the total.

CENTRAL COM. ELECTED IN	NO. OF CENTRAL COM. MEMBERS	NO. ELIMINATED	%
1945	69	9	13
1947	84	29	34
1950	77	21	27
1954	71	3	4
1956	99	17	17
1959	93	10	10
1961	99	31	31
1964	93	8	8

If we accept the somewhat arbitrary criterion for permanency—election at least four times—we find that of the 214 militants who were members of a central committee between 1945 and 1968, 88, or 41 percent, were permanent members, compared to 10 percent in 1939.

Of the ninety present-day members of the central committee (elected or reelected in the Eighteenth Congress of January, 1967):

three have been members since 1926, in other words, for forty-two years (Billoux, Duclos, Frachon);

three have been members since 1932, for thirty-six years (Fajon, Guyot, Mauvais);

one has been a member since 1936, for thirty-two years (Waldeck Rochet);

six have been members since 1945, twenty-three years (Ballanger, after a lengthy interruption from 1947 to 1961, Figuères, Garaudy, Villon, Marie-Claude Vaillant-Couturier, Jeannette Vermeersch);

four have been members since 1947, twenty-one years (Yvonne Dumont, Léon Feix, Victor Joannès, Fernande Valignat).

All in all, therefore, seventeen of the ninety members of the central committee have been there for more than twenty years. Twenty-five have served for more than ten years.

One might also wonder about the extent to which the problem today is one of artificially revamping an organism that, if left alone, tends to become rigidly fixed. This concern about an overhauling of the body seems to be borne out by the relative suddenness with which the percentage of new members increased, in 1956 and again in 1964, as the following table shows.

YEAR	NO. OF TOTAL MEMBERS	NEW MEMBERS	%
1945	69	44	62
1947	84	24	28
1950	77	22	28
1954	71	15	21
1956	99	30	30
1959	93	11	11
1961	99	16	16
1964	93	25	26
1967	90	5	5

All this enables us to show how much more restricted was the body represented by the political bureau.

At the Fifth Congress, in June, 1926, the French party, under the direct control of the executive committee of the Communist International,[13] was called upon to reorganize its administration by inviting the central committee to designate a homogeneous and compact nucleus within it. Originally envisaged as comprising about a dozen members, this new body, which was named the political bureau, has always varied considerably in size. Reduced to nine members in 1937, it has tended to increase ever since 1945. Today it consists of nineteen members.

From 1926 to 1932, its political composition was

13. Three members whose identities were not revealed were eliminated from the official total.

varied. This is accounted for by the fact that it reflected closely the trials and errors that accompanied the search for strength upon which to build a Bolshevized party.

At the outset, the first political bureau did try to make itself the mouthpiece of the two forces upon whose solidarity the International eventually hoped to rely. Communist members of the trade unions represented one of these forces; militants trained in the communist youth organizations, especially the sections carrying on "anti-militarist activities," represented the other. As a consequence, alongside a few militants who, accustomed to the way things used to be done, were adjusting to new ways, were such men as Monmousseau, Frachon, Racamond, in the first category; Doriot, in the second. Maurice Thorez already occupied a special position. He was one of the young men—only twenty-six at the time—but he did not belong to the youth group that emerged from the *Jeunesses communistes*, because "youth" in this case signified not age but political policy.

Three years later, in April, 1929, the Sixth Congress, convening at Saint-Denis, eliminated from the political bureau those members who were part of the pre-Bolshevization generation (Bernard, Sellier, Renaud Jean), as well as two other militants who meanwhile had suffered "accidents along the way": Dudillieux and Crémet. Simultaneously, the political bureau suddenly welcomed five "new" members: Barbé, Ferrat, Billoux, Lozeray, Célor. This action was evidence of the triumph won by the group that had emerged from the *Jeunesses communistes*. During the ensuing period, which was a terribly confused one, the political bureau was again thoroughly shaken up. This occurred on three separate occasions.

In June, 1930, the political bureau was suddenly reduced from thirteen to seven members (Barbé, Cachin,

Doriot, Frachon, Monmousseau, Sémard, Thorez); in March, 1932, the central committee elected at the Seventh Congress designated a political bureau of eleven members. After the twelfth plenary session of the executive committee of the Communist International in September of the same year, four candidates were added to the political bureau, in the following order: Vassart, Tillon, Martel, and Arrachart.

This decision taken in the autumn of 1932 marked the final point of the process that culminated in the establishment of a political bureau. Thereafter the political bureau changed very gradually as a few new members were periodically added: two at the Eighth Congress; none at the Ninth; two at the Eleventh; two at the Twelfth; three at the Thirteenth; three at the Fourteenth; one at the Fifteenth; one at the Sixteenth; two at the Eighteenth.

On only two occasions were new elements brought in. The first of these occasions coincided with the immediate post-Liberation period preceding the Tenth Congress in July, 1945. In January of that year, the central committee (composed of members elected in 1937, prior to the war) added six "new" members (Dupuy, Fajon, Guyot, Mauvais, Rochet, Tillon) to the eight "old" ones (Thorez, Duclos, Marty, Frachon, Cachin, Monmousseau, Billoux, Ramette). Its action was dictated solely by the need to conform to regulations that had not been acted upon earlier because of circumstances. Then, at the Seventeenth Congress, in 1964, the addition of four new members marked the end of the Thorezian period.

The present attitude on the question of revamping the political bureau is a continuation of the one that has prevailed for thirty-six years. It accounts for the fact that in forty-one years (between the Fifth and Eighteenth Congresses, or from 1926 to 1967), a total of only forty-three militants have joined the political bureau, nineteen of whom are still members today.

It is therefore not surprising that the members of the political bureau should have been carried over from one congress to another. Although eleven out of forty-three were elected only once (during a period that spanned two congresses), six were elected twice, five three times, five four times, four five times, two six times, three seven times, four nine times (Cachin, Fajon, Guyot, and Rochet), one eleven times (Billoux), and two twelve times (Duclos and Thorez).

The great stability of the leading body has posed a serious problem: how can such a body attain the mobility it so sorely needs? To augment its size is an unsatisfactory solution because the group will lose its effectiveness if it becomes too large. Today there are nineteen members in it, and this apparently constitutes the outside limit. Consequently, should new elements be introduced into the political bureau, some of its present members will have to be eliminated. But on what basis should this be done?

Of the twenty-four leaders who, over the past forty years, have ceased to be members of the political bureau, three died natural deaths (Thorez, Cachin, Monmousseau). Ten others left for a variety of reasons: age, illness, ineptitude, or because they were assuming other party responsibilities. This is a small number. One soon becomes aware in this connection of the impact of "party affairs," as the communists call them, meaning serious political crises, on the movement as a whole. Actually, ten members of the political bureau left because of basic disagreement. In the midst of the upheaval caused by Bolshevization, Sellier and Renaud Jean resigned. Doriot and Ferrat quit, for opposite reasons, during the ripening of the Popular Front policy. When the Nazi-Soviet Pact was signed, Git-

ton left. After the war there were three major "affairs:"
the "Marty-Tillon affair" in 1952; the "Lecoeur affair" in
1954; the "Casanova-Servin affair" in 1961. Among other
things,[14] these crises served to reestablish a certain degree
of mobility at the top of the communist hierarchy. Interesting in this connection is the fact that the notorious trials
of the stalinist era, although marked by more violence,
had an identical effect.

Differentiated Competition. The relative waste of talent
among cadres competing in the selection of a stable administrative nucleus (at every level, but especially in the
lower echelons), together with the relative rigidity at the
top of the communist hierarchy, should have been conducive to the arrival of new men, of individuals of outstanding ability, since they had triumphed in the face of
open and fierce competition. Nothing of the kind, however occurred. Competition was largely distorted for two
reasons: the *real* nature of power in the communist apparatus; the party's general conception of the decision-
making process. As a result, administrative bodies at
every level were set up in such a way as to make them as
"representative" as possible. Such representation was
visualized as a process that moved in two directions:
from the outside world to the party; from the party to the
outside world.

The central and federal committees were less intent on
selecting the most capable, gifted candidates—the criteria

14. I have attempted to deal with these three French "affairs"
in an overall analysis of the Stalinization of the French communist phenomenon. Cf. A. Kriegel, "Les Débats théoriques et
idéologiques dans les PC français et italiens depuis 1956," Report to the Table Ronde of the Association française de science
politique (May 1968) on "Les problèmes du communisme dans
le monde contemporain" (in the process of publication).

for this were subjective and questionable—than on gathering together men who, because of their functions and positions, were best equipped to understand and interpret the profound currents of opinion in circles whose views would markedly affect the party. And, inversely, the movement wanted men who, within these circles, were living symbols of what the party hoped to accomplish in the present and in the future.

Thereafter everything occurred as if a theoretical model of the central committee were being adhered to. Actually, a theoretical ideal of the party is operative. It controls in part the image provided at every congress by the report of the "commission on mandates," a document that indicates the number of delegates and their distribution according to sex, occupation, age, and seniority. This image is in fact *real* because it is patterned on actual, flesh-and-blood individuals working together. At the same time it is also *theoretical* since a good number of these real individuals are selected as delegates only because they approximate the theoretical, idealized conception which the party has of itself.

The basic objective in choosing delegates, therefore, is to make the real conform as closely as possible to the theoretical model. The following categories *must* be given maximum "representation": the different "generations"; women as well as men; various socioprofessional affiliations; principal regions; key sectors for mass action. In the end, then, the administrative body *must* represent a microcosm of both the party and the country—at least that segment of the nation which the communists regard as their "real country."

Given these circumstances, competition is not all-encompassing. It is not true that anyone can compete against anyone. Competition is uneven and occurs sector by sector; its intensity varies according to the urgency of needs.

Thus, the need to include women who "represent" the female masses makes it imperative to carry out an exhaustive program of recruitment and to train female cadres. The fluctuations of these cadres are as considerable as those that affect female members of the party generally.[15] In 1966, out of 589 female members of federal committees, 135 were not reelected; of the 576 females elected, 122 were elected for the first time.[16]

Similarly, since 1945, the majority of party members elected to the central committee and quickly eliminated—despite the absence of serious disagreements or defections—were workers. They had been promoted rapidly precisely because of their satisfactory social origins, but they were not able to adapt themselves to the requirements of their new positions.

All in all, the uneven competition between sector and sector evolved within a context that helped to reinforce further the influence of the theoretical model. This definitely explains why the communist leaders conformed so rigidly to their conception of the model. They were at once very aware and very ignorant of what they needed to know —ignorant of everything that was not embraced by a theoretical model the fashioning of which goes back several decades. It seems increasingly clear that individuals belonging to categories whose particularly valued "image" was threatened were the only ones who would take the risk of vying for rapid promotion. For everyone else, promotions were the carefully considered and long anticipated result of the exercise of functions in which the

15. See above, chapter 4.
16. J. Thorez-Vermeersch, *France nouvelle* (September 28, 1966).

recipient is confirmed a posteriori by a regular "election." The last three central committees were exemplary from this point of view: the new "alternates," elected at the Sixteenth Congress (1961), the Seventeenth (1964), and the Eighteenth (1967) were, respectively, thirty-six, thirty-seven, and thirty-seven years old. More important, the average amount of time required to attain seniority— that is, the length of the period during which they were party members—was sixteen and nineteen years (we don't yet have the figures on this for the Seventeenth Congress). We have here evidence that, in most cases, election to the central committee represents the crowning achievement of a candidate's party career. It would of course be interesting to know the average amount of time needed by functionaries, as distinguished from length of time as party members, to attain seniority, but unfortunately we do not have statistics for this. Apparently, almost all newly elected members already were part of the apparatus. They were called upon to become part of the party's administration precisely because of the functions they fulfilled. Thus we begin to understand how the mechanisms of selection come to be confused with the training process.

11 | The Training Process

Down with communist pedants!

Far be it from me to deny the need for a popular (but not a vulgar) literature for the most sincere workers. But what strikes me as revolting is the constant juxtaposition of pedagogy with questions of policy and organization.

LENIN[1]

We must say not only to the Russians but also to foreigners that the most important thing in the period now beginning is to learn. We do learn, in a general way; they will have to learn, in a special way, in order really to understand the organization, structure, methods, and nature of revolutionary work. If this is done, I am certain that the prospects for worldwide revolution will be not only good but excellent.

LENIN[2]

The process of training communists is obviously complex. The old, worn-out, oft-reiterated phrases are significant: "Impatience is not a revolutionary virtue." "One learns from life as well as from books."

Using different terms, Jesuits and communists, cautious educators that they are, concur on one fundamental point: people are powerless against time and experience. In regard to such things as aptitude, dedication, vocation, only

1. Letter to Bukharin, dated February 4, 1922, vol. 25, p. 335.

2. Speech to the Fourth Congress of the Communist International, November 15, 1922, published in the *Bulletin* of the Fourth Congress, no. 8, November 16, 1922.

duration is a valid yardstick and only practical experience is decisively revealing:

> Cadres are created by selection in action. This selection takes a long time. It can only come about as a consequence of continuous experience in the struggle. . . . The communist organizer must be schooled in the idea that he should not busy himself with revolution as if it were a pastime, that he must devote himself entirely to the revolutionary struggle, that he is entirely at the disposal of the Party.[3]

Hence the extension of the probationary period, whenever an abundance of resources makes this possible. As we have seen, the recent promotions announced by the central committee are noteworthy less for their relatively restricted nature than for the length of the probationary period and the amount of experience that had been acquired by the newly-elected members.

From this point of view—which coincides with the modern attitude toward the training of the functionary—every activity is of some pedagogical value: reading *l'Humanité*, discussions at the section conferences, participation in an election campaign or in a strike. The annual party at Vincennes for *l'Humanité* is not the least important of those activities whose purpose is basically pedagogical.

But the party is not merely a source of information derived from the vicissitudes of daily life. Its aim is to proceed very systematically in the training of cadres.

Various methods have been tried—correspondence courses, monthly educational conferences, graduated reading lists, encouragement of "individual efforts"—

3. *Cahiers du bolchevisme*, special no., "La Bolchevisation et le problème des cadres," May 23, 1925

which are then gone over for mistakes.[4] For example, almost six hundred students took the correspondence course in 1932–33. Of these, thirty-nine were women; fifty-four belonged to the party's youth organization. Fifty percent of the students worked in private industry; 55 percent, mostly young people, were ordinary party members. The course was divided into two parts: lessons in theory ("capitalism," "socialism," and the like) and instruction in practical politics. The courses in practical politics included such assignments as the following: "Write an article"; "Write a tract for socialist workers"; "Draft an outline for a speech"; "Draw up a list of workers' demands."[5]

The most widely used technique, which has persisted until the present, is that of establishing a network of schools whose objective is to give carefully picked militants "a systematic introduction to communist doctrine."[6]

A mere enumeration of the various schools will probably not shed much light on how they actually function. First there are the *elementary schools* for sectional cadres. They offer a series of night courses. Then, at the departmental level, there are the *federal schools* that operate during the day as well as at night. The courses given during the day are part of the program of the "permanent federal schools" whose students quit their jobs to attend school for two consecutive weeks, approximately. Lastly, there are the *central schools* run by the party's Central School at Choisy, formerly the home of Maurice Thorez. The courses at this school last anywhere from one to four months and are given either to people in specialized cadres

4. Cf. in 1952 the campaign for "individual study."
5. See *Cahiers du bolchevisme*, nos. 22 and 23, 1933.
6. *Cahiers du bolchevisme*, no. 13, February 15, 1925.

—women workers, trade union militants, peasant militants—or to a group of students whose activities and indoctrination vary considerably. The common denominator, identical for all of them, is the level of responsibility attached to their respective functions in "civilian life"— meaning the jobs they held before they were chosen to attend the school. The reports made by the central committee's services the day before the meeting of each national congress contain extensive, concrete statistics for which the central educational section, organized in 1930, is always responsible.

The large numbers that attend this network of schools is a measure of the importance attached to the training of cadres. It is also an indication of the human, financial, and organizational investment involved. Nevertheless, it does not shed light on the content of the courses. Obviously the curriculum has changed throughout the years, changing circumstances and events having determined the political themes. Courses have also varied in accordance with the kind of students enrolled and their intellectual level. Generally speaking, the curriculum comprises five major subjects: communist theory, economics, history, general politics, and political techniques.

In 1930, for example, courses in communist theory were reduced to a minimum because "theorizing" was looked upon with some suspicion. The program included courses in the Marxist methodology, the relationship between capitalism and imperialism, the state. The course in history dealt with the "Second International and opportunistic degradation, the history of the Russian Communist Party, the Communist International and its French section." The courses in general politics covered the following topics: structure and operation of the Communist party; strategy and tactics; the peasant problem in France; the national and colonial problem in France. Courses on current political problems were concerned with the situation in France and in the USSR; the danger of war; parliamentary and municipal politics; party tactics. Lastly, the course on political techniques dealt with various forms of the so-called agit-prop (agitation-propaganda) of the organization.[7]

In 1936, when the influx of new members posed the problem of education on an unusually large scale, the central educational section published a series of five handbooks designed for the elementary schools. They were entitled: "What is the Crisis? How Can we Solve it?"; "The State, Fascism and Democracy"; "The Party"; "The Party's Political Policies"; "France from 1789 to the Present."

Also in 1936, the curriculum of a regional school (there were eight such schools, one in each of the following places: Paris, Nice, Marseille, Alès, Bordeaux, Rouen, western Paris, Alsace-Lorraine) contained courses on the principles of economics, the state, imperialism, the economic crisis, fascism, the proletarian revolution, the construction of socialism, the history of the pre-1914 workers' movement, the founding and growth of the French Communist party, the role and principles of the party, and others. As for the Central School, its 1936 curriculum for an eight-month session comprised the following: eight courses on economics; three courses on the problems of government; four courses on materialism; eight courses on the party and organizational problems; nine courses

7. Cf. Victor, "Une année d'expérience des écoles régionales," *Cahiers du bolchevisme*, no. 9, September 1930. It is altogether possible that the signature "Victor" stands for Victor Bur (Victor Fay), the director of the educational section in 1932.

on the policies of the party; and four courses on current affairs.[8]

At present the curriculum for the elementary schools is condensed into six pamplets: "Social Classes and Capitalist Exploitation"; "The Struggle for Peace"; "The Nation and the National Role of the Working Class"; "The Struggle for Democracy"; "The Communists' Ideal"; "The Communist Party." In 1956, Maurice Thorez, addressing the teaching staff of the Central School, suggested a number of topics for study: important changes in the international field and the role of the USSR in world politics; pauperization; various forms of transition to socialism; the significance of the fact that war has ceased to be inevitable; the unity of the working class.[9]

All this, however, is merely descriptive; it does not help us to understand the nature of these schools.

The instructions issued prior to the opening of the schools were clear enough. The schools were not to be centers for the formulation of doctrine or for research. The directives sent to the teaching staff of the first central school read in part: "The Communist Party hopes to avoid the 'eternal' error made by earlier Marxist or socialist schools that educated only local militants or else grounded people so thoroughly in theory that they were lost when they had to engage in practical politics."

Not that the party was opposed a priori to the establishment of research centers. This is borne out by the fact that such centers did and still do exist. But this in itself

8. P. Bouthonnier, "A propos de la formation des cadres dans le Parti," *Cahiers du bolchevisme*, 1936, nos. 14–15. See in the following number (16–17) the article on "L'Organisation des écoles du Parti."

9. Maurice Thorez, "L'Enseignement du marxisme-léninisme dans les écoles du Parti," *Cahiers du communisme*, November 1956, pp. 1198–1214.

does not mean that they are bastions of dogma or, inversely, that they are enterprises overflowing with fire and fury.

In November, 1930, the CEM (*Cercle d'études marxistes*) made the following suggestion:

> The party should study from a theoretical point of view all the problems that confront it; it should also provide the central committee and our regional cadres with the theoretical elements that are required for an elaboration of our policy.

This was an ambitious program. It was conceived in accordance with the idea that "the main cause of all our weaknesses and faults lies in our inadequacy in the domain of theory and even in some instances in our disdain for theory."[10]

Under the guidance of the central committee, the CEM was to be divided into study sections. The first ones to be formed would be an "economic section," a "section for the history of the party," and a "section for the history of the trade union movement." The work to be undertaken would focus on the following topics: "aspects of the economic crisis in France"; "the history of the party and the trade union movement."

The CERM (*Centre d'études et de recherches marxistes*), under the direction of Roger Garaudy,[11] and the Institut Maurice-Thorez, under the presidency of Georges Cogniot, have developed in less than ten years into a complex endowed with considerable working facilities: archives, library, documentation center. The CERM, whose

10. C. Servet, "Un cercle d'études marxistes est créé," *Cahiers du bolchevisme*, no. 11, November 1930.
11. Since expelled from the party for political and ideological differences.—Trans.

internal activities are carried on by groups working together on interdisciplinary or single-discipline subjects, aims to explore new or controversial problems which both Marxism and the developing sciences are bringing to light. The results of individual or collective research conducted by these groups are published in topical cahiers. The CERM also is responsible for publishing the *Semaines de la pensée marxiste*. Based on a network of departmental sections, the Maurice Thorez institute, the "center for the study of the history of social thought and the workers' movement," resembles the institutes of party history attached to the central committees of all socialist countries. It supports the entire range of activities connected with its purpose: lectures; exhibits ("The Paris commune," "Marx and the International Movement," "The International Workers' Movement from the First International to the Present"); French and international colloquia ("The Popular Front," "The October Revolution and France"), the essential points of which appear in a monthly periodical, the *Cahiers de l'Institut Maurice-Thorez*.

Whether we are talking about the CERM, where the personality of the director determines its readiness to organize colloquia and try out new approaches, or the Maurice Thorez institute, where the spirit of the "faithful old grumbler" of the Invalides Museum reigns, the cultural and intellectual aims of these institutions must be seen within the context of the "ideological struggle." They are but part of the movement's ideological weaponry stationed strategically on its battlefield.

The schools are an entirely different matter. They are intended to be and are schools for the cadres, unswervingly dedicated to the training of political leaders needed by the party to direct its various organizations. There is therefore not the slightest inclination in them to dispense culture, even working-class culture. Nor is there any thought of communicating knowledge, even Marxist knowledge. These are schools for the cadres and not at all centers for the development of ideas. The schools have to mold *professionals*, in the sense that Lenin used the word when he spoke of professional revolutionaries: "The Party needs leaders for the struggle, not bookworms. We must organize schools for the cadres, schools that go beyond the elementary level but are also closely connected to practice and to action."[12]

Historically, a precedent was set in 1924–25; precisely at the time of Bolshevization, the first central school was established. Its avowed object was to sift out candidates for the first of the permanent cadres.

The teaching methods employed show that the precedent still holds. Although not particularly novel or innovative, they do at least represent an attempt to guarantee "the unity of theory and practice." The first experiments along this line were spectacular. At the central school of Bobigny, the students had to "apply" in the afternoon or evening what they had learned only a few hours before in the morning. The pace, however, had to be slowed down. It was too risky.

In the elementary schools where classes met at night, two-hour sessions were scheduled. The first half hour was spent quizzing students about what they had learned the night before. There followed an hour of regular classroom work. The final half hour was devoted to memory drills. The "permanent" federal and central schools employed more complex methods. Authoritative courses or lectures were given along lines laid down in advance. These were prescribed for teachers as well as students by the educa-

12. E. Fajon, "Apprendre pour mieux comprendre et mieux lutter," *Cahiers du bolchevisme*, 1935, p. 1420.

tional section. After the lectures, there were classroom discussions, especially a general review that enabled each teacher to ascertain whether his students had digested the material. This method served primarily to "teach the students to learn" by creating an atmosphere of collective research and study. With the same objective in mind, a very significant ceremony was staged during the closing period. This comprised, in addition to a small celebration, a critical and self-critical discussion in which both students and teachers evaluated their respective performances.

The method of recruiting both teaching staff and students typified the party's schools.

The teaching staff was not selected from the masses of professional instructors. They were so numerous that if the party had wished to do so, it could have provided all the teachers needed for the network of parallel schools. But the party did not want to do this. Indeed, it went so far as to make sure that there would not be too many professional teachers who, like all other members, were constantly being asked to donate their services to the party's schools. The party wanted a teaching staff selected on the basis of each individual's role as a leader in the movement's apparatus rather than on the basis of his pedagogical qualifications. It is of course true that Étienne Fajon, the man who did so much to promote professional education in the central educational section, was himself a teacher. However, the present director of the party's Central School is a steel worker.

In this connection, instruction was to serve as a channel for the transmission of specialized knowledge to the specialists of tomorrow. As in all trade schools, it was up to the established cadres to lay the groundwork for future cadres. The job of teaching was an integral part of the routine internal tasks that a leader must know how to perform. As early as 1935, Fajon had written: "Militants to teach courses? There are militants at every level. And the best teacher is usually not the one who talks the most but rather the one with the greatest amount of experience as a militant."[13]

As for the students, recruitment was based on one fundamental principle: selection.

The students were not volunteers. Had they been, the schools would have been filled with very worthy individuals but who nonetheless were not the right people for the kind of work the schools were designed to perform. They would have been people concerned, to be sure, with the problems of Marxism, socialism, and revolution, but not necessarily with practical politics. The students were a lively group. Although all of them were seeking a "socialist culture," the group was socially and intellectually very heterogeneous. By establishing a working-class university (today called the New University), the party was attempting to meet the needs of this disparate group and to adhere to the tradition of a people's university.[14] The undertaking was ambiguous and rather disappointing, presenting as it did the difficult problem of specialization based on self-education.

In any event, further distinctions must be made here

13. Ibid.
14. *L'Université ouvrière* was founded in 1932. Between 1933 and 1936 7,600 students took courses from Cogniot, Politzer, Wallon, Prenant, Friedmann, and others. After the Liberation, the establishment continued under the name of *Université nouvelle*. Similarly, and during that same period, the *Cahiers du contre-enseignement prolétarien* proved an interesting attempt to pit a "contre-enseignement" against public, "bourgeois" instruction. Very quickly the impasse of bourgeois science versus proletarian science made itself felt.

too: students in the party's schools were selected by sectional cadres. One of the major tasks confronting the cadres in their recruitment of students was to obtain quality. Moreover, at every level, the secretariat of the corresponding bodies had to ratify the sectional cadres' recommendations before the date and conditions governing the candidate's enrollment in the courses could be determined.

Thus, from the students' point of view, "to go to school" had all the earmarks of a mission—a political one at that—and was deemed both an honor and a responsibility. From the point of view of the party's apparatus, it was one of the most effective ways of preserving the party's "social purity." A major criterion of selection was, in fact, the socioprofessional status of the candidates. One illustrative example is the social composition of a regional school at Lyons in 1936. Of its thirty-two students, twenty-one were factory workers, seven were ordinary employees, two were employees in the public services; two were artisans, three small businessmen. This predilection for students of working-class origin gave the schools one essential function: to help the students learn to read a text, to write, and to familiarize themselves with works that they would not have ventured to tackle on their own. Thus they acquired a basic foundation that would thereafter enable them to gather data on their own and to think for themselves. In this modest but important way, the party avoided amassing a preponderance of intellectuals—something that had been traditional in workers' parties—who can talk and write well.

But this rigorous selection was not a sociological venture of lasting influence. Again, in order to insure the "social purity" of the party's cadres, so that the workers could execute this kind of intellectual "take-off" and acquire the techniques indispensable for the assumption of administrative duties, it was not enough to give them these advantages, to launch them by means of a school system. They also needed to work on their own, without the strain of competing with groups better prepared than they from the very outset. This is what selection accomplished: it limited the number of students and guaranteed a uniform level of competence, at least in the beginning. The instruction proved efficacious.

In addition, this vigorous selection made it possible to observe the students and to evaluate them. The report compiled after the termination of the course was invaluable in determining the kinds of jobs the graduating students might take.

It would be a mistake, however, to believe that the professional training of adults by pedagogical methods was always successful—even in relation to its objective. Actually, there was enormous "waste." The first central school established in Bobigny in 1924–25 had sixty students. It became so famous that instead of talking about the Bolshevization of the party, people referred to its "Bobignization." Of these sixty students, thirty left the party less than five years later, and eight quit it in the thirties. Up to the outbreak of the war, only about ten former Bobigny students were still members of the party. But these ten included Jacques Duclos, still a member of the political bureau today, and Fernand Grenier who, until his recent retirement, was a deputy for Saint-Denis and a member of the central committee.[15]

To be sure, Bobigny was the first experimental school,

15. See the very colorful account of "Bobigny" (mid-November, 1924 to end of January 1925) by Albert Vassart, who was a Bobigny student. See also, *Cahiers du bolchevisme*, no. 29, April 1, 1927.

and the problem of how to select the individuals to be trained had not yet been solved at that time. By the start of the thirties the waste was considerably greater, because from 1927 to 1930 repression and the internal problems of the French party made it impossible to continue the schools in France. Students were therefore sent to the international Leninist school in Moscow where the course of study lasted two and a half years.[16] It was a difficult school to run because of vast national, intellectual, and cultural disparities among the students. From the first two French groups that studied there after 1926 (the second group included Marion, the future Vichy minister!), not a single outstanding leader emerged.[17] Nonetheless the school did contribute effectively to the training of a "basic generation," at least until 1935 when it was suppressed. The list of former students includes such individuals as Waldek Rochet, Raymond Guyot, and Claudine Chomat.

Today it appears that most members of the current cadres have gone to one of these schools, whether federal or central. In a single school year, 1962 to 1963, 521 students took courses at the central school; 1,286 attended for two school years, during 1964–66.

All in all, it is quite possible that the network of schools represented for the party what the network of primary schools represented for the Third Republic: a powerful instrument for the creation of a sense of cohesiveness, a training agency of exceptional quality. By giving priority to the training of cadres, the schools performed a three-fold function within the communist subsociety: they insured "social purity" within the party leadership; they

16. In 1932 the length of study was reduced to one year.
17. On the Komintern's schools, see B. Lazitch, "Les écoles de cadres du Komintern," *Contributions à l'histoire du Komintern*, ed. J. Freymond (Droz, 1965).

encouraged widespread mobility within the movement so
that the leaders were constantly stimulated by fresh contributions from below; lastly, they insured the transmission and circulation of collective archetypes of tradition.
This threefold role had one common feature: the aim of
conserving, using the word in the sense indicated by Jules
Ferry when he said: "Conserving? All right, but conserving the Republic." In this case, the aim was to conserve
Bolshevism and its derivative, Stalinism. In any case, it
aimed to conserve a revolutionary perspective, a certain
spirit and language, all of which contrasted sharply with
the reformist practice employed for the handling of everyday affairs. If such Leninist themes as the revolution to
come, the dictatorship of the proletariat, the Soviets, and
the internationalism of the proletariat continue to attract
so much sympathetic interest after fifty long years, the
reason is to be found in the fact that Lenin's followers had
been *taught*, although abstractly and haphazardly. They
nurtured in depth a current of eschatological and millen-
nial fervor that some fortuitous event, shattering the thin
shell of everyday platitudes, could bring out into the light.

12 | The Centers of Power and Mechanisms of Decision-making

Who decides and how? Where, at which levels and in which bodies, does power reside?

At this point, a chronology is necessary; without it our analysis will remain theoretical and speculative.

During the Days of the International

From 1920 to 1940 the French party was a section of the Communist International. To overlook the precise significance of this fact, to treat the history of the French Communist party as if it were a totally independent body, makes even less sense than to place parentheses around the fact that French Catholicism is but a segment of the universal Catholic church.

At this juncture we are not—at least not yet—concerned with the following question. Is the policy of French communism determined in Paris or in Moscow? Rather, we are interested in another important issue: the global dimensions of communism of which French communism is but one part. This is the only way to deal seriously and in depth with the origins of the communist phenomenon.

To define Bolshevism as a strategy for revolution is an approach that may serve as a beginning but one that does not embrace all the facts—far from it! In essence, Bolshevism must be defined as a *worldwide* strategy. For Lenin, the October Revolution was merely a prelude, without any definitive character of its own. It could not constitute an event in itself. Rather, it was a minor, circumstantial episode that could not acquire a meaning, a destiny, or perhaps even a distinctive character until the Third International—the institutional expression of a plan for worldwide revolution—was founded. Thereafter, proletarian internationalism ceased to be what it had been initially when concretized by the First International: a form of collective feeling that included the sense of belonging to a limitless community where people were no longer oppressed and exploited. Proletarian internationalism is no longer what it once was when it shook the socialist elite of the Second International: largely a way of being, an ecumenical attitude, humanist in nature, with ethical principles of its own. Instead, it has become primarily a strategy: a definite, concrete formulation of the technique by which established global society can be destroyed.[1]

These remarks are not purely doctrinaire. Lenin's International was in effect, and quite concretely, a "world" party. It was conceived from the start as a short-term instrumentality for the proletarian takeover of power on a worldwide scale. It became the headquarters for a gigantic international army, with each national party constituting a detachment assigned to one of the sectors of the revolutionary front.

But how are we to interpret this military vocabulary? Metaphorically? Not at all. It must be interpreted liter-

1. I am summarizing here in a few words some classical analyses. Naturally they need to be developed. To do so, I take the liberty of referring the reader to two of my works, *Origines du communisme français* (Mouton, 1964), vol. 2, *Le bolchevisme en 1920 et la question du pouvoir*, pp. 655–701; "Vie et mort de la Ire Internationale," *Le Pain et les Roses* (Paris: PUF, 1968).

ally. This martial terminology is not just the Bolshevik style of writing; it represents a mode of thought.

The International's relations with the French Communist party served to link various hierarchical bodies within the unified, centralized organization. At this point we must provide the kind of detail that will enable us to find our way among problems deliberately obscured by polemicists.

The relations between the Communist International and its French section were twofold. One category comprised the nonperiodical meetings in Moscow between the French leaders and those of the Komintern. The other involved the two permanent delegations, one in Moscow, the other in Paris, that insured a continuity of contact during the intervals between "summit" meetings.

The meetings were nonperiodic but frequent. The congresses, supreme organs of the International, assembled seven times during the interval from 1920 to 1935. Each meeting lasted several weeks. The French delegations were large. At the time of the Second Congress (July-August, 1920), the French delegates constituted a very heterogeneous group.[2] The thirteen French delegates who attended the Third Congress in 1922 represented a cross-section of the conflicting tendencies that were tearing the party asunder. After the Fifth Congress almost the entire political bureau and the executive committee of the CGTU went to Moscow, leaving a very small and rather inexperienced team behind them in Paris. In addition there were the plenary sessions of the International's executive committee—thirteen in all between 1922 and 1933.[3] The plen-

2. On the French delegation to the Second Congress of the Communist International, see "Aux origines," vol. 2, pp. 620–26.

3. See the chronology of the congresses and plenary sessions of the executive committee of the Communist International, A.

ary sessions—this was the term always used in alluding
to them—which met during the intervals between meetings of the congresses, were in actuality small congresses.
They were attended not only by accredited nominees of
the preceding congress, but also by invited guests, chosen
because they were on the agenda and had some interest in
or connection with the controversial questions that arose.
For this reason the gatherings were referred to as meetings of the "enlarged executive."[4] The French delegation
usually comprised seven persons. In 1925, the Fifth Congress of the Communist International elected three French
nationals as regular members (Sémard, Treint, Sellier)
and three others as alternates (G. Jerram, Suzanne Girault, and Doriot), plus a seventh representative of the
Jeunesses communistes (Chasseigne). In 1928 the Sixth
Congress elected Barbé, Sémard and Thorez as regular
members of the executive committee and Billoux, Doriot,
Frachon, and Monmousseau as alternates. In 1935, at the
Seventh Congress, Cachin, Duclos, and Marty (the latter
was also a member of the secretariat) were elected regular members of the executive committee. Thorez was
elected to the presidium, while Frachon was chosen as a
substitute. At the same time Monmousseau was appointed
a member of the international commission. The number
of invited guests varied.

Occasionally the secretariat of the Komintern would
also invite for consultation certain French leaders, sometimes all of them, without awaiting the semiannual meeting of the executive branch. At times this was done because urgent problems had arisen; occasionally, however,

Kriegel, *Les Internationales ouvrières* (Paris: PUF, pp. 115–16.
4. But the enlarged executive committees, unlike the regular
congresses, cannot revamp the leading organs of the International, at least not the executive committee itself.

the meeting was called in order to deal more closely, and therefore more thoroughly than was possible in a multinational colloquy, with problems affecting the French section. Sometimes Russian or non-Russian experts were called upon to help the French in coping with their difficulties. In the early twenties, Trotsky was called in;[5] in the early thirties, the help of Manouilski, Lozovski, Stepanov (Chavaroche) was sought. All these men had become familiar with the French workers' movement (and with the French) during their stay in Paris before and during World War I. It was in the course of one such meeting devoted to French affairs (for which, in July, 1930, Barbé, Célor, Thorez, and Doriot had been especially summoned), that it was decided to reduce the secretariat of the French Communist party and the political bureau. The object was to enable the central committee to play a more significant role. The secretariat was limited to a single individual, Maurice Thorez.[6]

Lastly, one must not forget that the world congresses of "parallel organizations" also met in Moscow: *Profintern* (the Red labor international); *International communiste des Jeunes* (the international youth group known as the ICJ in France and as KIM in Russia); *Secours rouge international* (international Red Aid); *Confédération générale des paysans travailleurs* (general confederation of agricultural workers); *Union internationale des écrivains révolutionnaires* (international union of revolutionary writers), and others. Frenchmen were also elected to positions on these administrative bodies and therefore

5. See Leon Trotsky, *Le Mouvement communiste en France (1919–1939)*. Texts chosen and presented by Pierre Broué (Paris: Ed. de Minuit, 1967), 724 pp.

6. See André Ferrat, "Contribution à l'histoire du PCF," *Preuves* (February 1965), p. 58 and Albert Vassart, *Mémoires*.

had to come to Moscow for meetings of their executive or central committees. Let me cite a typical example. Albert Vassart went to Moscow early in February, 1928, to attend the ninth plenary session of the Komintern's executive committee as a representative of the French political bureau. He stayed in Moscow for quite a while, until the latter part of March, in order to attend the Fourth Congress of the ISR (*Internationale Syndicale rouge*) as a delegate from the CGTU.

It is plain, then, that occasions for high-level meetings were numerous. In 1932, an "average" year, Maurice Thorez went to Moscow in January to discuss the report he was to present to the party's Seventh Congress in March. It was entitled: "In Favor of a Revolutionary Solution to the Crisis." After the general elections in the spring, he returned to Moscow for the twelfth plenary session of the executive committee. He remained in the Russian capital for almost two months.

During the intervals between such trips, contact was maintained with the aid of a permanent representative.

In Moscow there was usually only one official French delegate to the executive committee of the Communist International. The post was held by Souvarine in 1921–22. He was followed by Treint, then by Crémet, who was elected member of the presidium at the seventh plenary meeting of the executive committee in December, 1925, and stayed on in Russia after 1927.[7] Next came François Billoux. Sent to Moscow as the representative of the French Communist Youth to the Communist Youth International, he was promoted in Moscow during the summer of 1927 and became the French party's delegate to

7. The presidium is a permanent body that directs the work of the executive committee in the intervals between plenary sessions.

the Communist International. His successor in 1928–29 was Henri Barbé. André Ferrat held the post from the end of December, 1929, until early August, 1931. André Marty, who had been released from the Santé prison in January, 1931, and had then resided for a short time in Spain (from which he had been expelled in June, at the same time as Duclos), represented the French section from August, 1931, until the thirteenth meeting of the executive committee in December, 1933. He was succeeded by Albert Vassart. It was during Vassart's stay that the major decisions of June, 1934, were reached.[8]

The delegate of the French party to the executive committee of the Communist International was not the only Frenchman who resided more or less permanently in Moscow. In addition to the special correspondent of *l'Humanité*, and in addition, too, to the French students enrolled in the schools of the Communist International, there were Frenchmen in the central apparatus of the Komintern. They served in a variety of capacities—journalists, editors, translators, specialists in colonial or trade union affairs. Still others were employed in the central agencies of parallel organizations (one example was the CGTU's delegate to the central committee of the Profintern).[9]

All in all, although it was not as large as the colonies encountered elsewhere—especially in countries where the party fared disastrously—the French communists who lived in Moscow constituted a rather sizable group.

8. See Albert and Celie Vassart, "The Moscow Origin of the French 'Popular Front,' " in *The Comintern Historical Highlights*, ed. by Milorad M. Drachkhovitch and Branko Lazitch (New York: Praeger, 1966), pp. 234–52.

9. To take one example among a hundred, Paul Nizan worked in Moscow in 1934–35 on the French edition of the *Littérature internationale*, an organ of the International Union of Revolutionary Writers (UIER).

In the early days, from 1918 to 1920, the Bolshevik emissaries in Paris were charged solely with discovering, contacting, and bolstering those elements in the unified Socialist party—specifically youth groups and the CGT— that leaned toward Moscow. These emissaries came from Switzerland, where the first official Soviet mission had been established; from Amsterdam where, for the space of a few months, the subsidiary bureau of the Third International had operated; from Berlin, which as early as 1920, became the headquarters of the party's secretariat for Western Europe.[10] It was this last organization that had mandated Klara Zetkin whose greetings in the name of the Third International had caused a sensation at the Congress of Tours.

During the subsequent years, from 1920 to 1923, when contacts were much more easily made in the material if not the political sense, the Komintern hastened to send representatives to Paris on brief reconnaissance missions. Their task, especially when the party congress met and conflicts arose, was to support the left wing. It was around the latter, naturally, that a truly Bolshevik party would be constituted. In addition, the representatives of the International were, under certain circumstances, to encourage at least a temporary alliance between the left and the center.[11]

After 1923 the executive committee of the Interna-

10. See *Aux origines*, vol. 2, "La précarité des liaisons Paris-Moscou," pp. 555–74.

11. See the decisive testimony of J. Humbert-Droz, *"L'Oeil de Moscou" à Paris* (Paris: Juillard, 1964). "The alliance of the left with the center" is the result of the "united front" tactics which the Communist International stressed in 1922 within the framework of their wait-and-see policy after the failure of the worldwide revolutionary offensive during the years immediately following the war.

tional, gradually strengthening the control over the revolutionary center despite the pressure of the national sections, began to send more important figures rather than mere emissaries charged with limited missions. The new men were permanent delegates whose job it was to gather information about the overall activities of the local leaders. Among them were Auguste Guralsky (sent to Paris in 1924 to launch the "Bolshevization" of the party and known as "Lepetit," he taught at the central Bobigny school); Mikhailov-Williams (who served from the end of 1924 to the end of 1925); Petrovsky, who was subsequently sent to England in 1926, where he was known as "Bennet"; Schueller, who held the post early in 1928; Pourmann (a Polish member of the Communist party's bureaucracy who committed suicide in Moscow sometime in the thirties); and lastly, Manouilski and Humbert-Droz who, toward the end of the twenties, made rather lengthy trips to Paris.[12]

The delegates of the Komintern to the central committee of the French party were destined once again to undergo a change both in character and in size. In 1931, in an effort to counteract the profound crisis that was upsetting the French party (and which Moscow refused to believe was due to the general ultraleftist line laid down by the Communist International in 1928 and by the executive committee in subsequent years), Moscow hurriedly dispatched an entire international team to Paris instead of a single delegate. The mission of the team was to super-

12. This is what I attempted to demonstrate in reference to the Popular Front and the episode relating to the communist decision not to participate in the Léon Blum government (May-June, 1936). See "Les Communistes français et le Pouvoir," in M. Perrot and A. Kriegel, *Le Socialisme et le Pouvoir*, (Paris: EDI, 1966), pp. 111–45.

vise and also to back up if necessary the group that was officially in control of the French party. Fried (Clément), who arrived in August 1931, headed the international team. He participated in the deliberations of the political bureau and the central committee, and was even arrested at one of their clandestine meetings. His assistants included Ernest Geroe (the future minister of the pre-1956 Hungarian People's Republic), Anna Pauker (the future minister of Socialist Rumania from 1947 to 1952), George Kagan (Constant), the "young and brilliant" Polish intellectual in charge of the agit-prop section and an editor of the *Cahiers du bolchevisme*.

By and large, this international team managed to perpetuate itself until 1939, although there were many changes in personnel. It was a complex apparatus that served as a link between various countries and facilitated clandestine communication. After the German catastrophe of 1933, the Austrian disaster of 1934, and the dismemberment of Czechoslovakia in 1938, its importance increased. As Paris became flooded with émigrés and political refugees from all the countries affected by the Nazi holocaust, various new tasks devolved on the international team: housing "illegal" communists and procuring false papers for them; arranging the many trips made by agents across several frontiers; safeguarding the archives and transmitting information and directives by coded telegrams, to say nothing of the transfer of funds. Called the "OMS (*Otdiel Mejdounarodnoï Sviazi*) Paris section," it was strictly isolated not only from exclusively Soviet agencies in France, such as the embassy, but also from the political apparatus of the French party. The "OMS Paris section" was in contact solely with the French delegate to the Komintern (or with the French "technician" of the specialized party apparatus) or with the "OMS Center" which in turn communicated with the secretariat of the Komintern.[13]

This analysis, although too brief, shows that relations between the Communist International and its French section can in no way be compared in frequency, intensity, or complexity to the warm but flexible and intermittent relations that existed between the unified Socialist party and the pre-1914 Second International. The ties that united the pre-1914 Socialist party and the Second International were virtually devoid of any institutional backing, save for periodic congresses and the subsequent support given by the international socialist bureau.

This, however, fails to afford an adequate description of the kind of relations that joined the French Communist party to the Muscovite center. How far did the center concern itself with the French section? Was there a special domain that constituted the exclusive concern of the French party's bureaucracy? Was the role of the center confined to providing some sort of political impetus? Was the center content to define general strategy, leaving the French militants to work out their own tactics, in accordance with the dictates of the national situation?

The executive committee of the International had no intention of merely being kept *informed* about the political, ideological, and organizational policies of the French party. It intended to *determine* them. One can hardly pretend otherwise.

Strategy, naturally, came first. This was the specific

13. The most detailed work on the political structures and techniques of the Komintern's apparatus is without doubt the book now being written by M. Drachkhovitch and B. Lazitch, *l'Internationale communiste sous Lénine.* I hereby thank the authors for having allowed me to read chapters of their manuscript.

responsibility of the congresses. It is impossible to give here, even briefly, an analysis of the seven congresses that punctuated the short history of the Communist International. We must simply recognize the fact that it would be theoretically meaningless, and therefore a flagrant methodological error, to entertain the slightest hope of perceiving any rationality or coherence in the French Communist party's policy without at the same time tracing it to its source: the decisions of the International, the documents, declarations, and publications that emanated from it.[14] These are voluminous; they constitute the kind of reading that is certain to put you to sleep or make you smile: official minutes of the congresses; records of the meetings of the executive committee; theses, edited and assembled into booklets; resolutions; periodicals such as *l'Internationale communiste* and *La Correspondance internationale*. Together, they come to tens of thousands of pages. They were often repetitious, redundant, dull, full of jargon, uneven in argumentation, stuffed with false perceptions, false evidence, abounding in lacunae, very cautious in spite of attempts to simulate frankness, arousing distrust by their eschatological tendency to cry catastrophe; yet these tens of thousands of pages were nonetheless read with the keenest attention and discussed with the liveliest interest. They gave rise to so much debate, opposition, and uncertainty that they were never completely lifeless.

The executive committee also had every intention of determining electoral tactics. The disasters suffered in the elections of 1928 and 1932 were the direct consequence of the tactics elaborated by the Komintern,[15]

14. See below, the Bibliographical note.
15. Bear in mind the crucial testimony given by Humbert-Droz in 1928: "We were busy preparing for the 1928 elections.

which had also determined trade union tactics.[16] The
executive committee had every intention of deciding
organizational problems, particularly those relating to the
cadres. Administrative problems were discussed in Moscow, and decided there. It was in Moscow, as we have
seen, that in July, 1930, at a special meeting of the French
delegation to the Komintern, Maurice Thorez was suggested as the only possible secretary. It was in Moscow,
at the twelfth plenary session of the executive committee
(September, 1932), that this same French delegation decided, for example, that Frachon should yield the administration of the party's union section to Gitton, and that

---

. . . I asked Bukharin to present the question to the presidium.
A very representative committee, including Stalin himself, was
appointed. It assembled in various Russian party locales and
held lengthy meetings. Arguing against Petrovsky, I spoke in
favor of the 'class-against-class' tactic—a tactic aimed at forcing
socialism to choose between the petty bourgeois leftist bloc and
the worker-peasant bloc.

"I won out. But when Moscow learned the results of the
first round in the elections of 1928, the wind of panic swept over
the Kremlin. . . . Not a single communist elected! Stalin immediately ordered a reversal of the strategy, saying: 'The Soviet
Union cannot accept the fact that no communists are represented
in the French chamber.'

"We had a long and violent debate in Bukharin's large office
at the Kremlin. Stalin wanted a telegram sent to the French
Communist party that very night ordering it to communicate
with the socialists and to ask them to support the communist
candidates in the Paris region. In return, the communists would
support the socialists in the Nord and elsewhere. I was violently
opposed to the adoption of this abrupt change of strategy between two rounds of balloting, pointing out to him the confusion
that would result within the party. . . . In the end Stalin very
ungraciously said: 'You know the French situation better than
I do—so say nothing in the telegram.' That was the one and
only time I saw Stalin give in" (J. Humbert-Droz, *"L'Oeil de
Moscou" à Paris*, pp. 241–42).

16. See above, chapter 6.

he should replace Monmousseau as head of the CGTU.

Is this to say that until decisions were made in Moscow, the French section had merely to await orders, and that after the orders were given, it had merely to acquiesce? Such an assertion would give a very false and very schematic view of the communist world, or of any world, for that matter, even of one in which power is absolute and authority infallible.

The game is far more complicated. For one thing, Moscow was not a solid entity. There were cracks in its structure. The struggles within the Russian party during the twenties, the uncertainties of Stalinist policy during the thirties, the ambiguity of world events whose meaning and importance were still partially masked—all this was reflected in the administration of the International. Besides, it was a complicated game because "Paris" was not a homogeneous entity either. The very diversity in tradition and in mentality that had contributed to the establishment of the party, together with the crumbling national edifice that made France during the interwar period a perpetual prey to false promises, resulted in a chaotic circulation of currents of thought and opinion, in a centrifugal agitation so great that it was risky to draw a firm conclusion about the reasons for successes or failures.

In short, the power of the International had all the majesty of the Revolution. It penetrated into the far corners of the huge phenomenon that the world knew as the global communist movement. Moscow's wishes carried the weight belonging to a country where socialism had been constructed. Impressive, far away, perplexing, experimental, excessive, informed, and complicated, the Komintern's authority was somewhat akin to "the law and the prophets," absolute but hermetic.

Direct Soviet Administration

Did the dissolution of the Communist International in 1943 signal the genuine emancipation of the French Communist party? Actually, the very reverse took place. Does this mean, as has often been said, that the decision to dissolve the International was only a political ruse, a snare and a delusion?

Two international communist organizations had already disappeared: the *Profintern* folded in 1936; the Krestintern, headed by a Bulgarian, Kolarov, was dissolved in 1939.

The war had naturally made it more difficult to operate the international organization. For one thing, the administration and control of the national sections located beyond the firing line inevitably loosened, and it took a long time for communications to reach their destination. Even if these sections were not altogether inaccessible, if some liaison between Western and Eastern Europe had been maintained through contact with the British, through nearby countries, or by radio—save for a few brief interruptions of a technical nature—the complications were nonetheless endless.

In addition, conditions that developed in the Soviet Union after the German invasion made it difficult for the central apparatus in Moscow to function. In July 1941, after receiving a new title—Institute No. 301—the Komintern was transferred to Ufa. Later, its services were renamed "Institute 205." Apparently, life in Ufa was sinister; here groups of foreign communists had sought refuge in the wake of Hitler's successive conquests and victories.

At that time the issue ceased to be that of defending or saving the Soviet Union. The Montenegrin communist Veljko Vlahovitch pointed this out when he said:

"The reasons for Stalin's decision to dissolve the Komintern must be sought in the international situation at the time of the Second World War. The determinant was the creation of the anti-Hitler coalition rather than any profound analysis of conditions within the workers' movement, or of the movement's needs and prospects."[17]

In any event, the worldwide reactions were exactly what the communist leaders had expected them to be. Speaking its own language, every country, the Western democracies as well as the Nazis, took the new Soviet developments to mean—whether they had desired this or not—that communism was not committed to renouncing its erstwhile interest in worldwide revolution.

A good example is an official American reaction, that of Senator Connally, chairman of the Senate's Foreign Relations Committee. The senator declared that Moscow's decision, giving as it did assurance that Russian communism would no longer interfere in the affairs of other nations, afforded proof of the solidarity that existed among all peoples who were fighting Hitlerism.

French "collaborationists" reacted as follows. "The suppression of the Komintern is fully characteristic of a vast political and diplomatic operation whose purpose is to facilitate the activities of the Bolshevist-plutocratic

17. Veljko Vlahovitch joined the International Brigade while he was still a student. He lost a leg in Spain and, after the defeat of the Republic, returned to Moscow where he served as the Yugoslav member of the Communist International for youth. It was as the coopted secretary of the ICJ. (Internationale communiste des Jeunes) that he attended the meeting of the presidium of the Komintern at which the question of dissolving the Third International was discussed. Veljko Vlahovitch is at present the number-four man in the Yugoslav Communist party. He tells his story in *Est-Ouest*, no. 216 (May 16–31, 1959), pp. 7–8, where it is translated.

bloc and to weaken Germany's position by depriving the Nazis of the pretext of an anticommunist crusade."[18]

Although the Allies and the Nazis were in agreement about the significance of Moscow's decision, there was some difference of opinion as to its actual impact.

What was the real situation?

The activities of the Komintern did not of course miraculously cease. A direct witness, Castro Delgado, has written: "The Komintern subsists in actuality. To be sure, many of its activities have been modified, yet it still constitutes the external instrument of the Russian Communist party."[19]

The dissolution of the Komintern was nevertheless effected. For example, its school was closed and its students were sent to Moscow where they were assigned to committees representing their respective countries.[20]

Although the Komintern as such no longer existed, its functions were *transferred*, not suppressed. Its operations ceased to be the responsibility of an autonomous organ such as the political bureau of the Communist International. Instead, they were handled by the Soviet party's central committee. Castro Delgado explains this in concrete terms:

18. *La dissolution du Komintern* (N.P. éd. des Cahiers du monde nouveau, 1943), 32 pp. (facts and documents).

19. Enrique Castro Delgado, of working-class origin, joined the Spanish Communist party in 1925. In 1936, as a member of the party's central committee, he headed its central organ, *Mundo Obrero*. Having sought refuge in France in 1939, he went to Moscow as the representative of the Spanish Communist party to the Komintern's executive committee. In 1944 he lost his seat in the Spanish party's central committee, managed to leave Soviet Russia in 1945, and settled in Mexico. His book *J'ai perdu la foi à Moscou* was published in France by Gallimard in 1950.

20. See Leonhard, *Child of the Revolution*, p. 223.

Dimitrov's office is no longer in the building that stands to the right of the Agricultural Exposition where the Komintern was located before its dissolution. Now he is on the third floor of one of the buildings used by the central committee of the Russian Communist party. The other secretaries have also moved their offices. For instance, the offices of Dolores Ibarruri, Rakosi, and Anna Pauker are located in Red Square, opposite the Kremlin.

Castro Delgado does not limit himself to pointing out that the *forms* of the Komintern's activity had changed. He likewise indicates similar but deeper changes in the *definition of objectives* which the communist movement had set for itself:

Under orders from the central committee of the Communist party of the USSR, the Komintern is preparing its teams for those countries which, it is sure, the Red Army will enter before the Allied armies arrive—Poland, Czechoslovakia, Rumania, Bulgaria, Hungary, to say nothing of East Germany.

Castro Delgado's statement is confirmed by that of Jesus Hernandez. During the evening of the day on which the decision to dissolve the Communist International was publicized, Hernandez was called to Komintern headquarters where he encountered Togliatti, Manouilski, and Dimitrov. Thereupon Manouilski reportedly spoke to him as follows:

In the present situation, the various parties cannot consult Moscow about questions that require an immediate answer. Since Moscow can no longer provide centralized leadership, it seemed better to allow the national sectors a certain flexibility. . . . Each national representative will, like yourself, retain his present functions. "The apparatus" will be less important and above all less visible, but you will all remain in touch with Dimitrov, who will carry on from headquarters in the foreign section of the Bolshevik party.[21]

This constituted a return to the state of affairs that had existed prior to the founding of the Communist International. In 1918 and at the start of 1919, international revolutionary activities had been directed from Moscow by militants grouped according to nationality.[22] Leadership was provided by the foreign section of the Communist party.

In the light of all this, it seems clear that the dissolution of the Komintern was dictated by the circumstances that had arisen as a consequence of the new war situation. This is precisely what the official version maintains. The move had two aspects. First, the dissolution had immediate and important advantages from a political point of view: it facilitated the establishment of relations between the USSR and its allies and engendered an atmosphere of mutual trust; it also paved the way for a rapprochement between the communists and other political groups within

21. J. Hernandez, *La Grande Trahison* (Fasquelle, 1953), p. 249. Hernandez, born in Murcia in 1907, was the son of very poor peasants. He became Minister of Public Education in the government of Largo Caballero. Having sought refuge in the USSR after the fall of the Spanish Republic, he was named a member of the Komintern's executive committee. Dimitrov sent him to Mexico to reorganize the Spanish Communist party there. It was then that he told his compatriots the truth about the living conditions of Spanish revolutionaries who had emigrated to the USSR.

22. See A. Kriegel and G. Haupt, "Les Groupes communistes étrangers en Russie et la révolution mondiale (1917–1919)," *Revue d'histoire moderne et contemporaine* (October-December 1963), pp. 289–300.

each country. In short, it tended to bolster the strategy of national union which everywhere led the communists to emphasize the need for antifascist patriotic unity. Second, so far as structures were concerned, the dissolution of the Communist International, by suppressing all intermediaries between the Russian Communist party and the leaders of the most important national sections, enabled the Politburo to follow very closely the ups and downs that could lead to the seizure of power in countries abandoned to Soviet influence.

Thus, with the dissolution of the International, a certain kind of allegiance had disappeared. But it was replaced by another, one that was, all in all, less contractual in nature. The various forms of close cooperation and unity that, whatever their value, had survived within the International, were destroyed. Even the myth of world-wide revolution was exploded. It had become largely fictitious anyway. The Soviet Union had, of course, been its point of departure, its anchorage, its unfailing inspiration. By fulfilling such a role, the Soviet Union, without any mediation or preparation, had absorbed within itself all the virtues of worldwide revolution. This was in accordance with the theory launched at the Sixth Congress of the Communist International in 1928. The loyalty sworn to the International was converted into loyalty to the Soviet fatherland as the only workers' fatherland.

Those were precisely the days when one could speak of a Stalinist party, in the fullest sense of the term: a party that was also a province, a "colony" in the ancient sense of the word, an empire whose Caesar was Stalin. All the hierarchical functions were visibly affected by this deterioration. Thereafter Maurice Thorez possessed the majesty of a proconsul. He served an immense state, a power that was epitomized by the man with whom he had a direct, exclusive relationship that was subject to no external control. As proconsul, he wielded a power that had all the classical attributes of this kind of authority: rigidly restricted in all essential matters, it was discretionary in matters of detail. At the same time it tended toward a decisive end: the elimination of all possible competition. It is interesting to note here—this trait illustrates Thorez's intelligent circumspection—that the secretary-general of the French party was clever enough to imitate Stalin in all matters save one: he continued to convoke and assemble the regular organs of his party. His purpose, to be sure, was not to allow them to function as decision-making bodies. He wished to make sure that they would confine themselves to the task of collecting information. Here we touch upon one of the essential mechanisms of power. We will return to it.

The Socialist Camp and the Kominform

The disappearance, however, of all institutional forms of liaison between the supreme leader and his delegates either at home or in the barbarous lands abroad did have some drawbacks. Taking advantage of the fact that they were far away, the proconsuls could relax. No longer were there regular agencies to which they had to report at fixed intervals, as they had done in the past. We have seen this in the case of Tito, to say nothing of Mao. Besides, as everyone knows, a person who monopolizes responsibility always needs a screen behind which to hide in case of failure, or to vent his wrath. We have also seen this in the French and Italian Communist parties. During the cold war they were accused of having followed an "opportunistic" line after the Liberation.[23] And lastly, the integration into the apparatus of the Soviet party of informa-

23. See Eugenio Réale, *Avec Jacques Duclos au banc des accusés à la réunion constitutive du Komintern à Szlarska Poreba* (Paris: Plon, 1958).

tion services charged with following closely the activities of national foreign parties rendered sectional or general confrontations, which at certain times were necessary, extremely uncomfortable. Besides, this integration did not conform to the internal legality of the international communist movement. A good example of this kind of awkward confrontation occurred in 1947 when the official attitude toward the Marshall Plan occasioned false and regrettable moves in France as well as in Czechoslovakia. As so often happens, direct administration failed to insure greater unity and homogeneity in the general struggle. Instead, it resulted in a wave of uncertainties. The party had to return to some institutional form that would be more flexible than the old International and less "direct" than the Soviet party's direct administration.

Moreover, the military and political victories of 1944 to 1947 had helped to bring about a new distribution of forces in the world. Operating under the aegis of the Soviet Union, these forces represented a Bolshevik model of the kind envisaged by Stalin. The theory advanced to justify such a redistribution of forces was based on the notion of a "socialist camp." This was not merely a notion about territory; rather, it was a complex notion, comprising a system of states—the Soviet Union, China, and the peoples' democracies; a system of parties—the communist and workers' parties, whether in power or not; and lastly, a dual system of qualified anti-imperialist alliances (embracing all peoples that were fighting colonialism) and a popular alliance for peace. These alliances were quite different. The anticolonialist alliance, to which Stalin seemed to pay but little attention and which was not always crowned with success (it was never embodied in a specific institution, for example), attempted to place under the sole control of the proletarian revolutionary movement various struggles that sprang from altogether dissimilar objective situations. The alliance for peace, on the contrary, was entirely "artificial." It was based on the thesis that only America's imperialist interests threatened world peace—a peace which socialism alone, guided by Soviet diplomacy, could guarantee.

To every "section" in the socialist camp a specific multinational institution was assigned. The president of each institution was not necessarily a Russian, nor was he always even a declared communist. Nonetheless, representatives of the Soviet Union's Communist party invariably played major decision-making roles in all these organizations: the Warsaw Pact; the *Kominform* or office of information; the worldwide movement of partisans for peace and its global council, flanked and supplemented by specialized autonomous apparatuses (the world trade-union federation—*FSM*; the world federation of democratic youth—*FMJD*; the international union of students—*UIE*; the international democratic federation of women—*FDIF*; the international association of democratic lawyers—*AIJD*, and so on).

Thus, the centers and mechanisms of the decision-making process were established, and they functioned as much as ever within the basic framework of a situation that in large part explained the extraordinary aura with which the public surrounded French communism. Wasn't all of France in the socialist camp? Wasn't the socialist camp all of France? This interrelationship explains the prominence of communist action. The party was endowed with a kind of depth that resulted from the fact that it was rooted in the national reality, that it had become an integral part of French working-class history. At the same time it enjoyed a wider horizon. This is attested by the fact that any communist traveling to any part of the world and presenting his credentials at the local party headquarters always received help. Having been accorded such a welcome, he was promptly initiated into the current realities of whatever country he happened to be visiting.

This does not mean that, in the making of decisions, the two factors always play equal and identical roles. The French party, in addition to providing a solid buttress for world communism (something that endowed the party with a special identity of its own), was able to bring its weight to bear on more than the destiny of France. After all, that is merely a French affair. The party's deep roots in the everyday realities of the nation—something which enabled the French party to promote international co-operation—also helped to discover those concrete evidences, those colorful manifestations, those exemplary allusions, that spring from the very quick of life, and that confer the power of persuasion on communist philosophy and influence.

Having conceded this much, I must add that the socialist horizon is the primary factor that determines the party's point of view—in other words, its "line." The same process whereby, at the local or provincial level, the responsible organs are given the task of interpreting the party's general policy in terms adapted to the requirements of minor objectives and situations, also serves at the national level. Of course there are good interpretations and others that are not quite so good. Some are inspired while others, not to speak of those that are completely contradictory, fall flat. Less enclosed in a network of international controls than during the time of the Komintern, less directly subject to the tutelage of the Soviet Communist party than during the years from 1943 to 1947, the French party gave proof throughout the

Kominform decade (1947–56) of its capacity to interpret Soviet socialism quite honestly. The major decisions it made at the time attest the influence of the Soviet attitude as it was reflected in and adapted to the collective institutions in which the French party participated and where its luminaries occupied flatteringly high positions: Saillant captained the *FSM;* Jacques Denis headed the *FMJD;* Madame Cotton was chief of the *FDIF;* Frédéric Joliot-Curie was the president of the world peace organization; Joé Nordman and J. M. Hermann were the heads of groups of lawyers and journalists, respectively. These are only some of the names but they suffice to show how deeply the French party was involved in the activities of the entire international movement.

Destalinization, General Meetings and Schisms
All this enormous, subtle machinery became involved in the turmoil which resulted when Khrushchev, drawing logical conclusions from all the new data turned up by technological discoveries, became convinced that peace could no longer be subordinated to the higher interests of worldwide social revolution. Peace, he felt, could no longer be used as a weapon to disguise Soviet aims, or even the aims of the socialist camp, to the extent that the one transcended the other. Peace would have to be preserved not only by fighting for it but also by assuring the peaceful coexistence of different social systems. Just as the exigencies of the war had forced Stalin to dissolve the Komintern, so the exigencies of the quest for peace compelled Khrushchev to dissolve the Kominform.

This was merely one aspect of the gigantic attempt to return to reality that represented a characteristic and basic feature of destalinization. Socialism willingly allowed itself to be contrasted with capitalism as a system that offered humanity shorter, less costly, more equitable and efficacious avenues to progress. It was quite natural that the specific problems raised by this kind of blueprint for progress should have awakened an awareness of necessary revisions and readjustments. This awareness sprang from diverse obstacles within certain internal mechanisms of the system. How, for example, could the energy of individuals and social groups be mobilized in a system where the spirit of the party was only a fragile deterrent to the opportunities afforded by a situation in which there was a political monopoly? This awareness also sprang from the differences that separated the various sections. The pattern of relations within the socialist camp was challenged at a time when that camp was impelled to revise all of its relations with the nonsocialist world.

For the past twelve years the French Communist party, together with other communist parties, has been faced with an unavoidable choice: the system that had established and subsequently extended one of the world's socialist sectors showed itself to be full of drawbacks and shortcomings that had to be remedied. This would have to be undertaken even if one accepted for a time what had already been accomplished and agreed to abandon temporarily the idea of universalizing socialism. The process of universalizing socialism would have to be carried out either gradually or all at once. With the aid of symptomatic or etiological remedies, whoever intervened would aim at curing the localized ills or effectuating a general recovery.

Thus the French Communist party found itself in an unusual situation. Some kind of decision would be required even if, as in 1956, it should conclude that there was nothing to be changed.

To be sure, from 1956 to 1962, the party drew attention to itself because of its extreme reluctance to give up even the slightest gains achieved with the aid of the Stalinist tradition.[24] It even went so far as to draw away glumly from the Communist party of the Soviet Union when Khrushchev engaged in a series of tumultuous undertakings—the reconciliation with Tito, the secret report of the Twentieth Congress, and others.

On the other hand, ever since 1962, the French party had been anxiously seeking a new formula for the socialist camp. In pressing this quest, the party had been especially concerned about the nature, purview, internal relations, and mechanisms of socialism. Recognizing the need to trim its own sails, it decided that the essential—the notion of a socialist camp—must at all costs be preserved. Many, at the 1960 conference, felt that the theme of the leading role of the Soviet Communist party was something that could be sacrificed. Some favored jettisoning the theme for purely tactical and circumstantial reasons; others rejected it definitively and for reasons of principle. But the French Communist party bent all its efforts to putting forth a formula that would be meaningless no matter what kind of logic you might use and no matter what kind of political universe you might choose. It is easy enough to spot the kind of trap the French delegate to the Budapest meeting of March, 1968, tried to set when he declared: "There is neither *one* center nor *several* centers in the international movement, and there can never be such a thing." This is literally impossible to comprehend. What

24. See François Fejto, *The French Communist Party and the Crisis of International Communism* (MIT Press, 1967). See, also, A. Kriegel, "Les Débats théoriques et politiques dans les partis communistes français et italiens depuis 1956" (Table Ronde de sciences politiques, 1968).

characterizes a structure is precisely that it has a center, even if this is only a storm center or a point of convergence moving toward the infinite via an infinity of centers.

Actually, no matter how slow the developments, no matter how dramatic the vicissitudes, certain consequences resulted infallibly from the dislocation of the unique, centralized, rigid system which the Stalinist formula for a socialist camp entailed (the Stalinist formula was directly derived from the Leninist concept of a worldwide revolutionary party).

The violence of the split that earlier had clearly severed the socialist from the capitalist sector cannot fail to become blurred. All sorts of intermediate realities, substitutions, mixed structures can multiply and prevent the tribunal of history from pronouncing its verdict on the gigantic debate between capitalism and socialism. This has happened often enough.

Instead of nationalist particularities serving merely to "color" the socialist reality, which they were supposed to do under Lenin and Stalin, the particularities of ideas, things, facts, and men have tended to triumph, thereby "nationalizing" socialism. In the socialist reality, everything diverse, heterogeneous, sectional has been systematically repressed or manipulated with the avowed object of enhancing the unity, homogeneity, and universality of the whole. From now on, the weight of national considerations will counteract the concern evoked by the socialist community; sooner or later, this community will triumph.

How is it possible to declare, in the words of the French delegate to the preparatory meeting in Budapest, that "the new conference must not condemn or exclude from the community of communist and workers' parties any other party, regardless of its nature and no matter how divergent its views might be?" How can one fail to see that what is valid on the international level cannot logically be declared illegitimate on the level immediately below it? Why should there be diversity at one level and strict unanimity at another?

Thus, the French Communist party is caught in a tight network of contradictions. Even if we allow for the abstract seductiveness that the universalist dream has always possessed—and not only for the old guard—a dream that constitutes the notion of a socialist camp; even if we allow for the internal and external risks of schisms, remorse, backsliding, intimidation, covering up, and the like, we cannot blink the fact that the French party was apparently carried away by the current of prevailing ideas. Basically, and paradoxically, because the party had made its decision, it was left with no choice. It could only decide to decide; once having decided, it could decide only for itself.

Now that decisions are reached in Paris, who actually makes them?

The Distribution of Power in Paris

Where, or rather how, is the decision-making power apportioned within the French party?

At every level—local, departmental, national—three collateral elements function side by side: committee, bureau, and secretariat. Should the last two be thought of as "puppet" elements since both the bureau and the secretariat are designated within the committee? Not entirely. Should we think of the committee as being privileged since it alone, in theory at least, emanates directly from the will of the congress, the supreme organ and expression of the members' will? To do so would be to forget that, as we have seen, the "election" is fictitious.[25] Or should we, on

25. See above, chapter 10.

the contrary, regard the committee as being purely decorative? To do so would be to treat as totally unintelligible or absurd the care with which ranks are conferred, and the nuances with which a complex course is defined.

Actually, relations between these three elements have always varied and are still evolving. The reason for this is to be sought in the fact that the comparative importance of each element is not based solely on its theoretical functions.

During the years when the Stalinization of the French Communist party was naturalized by the cult of Thorez, the power and the authority of the secretary-general were such that the three elements of central power were virtually merged into a single entity. This meant that the three elements were in a sense aligned in a row, in a false hierarchical order: secretariat—political bureau—central committee.

Initially, it was the secretariat that possessed the least amount of political prestige. In the old Socialist party, the secretariat constituted nothing more than an administrative post, and a very technical one. Because it did not rely on an apparatus, it demanded the time-consuming effort involved in writing letters and maintaining a correspondence.

In 1924, at the time of the party's Bolshevization, the International wanted to confer more prestige and weight on the functions of the secretariat. It wished to make the secretariat the keystone of a permanent, solid political apparatus, one that would be structured, stratified, centralized. Unfortunately, the man chosen in September, 1924, to inaugurate the secretary's new role (he was no longer to be called simply secretary but rather secretary-general, to give the office more importance) was really the least appropriate person to hold an executive post. Not that Pierre

Sémard was unwilling to conform with good grace; but he was a proletarian who hailed from the Midi. Devoted, combative, honest, a very good speaker, this railway worker from Valence had given proof of his dynamism during the widespread strikes in the spring of 1940. But he had such a natural aptitude for happiness, such a clear reserve of gaiety and simplicity, that he was soon made to feel very uncomfortable in the secret and complicated world of the International. In short, he was like the Curé of Ars at a time when a Loyola was needed.

Very quickly recognizing its mistake, the International nevertheless waited five long years, because it had no other candidate to take Sémard's place. Not until the Sixth Party Congress (Saint-Denis, April, 1929) was Sémard finally stripped of his title as secretary-general.

Although the Sémard experiment had not been conclusive, the general secretariat was abolished and replaced by a "collectively responsible political secretariat" consisting of four members: Henri Barbé, Pierre Célor, Maurice Thorez, and Benoît Frachon.

Unfortunately, a few months later the entire directorate of the Communist party and of the CGTU were accused of conspiring against the internal and external security of the state. Even before they had a chance to prove themselves, the party's new administrators were jailed or forced to go underground. An interim secretariat was chosen from among nonincriminated members. Meanwhile, from their hiding place in Belgium, the "illegal" members of the secretariat tried to supervise the functioning of their agency. All this was inevitably accompanied by a goodly amount of confusion. In July, 1930, in the wake of a special meeting in Moscow that had been called to examine the French situation, the central committee decided that "the secretariat would be transformed and only one comrade would be politically responsible and technically supported": Maurice Thorez.

It was at this time, July, 1930, that Maurice Thorez, although he had never officially been given the title of secretary-general (the title was not restored until January, 1936, following a meeting of the Eighth Congress of the French Communist party), began to exercise functions somewhat similar to those of a secretary-general. In August, 1931 (after the denunciation of the "Barbé-Célor group"), under the direct control of the International's delegates in France, the secretariat was once again given its full complement. In addition to Thorez, who was in charge of general policy and directed the antimilitarist apparatus, Frachon, chief of the central trade union section, headed the network of communist members in the CGTU. Duclos was made head of the organizational section. A year later, in September, 1932, further changes were instituted. Frachon, as we have already indicated, was assigned to the CGTU. Jacques Duclos, after his involvement in the "Fantômas affair," an episode that caused so much excitement at the time, was once again condemned to exile for having acted illegally. Marcel Gitton replaced Frachon; Duclos's place was taken by Albert Vassart. In 1933, Duclos was free to resume his post in the secretariat where he headed the agit-prop section. In 1934 Vassart was sent to Moscow. During the ensuing period of the Popular Front, the secretariat officially consisted of three men: Thorez (the secretary-general), Duclos, and Gitton.

This structure was of course destined to last until the fifties. However, there were some changes in personnel. Marty, for example, replaced Gitton in the postwar secretariat. Thorez' illness and his lengthy convalescence in the USSR accounted for the appointment of Jacques Duclos as interim secretary-general; Etienne Fajon was the third member of the now traditional trinity.

At that time the secretariat was the body on which everything converged and where everything was initiated. Here all the discussions about how to apply Stalinist strategy in France took place.

After Stalin's death, arrangements had to be made for a prudent process of destalinization. Thorez himself intended to define how this should be done. Accordingly, he set the pace. What followed was the dismantling of the collective political function of the small group that comprised the secretariat. It was Thorez' idea that the broadest possible "collective administration" should be encouraged by restoring a measure of power to the regularly "elected" organisms such as the central committee. The party's secretariat disappeared, but the party's secretary-general continued in the person of Maurice Thorez. Henceforward the secretaries would merely serve as secretaries of the central committee, a term that underscored the subordinate and purely technical nature of their functions. Thereafter there was no reason why this technical function could not be more widely distributed. Today, assisting the secretary-general of the party, Waldeck Rochet, is the central committee's secretariat, which consists of five members. It is noteworthy that despite its modest title the secretariat is once again assuming an importance to which it is not theoretically entitled. In fact, at the last congress, the five secretaries elected by the central committee were all members of the political bureau. Thus, the secretariat is once again becoming the core of the political bureau, just as the political bureau is the core of the central committee.

Even during the period when Maurice Thorez was sovereign, the political bureau had never been stripped of its lofty character as a princely council of sorts. Perhaps the fact that it was composed of a round dozen men may have contributed in some indefinable way to the pious respect with which this holiest of holies was regarded. Nor is it certain that the meal of which all these men, with the exception of Thorez, partook together ritualistically each day was devoid of importance. They ate in a dining room at party headquarters that was reserved exclusively for them.

The considerable reshuffling of the political bureau during the last ten years, its greater heterogeneity, the fact that Maurice Thorez, even when absent, could acquit himself creditably of his role as the central figure at this Last Supper (Waldeck Rochet is far too shrewd to risk staying away)—all these are so many factors that definitely contributed to the return to a more prosaic atmosphere.

It is hardly fruitful to speculate, as so many have done on the basis of trivial indications, about the divisions within the political bureau. Under the direction of Thorez, the members of the political bureau—because of the exalted nature of that body, as I have described it—spoke in fables, like Aesop. In a gathering of the Apostles no error is possible, whereas today the members of the political bureau are plainly less rarefied creatures. Under the presidency of Waldek Rochet, the political bureau has become a forum where discussions are generally more relaxed and wide-ranging. The clash of opinion, formerly necessarily disguised (a conflict was never brought out into the open until after the storm had passed and the thunder was over), is today less rare and more direct. On the other hand, clashes never degenerate into crises. But it is too early to say whether this new stability is temporary, whether it is connected with the transitory nature of the present-day communist phenomenon—the neo-Khrushchev version—and with the provisional character of the Waldeck Rochet leadership.

The evolution of the central committee is less clear. This large body does not play the decisive role of a center of power, any more than it did earlier. Such a role has devolved upon the political bureau and the secretariat. But this does not mean that the central committee plays no role at all. It remains an indispensable agency for the work of mediation, to begin with. Above all, it serves as a formidable network for the exchange of information. The major task of its one hundred or so members, who are chosen on the basis of the importance of the listening posts to which they are assigned, is to provide information, often of exceptional value, about the basic currents of opinion that agitate the working class, the militants, and the masses generally for whom the party takes responsibility. These men cite examples to "illustrate" the report presented to the committee by the secretary-general or a member of the political bureau. These one hundred men are capable of quickly spreading to all levels of society the ideas that the party's leaders wish to convey. The central committee also includes men who carry out the orders of the party's apparatus. Consequently, its meetings, which take place about three times a year, are designed not only to facilitate an exchange of information among its members but also to ascertain whether the execution of the apparatus's orders is proceeding smoothly.

It is not easy to understand the subtle division of power between the secretariat, the political bureau, and the central committee on the one hand, and the small team composed of the secretariat and the political bureau on the other. To succeed in doing so, one must take into account the role played by the apparatus in implementing orders. Two kinds of organs make up the apparatus: "central commissions" and the "work sections" of the central commissions. Since the 1930s, the duties of each member of the secretariat or of the political bureau have been channeled through a special administrative apparatus. In theory, this apparatus has no political competence and cannot give directives to hierarchically subordinate organizations. However, like the French public administration, it tends to venture beyond its "legal" competence. The members of the political bureau have maintained a certain stability thanks to their tacit willingness to refrain from stepping on each other's toes. During such a period, the services tend to function smoothly and the manipulation of the masses remains the primary task.

There are a number of "central commissions" each consisting of from twenty to thirty militants. Among these are members of the central committee, leaders of mass organizations, deputies, functionaries of the corresponding "sections." They are designated by the secretariat on the basis of their competence to handle matters debated by the central committee, matters which they would be expected to discuss in committee meetings. The committees meet once a month and function as a specialized agency which the political bureau and the secretariat consult about questions within its particular competence. It is expected to study the technical aspects and implications of the general directives and to check on the manner in which these directives are carried out.

In short, the "central commissions" are a collective administrative body that serve as an intermediary between the political bureau and the secretariat (to which they are connected through the members of the political bureau who preside over their meetings) on the one hand,

and the "work sections" on the other. These last are more or less a permanent extension of the central commissions. They see to the daily execution of the work to be done.

The number, size, composition, and competence of the "work sections" have naturally varied a good deal. The "central trade union section," for example, was extremely important during the thirties because it served as a liaison between all the communist minorities in the trade union federations as well as between those in the regional unions of the CGTU, plus a few in the CGT. In 1935–36 it disappeared along with the minorities themselves.[26] Similarly, the "colonial section," which had the task of linking the organizations of colonials residing in the metropolis as well as the various overseas territories, deserves a special monograph of its own. Tied to the Komintern prior to 1939 but virtually autonomous, it was supplied with special instructors who continuously combined their illegal activities with their legal work during the postwar period. Considering the magnitude of the movement to decolonize, this section behaved with great uncertainty, simultaneously reflecting and feeding upon the uncertainties of the metropolitan party itself. The least that can be said is that the *real* emancipation of the overseas communist parties from the metropolitan organization came shortly before the emancipation of the colonial peoples themselves, and that upheavals and clashes accompanied the process of emancipation.

Generally speaking, the large stable work sections— the organizational section plus the various bodies connected with it (cadres, mass organizations, immigrant labor groups); the ideological section, which at times was centralized and at others was subdivided into several seg-

26. See above, chapter 6.

ments that controlled, respectively, propaganda, the network of education, the press, and publications; the agrarian, female, and economic sections; the administrative secretariat in charge of financial affairs—all these constituted so many minor strongholds in which the play of forces became a part of the competing elements within the political bureau.

In any case, the important thing in this connection is to have some understanding of the mechanisms of equilibrium among the members of the political bureau as well as of the mechanisms of competition between them. At the same time, the notion of discipline tends to become clearer. Often this notion was either misunderstood or interpreted in a speculative manner. Applied solely to revolutionary dedication, it was exalted; or else it was caricatured as humble submission on the part of a robot-like being. In actuality, discipline was the spontaneous and natural consequence of a most tightly woven political fabric. Secretariat, political bureau, central committee, central commissions, works sections, mass organizations, administrative bodies attached to large federations, schools, cultural institutions, publishing houses, large press organs, periodicals, economic and financial institutions—all these dovetailed and combined in such a narrow, complex way that the party's overall cohesiveness could not fail to be superior to those centrifugal forces that are always active in every microsociety within a global society.

It is this tightly woven political fabric at the top of the hierarchy that encloses the responsible militant, that constitutes the framework and the pattern of his life and thought. It is this, moreover, that makes his life and thought "comfortable," so that it is hazardous to tear apart the intangible net that envelops him.

13 | Party Secrets and Party Secrecy

The general attitude of a bureaucracy is marked by secrecy, mystery: it is the hierarchy that guards this secrecy from within, and it is maintained from without because of the nature of the closed corporation. As a consequence, a bureaucracy reacts to any political manifestation or political interpretation as if it were a breach of its mystery.

MARX[1]

"We are a glass house." It was Jacques Duclos, with his small, cold eyes and quizzical smile, who thus proclaimed his innocent candor at the very moment when he was unluckily indicted for conspiracy.

An Explicit Policy

A glass house? Yes, that's true, if we mean by this that the communists' actual policy is really their publicly declared policy, both in form and in content.

We have already alluded to the major role played by language, as distinguished from privileged spokesmen, in the establishment of a subsociety.[2] No comments will be necessary if we fully understand this special language. The veracity of communist language is tied to theories about the party's relationship to the masses and to assump-

1. *Werke*, vol. 1 (1956).
2. See above, chapter 5.

tions about the active role of the masses in all types of political action. I am constantly surprised by the obstinacy with which so many observers persist in asking: what is it the communists really want? What is concealed in what they say they want? Actually, nothing. They always want exactly what they say, expressed in their own fashion, of course.

The following facts should be taken into account. (1) The terms they use are based on specific as well as explicit semantics. (2) The unquestionable ambiguity of their language is not of one piece with their intentions, which are inspired by a spirit of caution and dissimulation. Rather, the ambiguity goes hand in glove with the realities, which in effect are twofold because they are related to the way the political struggle is viewed. The charge of duplicity so frequently leveled at the communists is due not only to their language, but also to their concepts. They are here today and somewhere else tomorrow; they are fighting today for tomorrow. To put it briefly, they look upon the political world as a field of conflicting forces to be conquered by their combined strategy and tactics. This leads them to divide their program into small bits and pieces, aligning in depth their partial, successive objectives, which makes it seem as if there is no end to them. (3) The transition from the abstract to the concrete is their main method of "arranging" matters, in the optical sense of the word, on the basis of their political distance from the object in view—all this in order to minimize whatever remains vague or ambiguous.

Everyone is familiar, for instance, with the twin slogans, the "elimination of the power of the monopolies," and the "advent of a true democracy." The first involves the liquidation of the present system of government; the second signifies the establishment of a new system that would initially join the "family" of the people's democracies or, to be more precise, that would be the kind of regime which immediately precedes and "paves the way" for a people's democracy. Usually these two slogans are used among interlocutors who tacitly designate an indeterminate, intermediate period, since long-term aims are suggested once and for all by the two traditional formulas whose power has never lost its edge: "the liquidation of capitalism" and the "achievement of socialism."

This terminology is both abstract and ambiguous. *Abstract*: obviously, a whole series of interventions will be necessary to achieve the destruction of "the power of monopolies" in view of the fact that Gaullism constitutes its very embodiment. "True democracy" is, at worst, merely a metaphorical expression. At best, it is the reduction to a program of only one aspect of a system that in reality presents many others. *Ambiguous*: the "elimination of the power of monopolies" could mean the elimination of the rightist government or the elimination of the Gaullist regime, either of them being viewed as a contingent embodiment of the bourgeois or capitalist system; it could also mean the elimination of the capitalist system itself. As for "true democracy," the amount of socialism it would embody would eventually depend upon the relationship of the various internal forces of which such a democracy would be the expression.

It can therefore hardly be regarded as an accident that in the statement issued by the elected communists of the Paris region, these twin slogans, so abstract and ambiguous, should have appeared during the first days of the May, 1968, riots when the magnitude of the episode was still uncertain. We again encounter these same slogans, as well as others containing the usual variations on the same theme, in the political bureau's communiqués up to

May 17: "For a democracy that will pave the way to socialism" (May 14); "For an authentic, modern democracy, consistent with the interests of the French people" (May 17).

From May 14 on, identification of the enemy became more concrete. The enemy was no longer the "power of the monopolies" but "Gaullist power" or a "regime based on personal government." On May 17 the slogans grew even more precise: "The government and the present majority." As for a definition of the aim to be accomplished, it too became more concrete—the establishment of a "leftist majority." This transition from the abstract to the concrete is both a precondition and an expression of the transition from the level of the routine daily struggle (of indefinite duration) to the creative level of an exceptionally intense clash (its materialization to occur within a space of time that now tends to become definable).

Once the transition from the abstract to the concrete has occurred, the problem becomes one of reducing the inherent ambiguity of the objective. This must be done without discarding any hypothesis, not even the boldest. At the same time, care must be taken to dispense with hazardous calculations. This means returning blow for blow. Hence, between the seventeenth and the thirtieth of May the party adopted a series of formulas which, in accordance with the development of the situation, were not designed to dispel completely (to do otherwise would have been to resort to pure speculation rather than to tactical skill) the uncertainties conjured up by the prospect of a change of government (change of team, change of regime, transition to socialism). Rather the aim was to delimit and restrict these uncertainties within the bounds prescribed by a circumspect analysis of the convergent and relative strength of the country's real forces.

Thus, on May 20, the party declared that "the elimination of the government and of the Gaullist regime" must result in a new state of affairs; it must "pave the way for a new situation" bounded by two precise limits. The lower limit would consist in precluding "the patching up of personal rule," the mere substitution of a new set of ministers for the members of the Pompidou cabinet within the framework of the Gaullist regime. The country was at this moment about to witness a debate on a motion to censure the government. There thus existed the possibility (to be belied, however, by the immediate course of events) that the Gaullist regime might emerge intact from the difficulties that plagued it. The higher limit would consist in preventing the wave of strikes from developing into an "insurrectionary strike," which could bring with it the decisive seizure of power by a strategy which revolutionary syndicalism had devised early in the century and which a part of the socialist world of the Second International was determined to resume.

On the following day, May 21, *l'Humanité*, citing a communiqué issued twenty-four hours earlier by the political bureau, launched the slogan that expressed and crystallized the following objective, which from now on was to remain immutable: "For a people's government of democratic union."

What did the communists mean by such a government? In one communiqué after another issued up to May 30, the communists sought without cease to clarify for themselves as well as for others the nature of their stated objective. This they did, not in abstract language, but in terms of the initiatives taken and arrangements made by their adversaries and eventual allies.

First, clarification. A change of *government* must be nothing less than a change of *regime*. "More than before," Waldeck Rochet said over the radio on May 24 immediately after de Gaulle's first allocution, "the problem of personal rule remains to be resolved. The Gaullist *regime* has had its day. It must go." "The *indispensable* political change" (May 25 at 6:30 P.M); "a political change involving social progress and democracy" (May 28, an appeal issued by the French Communist party); "a *decisive* political change" (May 28, Waldeck Rochet to the French Press Agency); "a real change of regime," a "*fundamental* political change" (May 29, political bureau's communiqué)—all these formulas left no room for doubt as to the meaning of such popular slogans as "Ten years are enough!" "De Gaulle must resign!"

The second clarification, however, shows that when the question of succession arose, attention had to be focused increasingly on the short-term objective. The idea was put forward that the relative strength of the political forces at work *within* the ensemble of forces that were seeking to bring change must find expression in the future government and regime. This meant that any formulas (a government of the Third Force, recourse to Mendès-France as the "new miracle-man") that did not take this idea into account must be excluded. On May 24 Waldeck Rochet, speaking over the radio, had stated explicitly, although parenthetically: "The French Communist party is ready to take its place in such a government. . . ." But on May 28, in an interview reported by the French Press Agency, he was asked directly about the question of communist participation. His answer was italicized and printed in large type in *l'Humanité*.

> We have already said that we are ready to assume, within a people's government of democratic union, all the responsibility that devolves on a great workers' party such as ours. We now repeat this because we know that this is what the workers want.

On May 29, in the course of the evening that witnessed the demonstration "uniting 800,000 intellectual and manual workers," the political bureau sounded a solemn note in the following communiqué: "The people of France demand that the working class and its Communist party should be given *their proper place* in the new regime."

Finally, on May 30, the central committee that had convened that morning issued a resolution which indicated as precisely as possible the nature of the "people's government." At one o'clock that very day, three and a half hours before General de Gaulle's famous radio speech, the central committee stated that not only was this the end of Gaullist rule, not only did the formation of a people's government of democratic union exclude "the right,"—that is, the followers of Giscard d'Estaing and the centrists—but also and above all that it would lead to "communist participation *in accordance with the influence and authority of the French Communist party.*" It thus rejected all the formulas about which liberal anti-Gaullists had speculated, including the dream of a government going from "Giscard to Mendès" (a dream that was absurd in view of the distribution of political forces that Gaullism had furthered and that the crisis had not yet had time to liquidate). Five hours later, at 6 P.M., the political bureau, having drawn its own conclusions from the speech of General de Gaulle, returned to the abstract slogan of May 7: "Install a true democracy." This was sufficient to make clear that the episode was over.

Secrets

The party's policy is therefore explicit, whether it has recourse to legal or to clandestine means. From this point of view, the party's policy today is being laid down just as clearly and publicly as it was in 1943. On this earlier occasion, however, the party was forced to give its explanations through the intermediary of a clandestine and forbidden press.

This observation leads us toward a resolution of the very obvious contradiction between the explicit nature of communist policy and the secret nature of much of its practice and of its microsociety.

It is just as unreasonable to believe that the *true* policy of the communists is not the policy they seem to be carrying out as it is frivolous to imagine that one can learn everything about the communist apparatus by reading what is said about it in *l'Humanité*. Such a frivolous attitude can be likened to that of a navigator who does not know that the floating part of an iceberg is but a fraction of the rest, which is submerged.

In fact, although the party has *secrets*, it uses *secrecy* as an instrument of power.

Like any organization with a long enough past to have lost its innocence, the Communist party has secrets. Does it have more "skeletons in the closet" than other organizations? This is difficult to estimate; the number of disgraceful deeds is not easy to guess at—nor pleasant. To count the number of militants who disappeared with all the cash in the trade-union treasury, or with the wife of a friend; to compile a report on false revolutionary fervor or the shabby behavior of ambitious members; on base calculation or pitiful fears, on hypocritical displays of devotion or heroism—such enumerations or compilations would be no more meaningful than to write a history of the Catholic church by reciting the names of popes who failed to keep their vow of chastity.

The party also has secrets that can only be ascribed to the fact that its leaders found it advantageous to abandon certain practices that had been dictated by circumstances. It would be improper here, or any place else for that matter, to recall that what was once a pear tree is now the cross that bears Christ.[3]

Some incidents have had a dramatic impact at one time or another, but today they are remembered only as anecdotes.

Thus there was a time in the mid-twenties when the Russian espionage system, which admittedly had to create its infrastructure from scratch, took the easy way out by recruiting its agents from among responsible party and trade-union militants. Two incidents, the Crémet affair in 1927 together with its sequel, the Rabaté affair in 1928, resulted in the strict separation of the purely Soviet networks (no matter what their nature or functions) from organizations of the French and *international* communist movement, whether legal or not. As early as the mid-thirties, there was scarcely more contact between Soviet networks and the Komintern's communist apparatus than between Soviet networks and the French communist apparatus, save for very rare occasions during the years from 1940 to 1944.

The last serious snag in this connection goes back to 1932, the date of the affair of the *rabcors*, the Russian abbreviation, after the fashion of the times, for the "working-class correspondent" (*rabotcheskii corr*).

What kind of incident was it? According to Leninist

3. I apologize for this allusion, which is perhaps an obscure one for the reader. It's an old story whose equivalent I have never been able to find in French folklore. It takes place in Poland. An old Jew is about to be stoned because he failed to kneel when the Cross was carried by. This refusal to show his respect was not due to bravado but rather because the Cross in this procession had been made from the wood of a pear tree, which was familiar to him. "All the same, it's a pear tree," is an ironic way of referring to someone who wants to appear to be different from what he really is.

theory, a communist paper must not only epitomize the views of its particular editors, it should also directly reflect the working-class masses with whom it has privileged and exclusive relations thanks to the presence in the factories of a network of correspondents. And so, even prior to 1930, *l'Humanité* relied on several thousand *rabcors* who supplied material for a column called "Rotten Work Shops."

In 1932 the Soviet secret service apparently decided to employ this network, whose assignment it was to back up the editors of *l'Humanité*, for the purposes of economic espionage. With this end in view but without the knowledge of the correspondents, Soviet agents asked the editor responsible for the *rabcors* service, a steelworker from the Loire known as Philippe, to sort out the information that came to him. He was to give this information to an agent of Polish origin named Bir, who had assumed the picturesque alias of Fantômas. In June, 1932 this affair was discovered, and it caused a good deal of excitement. Following their arrest, Bir and Philippe were sentenced in December, 1932, to prison terms running from thirteen months to three years. Jacques Duclos, also indicted, managed to reach the frontier and went to Moscow. He subsequently proceeded to Germany, remaining there until he got the authorities to drop the charges against him.

Then there was an incident involving money. At one time, as we have already noted,[4] a goodly portion of the party's financial resources came from "international sources"—in other words, from the Komintern. Certain affairs that grew out of this were particularly scandalous. A good illustration is the fate of the Workers' and Peas-

4. See above, chapter 8. One could mention more recent affairs like those of the "Spanish gold" or of the "treasure of Villebon-sur-Yvette" in 1947.

ants' Bank which had to close its doors in January, 1930. During the anticommunist offensive launched by the Tardieu government in August, 1929, the police had occupied the bank's various branches and seized all its books. The liquidation of this bank was unpleasant in itself because the funds of various organizations and branches of the revolutionary movement had been kept there. To make matters worse, the bank's closure threatened the stability and therefore the very existence of *l'Humanité*. The initial capital of the Workers' and Peasants' Bank consisted of savings certificates guaranteed by *l'Humanité*. These were fictitious certificates, of course, but the public comptrollers could, in auditing the bank, demand payment. In addition, *l'Humanité* at that time had a considerable deficit, and these same comptrollers had every right to demand that the newspaper cover it.

In order to save *l'Humanité*, as the party likes to tell it, the leaders issued an appeal to the financial solidarity of the working class—this was the first large request for contributions—as well as to its vigilance. The result was the formation of the famous committees for the defense of *l'Humanité* (CDH) which subsequently became a powerful network that saw to the distribution of its Sunday edition. These measures produced tremendous political repercussions and unquestionably, were a great political success.

In parallel fashion and with the utmost discretion, financial and bookkeeping techniques were initiated that may have made smaller sacrifices on the altar of political morality and aesthetics but were superior in terms of effectiveness. While draconian economies were being achieved by an administrative reorganization of the newspaper, the discovery at the bank was gradually forgotten. Matters were facilitated by fresh contributions from the

Communist International to the central organ of the
French party. In this connection, the International pre-
tended that the money came from an advertising agency
that was dependent on a powerful press network managed
by the German communist Eberlein on behalf of the International.

These, then, are some of the party's "secrets." They
are not really so wicked after all. Rather, they are tales
from the past that the party would like to forget because
they call attention to a situation that prevailed long ago,
to an era when a very small, young, and inexperienced
French section got mixed up in a few outlandish mis-
adventures. All in all, such secrets are somewhat reminiscent of the bad conscience of a petit bourgeois thirsting
for respectability whose greatest fear is that someone will
mention his grandfather, the butcher.

But there are worse secrets, secrets tainted with blood.
Once again, I must evoke the difficult years from 1939 to
1945. They were punctuated by acts of revenge which occasionally stemmed from grave mistakes. But in view of
the fact that some information is lacking, one must not
reach hasty conclusions. Even in a period of great violence, however, not all violence is excusable. If victory
gives rise to contemptible forms of revenge, how is one to
assess, in the shadow and light of clandestine life, how
much of it sprang from individual initiative, haste, panic,
prudence, waste, or legitimate self-defense?

The most one can say is that it would perhaps have been
more instructive not to have cast a hagiographic veil over
these realities. Doubtless it is too much to ask that the experts should decide among themselves what was good and
what was not, but is it too much to ask that the Resistance
should not be treated as a period that was always serene
and unmarred? Just as the historian of the civil war during the initial years of Soviet Russia must assess without

cheating the fearsome price paid for the introduction of socialism, so the historian or the memorialist of the Resistance must make it plain that violence is a very bitter brew and that people should be aware of this fact. Unless, of course, one is writing an operetta.

It should also be brought out that bitterness and gall spoil the finest memories of any human undertaking. Yet, has any organization been more pitiless than the Communist party in making distinctions *among its own*, the good from the bad, the heroes from the outcasts, those whose praises should be sung from those that must be relegated to the scrap heap of history? Seen in this light, the party's secrets appear to be a refusal to accept the bittersweet reality. In the behavior of the party there was something that smacked of the cruelty of children who prefer to destroy, to demolish irretrievably rather than see their paradise marred.

This selection of communist memories by the elect reflects to some extent the elitist structure that is a characteristic of the party-society. These memories are curiously concretized for any atheist group by a corner inside the Père Lachaise cemetery where the party buries those judged worthy of its own Pantheon. Can one envisage anything finer than the life of some newborn infant wailing in a steelworkers' clinic, who one day will have his own bank account, a modest one, to be sure, and will eventually be buried not far from Maurice Thorez and Marcel Cachin, in the ninety-seventh section of Père Lachaise!

But alongside this happy soul there are others, the "unlucky ones," the real victims of elitist structures, to say nothing of the little people, the obscure, those with no rank or title. For example—and this time I am not speaking of an imaginary life—there is Maurice Tréand.

I don't know why Maurice Tréand was chosen to be a

student in Moscow, at the Komintern's special school for
the training of the "techniques" in its clandestine apparatus. At any rate, his first assignment proved unfortunate. In 1932, his training over, Tréand was appointed
"boss" of the liaison apparatus already referred to whose
mission it was to solve the security problems occasioned
by the presence in France of a team of international (illegal) militants.[5] He had scarcely begun to assume his
responsibilities when an "accident" occurred: at a meeting of the political bureau—a clandestine meeting because
two illegal members were present (Ferrat, who for the
past five years had been eluding arrest; Geroe, who had
replaced Fried)—the police broke in and arrested the two
clandestine members. This was Tréand's first mishap.
Even though he was not directly at fault, he could not help
suffering the consequences of such a setback.

He was formally absolved of responsibility for it, and a
little later, in 1933, was asked to head the cadres committee that had just been organized.[6] This was another
delicate assignment which he carried out creditably, as
evidenced by the fact that he was elected a substitute of
the central committee at the Ninth Congress in 1937.

But ill fortune overtook Tréand. In July, 1940, he, together with Jean Catelas, was asked to negotiate with the
Germans for permission to resume publication of *l'Humanité*. In the meanwhile, however, he was arrested by
the French police. Eventually he was released on orders
from the Germans. The steps taken by Tréand, which
could in nowise be interpreted as representing efforts on
his own behalf, proved embarrassing to the party in the
light of later developments. By 1940, Tréand's activities
were no longer in keeping with the image the party wished

5. See above, chapter 12.
6. See above, chapter 10.

to project of its overall conduct. Thereupon there was nothing for it but to resort to the kind of expedient that enables the party to meet all challenges:[7]

> Tréand was dumped. When Liberation came he was isolated like a person stricken with the plague. Someone in his outfit saw to it that he had everything he needed materially. When he died at Antony, neglected by everyone, the administration gave proof of its good taste: flowers were placed on his tomb by a delegation from the central committee, and *l'Humanité* issued a communiqué praising this "loyal militant."[8]

These sad stories do have one merit: they help us to understand why the communists adopt such a strange attitude toward history. On the one hand, they betray a very pronounced fondness for history, making use of it as if it were the most important of all the social sciences. And, in fact, they are constantly engaged in reconstructing the genesis of phenomena. In this way they oppose, on the basis of principle and of very serious argumentation, the structuralist method insofar as the latter is employed instead of the historical. This they do without making distinctions and regardless of changes that might have occurred within a given situation. On the other hand, French communists, at least until now, have shown themselves to be very allergic to historical research on matters of intimate concern to them, regardless of whether they themselves or others are conducting the research.

7. The materialistic manner of handling the situation was never acknowledged until the recent official history, *Le Parti Communiste français dans la Résistance*, p. 73.

8. Auguste Lecoeur, *Le Parti communiste français et la Résistance*, p. 95.

Secrecy

We finally come to the question of the role played by
secrecy in the communist world—not any specific or particular secrets, but secrecy in general.

One item that bears the communist stamp is the attitude
toward the writing of memoirs. Unless you have been
authorized or commissioned to do so, you break an unwritten rule if you compose memoirs or an autobiography.
For example, Thorez's autobiography, *Fils du peuple* was
written as a consequence of a political decision and not
because the author was inspired to write. The unwritten
rule is never to reveal to the outside world anything about
what is going on within the party even if, as is true today,
nothing illicit or illegal is taking place.

To put it bluntly, if orthodox communists, or even outcasts—those who have been excluded—rarely write their
memoirs (I'm not talking about angry outbursts or apolo-
gias, but genuine memoirs), this is because they really
have nothing to say. When they do write something personal, it means they have freed themselves inwardly or
have overcome a deeply buried repugnance that borders
on superstition. After reflecting about their experience,
many begin to realize how distorted their overall view of
things is. Although long accustomed to such distortion,
they also begin to realize how little they know—only a
few pieces of a widely dispersed puzzle.

This amazing dispersal, this splintering of the truth
into a thousand pieces which, to assemble, would require
the kind of systematic investigation that is virtually out
of the question, is due to the fact that specialization and
isolation are permanent fixtures, even in a period of total
legality. Nobody, not even the secretary-general, can
claim to know *everything*. Hierarchical relationships from
top to bottom and from bottom to top are abundant and

intimate, but relationships at a single level are, in practice, if not explicitly forbidden at least formally taboo. From cell to cell, from section to section, from federation to federation the intervention of a higher coordinating echelon is required in order to make contact. As for human relationships, it is an accepted fact that militants at every level, even the highest, do not talk to each other, save in a general kind of way, about matters that have nothing to do with their duties. Relations are often quite cordial, of course, although here as everywhere likes and dislikes play a part. Apart from "combat" situations where some genuine fraternity is experienced, feelings of camaraderie are rather tepid. As a consequence of all this, universal truth no longer exists because of the impossibility—unless precise permission is given from the top—of holding meetings whenever necessary at a given time and place without regard for the usual exclusions and hierarchies. We are left with only partial truths whose synthesis is hazardous and dependent upon personal interpretation.

When talking freely and investigating conflicting impressions, we must not deceive ourselves about the amazing efficacity of this overall proscription. It is efficacious in the sense that nothing from the past survives save the expurgated version, which is distributed by the appropriate agencies; it is efficacious too in the sense that any indiscretion is almost sure to be limited to whatever the leaders deliberately decide to leak.

As for the past, oblivion is not only a corollary of the rapid recruitment of new members; it is also the consequence of a form of behavior that casts suspicion on the type of interrogation that begins, "Tell me, Grandpa." To be sure, the older militants, who often say, "In my day . . ." are not free from the "old soldier" type of mentality. But generally speaking, it is not customary to indulge in telling stories about the past. Very few are those who encourage misplaced curiosity or trivial gossip. As a result, oral tradition is practically nonexistent (save in a narrow circle) and a written tradition endlessly repeated in condensed form easily prevails, having triumphed over imprimatur after imprimatur. All this explains the following well-known but dumbfounding fact: thousands and thousands of communist intellectuals living in a liberal democracy, people of perfectly normal intelligence, for several decades not only considered certain books to be taboo, but were totally uninformed about books that any public library or bookstore had on their shelves. The kind of secrecy that served to entomb these books was customary and tended to prevent members from reading any available outside material.

Today militants "discuss"; they do not "talk." Occasionally they let themselves go and tell each other their "secrets," but not without some feelings of guilt. They do not "gossip" irresponsibly. Yet their apprenticeship in discretion does not mean that they are all taciturn. Duclos, a jovial, eloquent lover of words, like so many politicians from the southeast of France, carefully guards most of the "party secrets," but this he does despite his volubility.

Auguste Lecoeur has reported a few significant examples of the extent and efficacity of the party's secrecy.

During the second half of 1951, Marcel Servin, at that time in charge of the party's cadres, had gone to the Soviet Union to visit Maurice Thorez, who was convalescing there. Upon his return, Servin, together with Léon Mauvais (who at the time ran the central committee for political control) formed a new committee to investigate the "political activities" of André Marty and Charles Tillon. This is what Lecoeur has to say:

As far as I was concerned, *even though I was party secretary at the time*, I had not heard the slightest rumor about any such affair. The same was true of the majority of the members of the political bureau, even though a committee had been established whose task it was to keep the political bureau informed. It was not until May 19, 1952, that Servin and Duclos mentioned it to me for the first time. At a meeting of the secretariat, they informed me of the conclusions that the committee had reached.[9]

One might concede in this connection that the reason for such secrecy was to be found in the need for "vigilance." But the following is even more curious because it has to do with information already known.

We know that in December, 1940, in the name of communist deputies who had been jailed and on explicit orders from the clandestine secretariat of the party, François Billoux, himself a prisoner, wrote a letter to Marshal Pétain. He asked to be heard as an *accusing witness* in the trial that the Vichy government was conducting in the Supreme Court of Riom against the "men responsible for the defeat"—Blum, Daladier, and Reynaud.[10] In 1952 Billoux was appointed president of the communist deputation in parliament. When he mounted the speaker's platform of the National Assembly he was greeted with cries and shouts that issued mainly from the socialist benches: "The letter to Pétain! The letter to Pétain!" As

9. Auguste Lecoeur, *Le Partisan*, p. 259.

10. See A. Kriegel, "Léon Blum vu par les communistes," *Le Pain et les Roses* (Paris: PUF, 1968). See the entire text of the letter of December 19, 1940, by François Billoux in *Histoire du PCF* (Éd. Unir), 2: 42–47 as well as the article François Billoux wrote in *l'Humanité*, May 18, 1951, to explain what happened. It is noteworthy that this episode is still not mentioned in the very recent official history, *Le Parti communiste français dans la Résistance.*

a consequence, Billoux asked to be relieved of his new duties. This is what Lecoeur has to say about the incident:

> The members of the political bureau were dining at the central committee's headquarters. Gaston Monmousseau, who was among those present, asked why "we didn't protest against those lies instead of giving in." Frachon answered that the letter had indeed been written and sent to Pétain. Monmousseau turned crimson. Although no latecomer to the party, he had known nothing about the letter. And he never asked for an explanation.[11]

In a world as "overinformed" as ours, it is inconceivable that such lack of information should fail to serve some purpose or have some meaning.

What is the sense of refraining from mentioning even the simplest matter? How are we to interpret, not only the lie of pretending that Thorez continued during the Resistance to head the party in his native land, but also the silence that still prevails about the date and circumstances of his departure—which today is of no further importance? How is one to understand the party's obstinacy in declaring "out of bounds" the publication of details about matters that are thirty or forty years old? The party's careful search for compromising documents further attests its need for secrecy. Even photographs are sometimes touched up or falsified.

Have such practices ceased to be the rule? How then is one to interpret the fact that basic data concerning, for example, the community of members remain a "party secret"? How is one to interpret the fact that the data obtained through investigations and examinations of party structures have never been made public save in the

---

11. Lecoeur, *Le P.C.F. et la Résistance*, p. 121.

form of percentages difficult to assess and collate? In short, how is one to understand why it is so difficult for men and ideas to circulate within the large hierarchical structure of the party?

These questions cannot be answered categorically. The party probably shares to some extent a certain timidity and discomfort that are very widespread in the Old World. It reacts to the idea of combining information with publicity as to a desecration, a rape. Our economic enterprises as well as our political organizations suffer in varying degree from an identical superstitious attachment to the protective workings of secrecy. They likewise suffer from an identical underestimation of the beneficial role that information can play in promoting a consensus.

On the other hand—this is doubtless true in all essential respects—one cannot deny that secrecy is an integral party of the worldwide phenomenon that communism represents. It is even possible to say that one of the most revealing features of a social democratic party as distinguished from a Bolshevik party is precisely the degree of the former's openness toward the outside world and of its susceptibility to penetration from the outside.

In a party inspired by Bolshevism, secrecy, that Leninist virtue par excellence, does not stem from the kind of external constraint due to circumstances such as existed, for example, in a police state like Tsarist Russia. But secrecy goes hand in glove with the theory and practice of the class struggle. To put it concisely, secrecy is the weapon of revolutionary warfare because it is a weapon of combat.

Secrecy, therefore, is not a superfluous element to be readily discarded. Rather, it is one element in a whole set of interrelated principles pertaining to the concept of revolution, from the march toward socialism by means of the class struggle to the idea of the party as a battle corps. Naturally, one might say that today the practice of secrecy has been perpetuated to serve as a reassuring but meaningless sign, an illusory guarantee for a whole set of principles that have long since collapsed. But that is another matter.

It is difficult to deny that secrecy retains at least a part of its initial purpose, given the extent to which information is held to be a hierarchical privilege. The mechanisms for the formation of cadres and for the creation of decision-making centers are so conceived as to permit information, emanating from groups and strata whose loyalties the party wants to capture, to move rapidly upward through the apparatus and to spearhead the movement. This, for example, was the principal asset of Maurice Thorez. He knew how to synthesize all the information that came to him from both within and without the party. He was also able to put his finger on the exact spot within the party where one could discover the average level of public opinion. He took into account the fact that the extremes of opinion about the various problems that are constantly arising and that are likely to be taken seriously by communist leaders are actually relatively limited in scope.

Moreover, the extent to which one shares both information and secrets defines the degree of responsibility assumed in any enterprise. This being so, the awareness that one is the object of a selective *initiation* reinforces the traditional reluctance to divulge a secret, since secrecy appears to be the result of a conquest. Secrecy is thus not only a guarantee of the revolutionary nature of a party involved in the class struggle; it is in addition a process that helps to enhance the party's homogeneity.

Such are the terms of the situation. This is not a trivial

matter; it is not merely a question of communist "style." I am not pleading for the right to gossip as over against the dignity of silence. The issue is one that transcends the question of socialism's relation to science. Doesn't secrecy sap the vitality of revolutionary science as much as it does the strength of other physical or humanistic sciences? And, more generally, isn't it true that the relationship of socialism to freedom is based on freedom of information?

The questions raised here cannot be answered hastily. The reader scarcely needs to be reminded that it was precisely on this point that Soviets and Czechs clashed, that traditionalists and partisans of innovation continue to confront one another.

To be sure, the generalized practice of secrecy contributed powerfully to the Stalinization of the worldwide communist movement. Secrecy plainly was one of the targets of those who denounced Stalinist crimes. The Twentieth Congress of the Communist Party of the Soviet Union constituted a fantastic flash of light amid the opaque darkness in which millions and millions of Soviets and others had been agonizing, without the slightest suspicion by their party brothers. Demands for free speech, for a purifying frankness, have been increasing uninterruptedly for the past twelve years in the people's democracies and even in the Soviet Union.

There is one thing no one as yet has learned: how to fight for a socialism that has not yet been achieved within the framework of a freedom that must be respected *now*. It is precisely on this point that conflict has arisen. No solution is possible until a new doctrinal position has been taken and until a certain amount of practical knowledge has been acquired. This calls not only for circumspection but also for imagination and daring, the objective being the gradual elimination of secrecy wherever it is not strictly necessary. To accomplish this, one must begin with the principle and conviction that secrecy will be the exception, that very seldom is it really necessary, that it inevitably degenerates into arbitrariness, obscurantism, and oppression.

Conclusion

"Back to Lenin." This doctrinal orientation, proclaimed on the morrow of the Soviet Communist party's Twentieth Congress, explains why the policy of destalinization was bound to fail at the level of theory. It explains why, for the last twelve years, it constantly gave rise to violent upheavals, outbursts, disunity, and schisms. The reason was not so much that the breaking of the Stalinist yoke freed national energies, encouraged cultural diversities, exacerbated economic inequalities, and revived old political traditions. Rather, the failure of destalinization was due to the absence of a guiding thread. This lack rendered the large multilateral assemblies basically futile, condemned as they were to fitting together short-term political solutions. Since no one of these assemblies knew what it was seeking or what was lacking, and didn't want to confess this to the world, how could all of this together provide an answer?

This lack, which makes it impossible to define intermediate objectives—the key to strategy—and therefore impossible to define short-term tactical ways and means, is intolerable in a movement where revolutionary theory is supposed to govern revolutionary action. There is no doubt that this lack was keenly felt, that it was humiliating at least to those in every sector of the front who were charged with major responsibilities.

The absence of a guiding thread is the result of a general refusal or inability, whether individual or collective, to analyze the Stalinist phenomenon in open language. Here is the very root of the neurosis whose ill effects are poisoning the worldwide communist movement. As long as this remains undeciphered in the memory of communists, as long as it is repressed in the unconscious of revolutionaries, as long as its significance, transcending its sinister manifestations, has not been explicated, the only course that can be followed is that of meeting contingencies one at a time. All that then remains is a futureless day-to-day struggle that can be likened to the life of a fireman who hastens to put out unforeseeable blazes.

The first thing to be done in this connection is not to reestablish a continuity between Stalinism and that which followed it, but between Stalinism and that which preceded it, Leninism. The break, artificially emphasized between the Leninist and Stalinist systems in order to guarantee the impunity of the former, has actually served to precipitate both systems into the endless complications occasioned by a false consciousness.

Of course one must mark out with precision those domains in which Stalin was clearly an innovator—at times the results were excellent but at others they were dreadful. In view of the very different situations the men and their regimes had to meet, a total absence of innovations would have been surprising. But the accusation that Stalin was unfaithful to Lenin in *essential matters* remains to be proved—essential matters, meaning the nature and leading role of the party in the revolutionary process and the maintenance of a proletarian dictatorship. However brilliant and devastating his indictment of Stalin's regime, Trotsky failed to demonstrate persuasively that things were different under Lenin. In the spring of 1920, Trotsky himself recommended "the militarization of the economy" as a solution to the problem of reconstruction. It is true, of course, that at that time excesses were justified by the civil war. But was the civil war the sole source? The physical liquidation of the Russian bourgeoisie was followed by that of the kulaks and subsequently by that of the "old Bolsheviks." How, then, can one be certain that insistence on bloody violence was due uniquely to Stalinist folly?

In other words, this "Back to Lenin," by stressing an anecdotal and biographical Stalinism, concealed the real question. It precluded reflection about the matrix from which Stalin had sprung: Bolshevism itself, as reified by a successful revolution. Not until now have a few disparate timid voices been raised to call attention to this matter.

How can one reflect on it without assessing the awesome compactness of the Leninist system? No purpose is served in this connection by dusting off Vladimir Ilich in order to remove with the greatest respect a few unfortunate minor flaws. What we need to know is why and how Leninism functioned. As a matter of fact, it functioned very well, very effectively, in a creative, positive way, at least until it reached a certain stage, a certain point of development, although at the cost of terrifying "inconveniences." Is it possible to avoid the price that was paid for the system and to overcome its limitations without cracking the system itself? Is it enough to remold this system in depth, or are the various parts of it too interdependent? If the price is too high, the limitations too narrow, will there be no other way out save that of abandoning it in turn to the "nibbling criticism of mice?"

One measures the power of a theory of political action

by its resilience, its capacity to adapt to new and extremely varied sectional and circumstantial situations.

In this connection, the case of Castroism should be excluded. (Its syncretism, by and large, loses all genuine credibility because of the insular nature of the experience and the fact that the Soviet Union assumed total economic responsibility for it. Consequently, one cannot even apply the criterion of internal effectiveness.) On the other hand, Stalinism, Titoism, neo-Khrushchevism, Trotskyism, Maoism—regardless of their differences and their respective grounds for complaint—all proceed from a single matrix: the Bolshevism of Lenin.

It is precisely this initial unity that renders their internal struggles so merciless. No war is bloodier than one in which the two sides make use of identical rules of warfare to come to grips with one another. But this is also why, in "pagan" territory such as the West, the pluralism of neo-Leninist variations, once they have accomplished their mission of liberating the movement from Stalinist rigidities, makes it impossible to recall who it was that criticized Stalinism in depth. Any complaints that logically justify a rupture with one faction justify a split with all of them, and these rivalries leave the factions open to a common condemnation, just as long ago the Chinese masses indiscriminately disregarded the rivalries between various Christian missionary groups.

Besides, orthodox communists, constrained to these debates about "true faith," can measure what the practice of secrecy has cost them, a secrecy which we have demonstrated to be unworkable. If these orthodox communists had not kept Trotsky "under wraps" and refused until very recently to resume any serious and informed discussions of his case (ever since they were convinced by his assassination that the reason for it was plain), they would not be obliged today to face revisions that seem all the more wonderful to Trotsky's defenders because they are "forbidden." If, according to a general consensus, the Maoists wielded less influence over the student movement of May, 1968, than the Trotskyites, the reason was doubtless to be found in the presence of several factors: a certain rigidity that prevented the Maoists from rendering more flexible their dogma of the revolutionary superiority of the working class; the failure of the "Chinese" to employ the effective but questionable techniques of "infiltration" which, in reality, degenerated into generalized conspiracy and trickery; the circumstance that Maoism, which is certainly a form of extremism but which in no way represents leftism, was therefore deprived of an important power of attraction in contrast to a movement in which a truly leftist appeal was essential; lastly, the continuous polemics waged against the "Chinese" by orthodox communists, which enabled even the uninitiated to recognize the former and to avoid being taken in by them.

Be that as it may, it is reasonable to believe (although in the summer of 1968 such speculation would have seemed hazardous) that the Leninist variations opposing Soviet orthodoxy—all of which are lumped together and improperly labelled "leftism"—have scant chance, despite their recent spectacular incursions in the French political arena, of becoming stabilized at a level that might enable them to become consistent and permanent elements in our political life. I say this because Stalinist indoctrination preceded the Leninist variations.

But it would be clearly incorrect to hold that "leftism" is devoid of significance or consequences.

Meticulous studies are needed to ascertain the significance of leftism. Such studies must make a careful distinction between what makes for extremism in these

Leninist variations and what, in effect, makes for leftism. These two political categories, *extremism* and *leftism,* do have certain features in common; nevertheless the lines of demarcation remain clear, even though leftism has a certain subjective, pejorative sound that leads polemicists to confuse it with extremism.

Whereas extremism is a radical option based on a strategy external to established structures—the varieties of extremism are related to the diversity of external levels and forms—leftism is the path to failure, favoring the revolutionary *movement* rather than its *objective*; the pattern rather than the goal.

This path to failure is often the result of the triumph of a vigorous subversive spirit over the rigorous requirements of a cool assessment of the contending forces. This subversive spirit, however, owing to frequent reversals and premature exhaustion, will soon degenerate into logomachy and harden into a form of doctrinairism. If my analysis is correct, this mechanism for the promotion of leftist deviationism makes one thing clear: although the mechanism itself has submerged almost completely the various Trotskyist groups (as distinguished from Trotsky himself, who constitutes a far more complex case), leftism is not to be identified with this or that sect; rather, it is a blend of all forms of extremism (including extremism of the right).

It is not difficult to *define* leftism in general. Lenin was very good at that sort of thing. His analyses are remarkably relevant in this connection. The problem is one of bringing to light, not the theory of extremism and its many variations, but its concrete, historical roots in a country like France. Related to this is the problem of exposing the leftist component that is contaminating some of these variations.

An imperturbable stability of French structure likely to foil all revolutionary plans regardless of their duration would redound to the advantage of a strictly leftist venture. Given the actual situation, it is therefore more satisfactory to think of some specific circumstances that, by precipitating a clash between universal stability and temporary fragility, would encourage recourse to extremist strategy.

Assuming such a clash, in which of society's privileged domains should we locate this fragility? To locate it at the level of "civilization" is merely to resort to empty rhetoric. The same "civilization" does not engender the same phenomenon in England, or at any rate not to the point where it becomes a serious political and ideological problem.

Are we to locate such fragility at the level of demographic structures where the numerical and qualitative imbalances between age categories in France are particularly marked because of France's special demographic history? This is especially true in university circles where during the school year the large numbers of lycée students and others are not included in the statistics compiled on the basis of legal domicile. It would be interesting to calculate the correlation in every urban center between the intensity of disturbances during the month of May, 1968, and the local age distribution—for example, the ratio of the student population to the total population; or to find out whether the differential rate of young workers in factories affected significantly the launching, duration, style, and objectives of strike movements.

Should we locate this fragility at the level of social structures and refer to the dossiers that have already been compiled on the new strata of the working-class world? Only a statistical examination of police records, for example, can enable us to decide whether the demonstrators

belonged to intermediate categories that form a part of
this "new strata," or to the so-called "dangerous classes"
that may gradually move from one category to another.
An inquiry aided by responsible members of strike committees might also provide valuable data about the categories that were the most active in each industrial plant.

Should we locate this fragility in the political domain
where Gaullism is a "baroque" hybrid that has no respectable precedent in French tradition and is therefore
vulnerable to sudden dislocation? It seems impossible,
especially in the political domain, to envisage an alliance
that will not be dominated by the communists, given the
relative strength of the noncommunist left. Such a situation definitely precludes any "leftist outcome," unless the
political situation should undergo a drastic change. Each
time, however, that the problem assumed a concrete form,
the majority of the electorate showed that it wanted nothing of the sort. To what extent did the May explosion
express a sense of despair over the "common platform"
adopted in February, 1968, by the Communist party and
the trade union Federations? Didn't the May disturbances
doom once and for all the old strategy based on the notion
that the left, such as it is, could represent an alternative?

Or should we turn to the profound and general crisis
of patriotism which, as we know, stands as a serious obstacle to the deployment of revolutionary energies? Besides nullifying the sense of belonging to a national community threatened by a measure of imperialism, the
process of decolonization that has come about as a consequence of successive military defeats served to put the
finishing touches on the sequence of developments initiated by the disaster of 1940. Just as the Louis Philippe
atmosphere of a country that lived in fear because it had
been defeated in 1815 led to 1848, so today—despite

the pathetic Gaullist gamble—the young generation, disenchanted with a country where the cement of national unity seems so greatly eroded, where virtually nothing appears capable of producing even a minimum amount of consensus, is staging a revolution. Under similar circumstances in the past, these young people waged war. To be sure, Jacobin centralization and the erosion of regional particularism, the refusal to integrate other than by rejecting the specific contributions due to the Frenchification of considerable foreign contingents—these have precluded the development of a diversified, complex national sentiment. Yet such a sentiment is more in keeping with the present one than the kind of all-out patriotism typical of earlier generations.

Or, to explain this French fragility, should we perhaps think about the equally profound and general crisis the church of France is experiencing in our ancient Catholic land? There is room here for a fine work on Christian extremism, which moreover is almost entirely riddled with leftism. The propensity of Christian extremism to yield to leftism calls for explanations whose elements one would be only too happy to receive from the hands of the experts.

In short, there are many directions researchers might follow in investigating the roots of extremism, directions that may lead to a situation in which, although nothing is really possible, not everything is entirely impossible. I have deliberately avoided mentioning hypotheses too sweeping to be documented: to wit, "hatred of father," or the "rejection of the consumer society." Yet it is impossible to refute them, because they do contain a grain of truth. We can only hope that all the ink that has been spilled over the May riots will soon give way to thoughtful documentation based on precise indicators and also on clearly defined hypotheses that are definitely consonant with the autonomy of human domains and mechanisms. In view of the fact that an event as complex as the disturbances of May is primarily sociopolitical in nature, this dimension should be carefully examined before an attempt is made to find the causes elsewhere—in questionable psychoanalytical fields, for example.

As for myself, I am inclined to think, at least at the moment, that this rupture of French stability—which, if not "typical" in degree, is at least exceptional in Europe—represents within the context of classical indifference to political institutions, the result of the specific and converging crisis that is buffeting the two main entities within which the nation's spiritual tradition is inscribed: Catholicism and socialism. With the exception of Italy, there is no country in liberal Europe that contains such large contingents of Catholics and communists. Nowhere else is the struggle quite so fierce that pits "progressives" and "conservatives," "liberals" and "integrationists," against each other within these two large bodies.

This fact may explain why the effects of the May upheaval were not confined even primarily to the government; rather, with disconcerting speed, the shock waves affected even the least "political" areas of the nation. The process is one that Marxism had predicted in connection with the course of economic crises. But in France we were given an interesting illustration of this process within the framework of a spiritual crisis. One might call it a "nervous crisis," but it would be a grave error to believe that it was not based on "reality," even though it was not materialistic at the start.

We still need to know why this extremism was so thoroughly tinged with leftism. The official answer is that the plurality and variety of hypotheses advanced regarding

France's vulnerability were in themselves sufficient proof that conditions were not yet ripe for a profound revolutionary crisis. The limited duration of a supposedly extremist outburst lacking major appeal was bound to lead to the triumph of leftism over radicalism.

Although the fact that conditions were not yet ripe explains the failure, it does not in itself account for leftism. What must be added is the flagrant absence of a revolutionary *model*. Save for a whisper of past, exotic memories linking the present adventure with great ancestors and with a universe beyond the oceans, the only model that seems to have exerted some sort of general influence is that of the Chinese cultural revolution. But it is not at all clear that credit for this belongs to Maoist groups, considering the enormous distortion of the French experience, if not its pure and simple contradictions.

Indeed, it seems that the adjective "cultural" in the phrase "cultural revolution" was generally interpreted to have the meaning attributed to it in speaking of "cultural" centers. Moreover, since in France the movement was primarily a student affair, the revolutionary emphasis was, curiously enough, placed on culture in general. Some students claimed that a humanist culture had deteriorated into a bourgeois culture; others proposed a radical death to all culture. Now, even if a receptive audience found the arguments interesting, it would have to admit that they had little connection with Peking's cultural revolution. Within the context of a *political* revolution that had been consecrated some twenty years ago by the seizure of power, that cultural revolution pitted two great powers, two institutions, against one another: the party and the army. This interpretation is based not on any culture, past or present, Chinese or non-Chinese, but on the thoughts of Chairman Mao—a phrase that has come to

signify the theoretical and strategic vision which determined international revolutionary action and its implications in China.

Leftism, insofar as it makes revolution a fetish, an
object of incantation, clearly embodies the *political* interpretation of two of the chief features of the May movement: the absence of any deep urgency or need and the
presence of a "culturalist" deviation which was the result
of a distortion due to an incorrect adaptation of the Chinese model.

As a corollary, the May events can be interpreted in a
playful fashion as a game, as if the "imagination in
power" were merely "imaginary power." This is not to
deny the magnitude of the chain reaction triggered by the
May movement, or the importance of the consequences,
positive or negative, it left behind it, even allowing for
the fact that things could have been better or worse. But
to regard this reaction and its aftermath as a posteriori
proof of a triumph over reality is to forget that some
games, *Revolutionspiel* as well as *Kriegspiel*, end trag-
ically. Besides, no game can be played unless it holds some
degree of reality for the participants. This is not to deny
that a starting mechanism was discovered which could
in the future be combined with some theory that would
launch the revolutionary process. The element of surprise
should not be underestimated in a revolutionary war, or
in war itself, for that matter.

Paradoxically enough, the spectacle of the streets lent
an aura of play to what was happening. Long weeks of violence culminated in an almost negligible number of victims. What is not surprising is the fact that revolutionary
themes were touted as if they were a virtual monopoly of
the nonadult population. Despite the efforts to demonstrate
how *serious* the young people were—"serious" was one of

the adjectives used with symptomatic frequency, especially in all allusions to the efforts of the lycée students—it was impossible for the adults to forget the age-old knowledge that the universe of children is a school and game universe. It is hardly plausible that a hierarchical authoritarianism which misunderstood the parental relationship should have been largely replaced, even in the sacred realm of politics, by a simple inversion of that relationship. Nor is it rational to emerge from the disturbances by proclaiming, as a certain number of generous but panicky professors did, that the sons had become the fathers.

At any rate, one may well ask oneself whether this leftism and this game, which delighted some people but discouraged many others, did not constitute convincing arguments for those who doubt that future extremist strategies have any chance of succeeding.

We now come to the possible consequences of the May events. In discussing the significance of May, 1968, it seems necessary to stress extremism above all else. Since the manner in which the internal debates were conducted typified the entire enterprise, it also seems unavoidable, when discussing the consequences of the disturbances, to underscore the leftist dimension.

Even if the episode amounts to nothing more than a mere "road accident"—this, though plausible, is not at all certain—leftism may nonetheless have important consequences. To begin with, we should not forget that it was a particular form of leftism (Stalinism) that, by paralyzing the German left, promoted among other things the rise of Nazism. There is reason, moreover, to fear that French leftism might accelerate the crystallization of right-wing extremism in Germany. Besides, Gaullist liberalism, which until now has withstood the most unfortunate situations, may yet degenerate into a kind of

Salazarism—the result of an unforeseen and unusual combination of undivided electoral power and General de Gaulle's Christian-social ideas. But above all what France experienced was a spectacular resurrection of the awesome experience used by the left in Spain during that country's civil war. This, together with other elements of weakness, contributed to a defeat that has lasted more than thirty years.

No purpose, however, would be served in this connection by listing the mistakes, failures, or crimes of the Spanish communists. Led by the delegates of the Komintern, they gave free rein to their unfounded hegemonic claims. Nor would there be any point in demonstrating how the adventures and excesses of the anarchists and "Poumists"[1] compromised the urgently needed unity of the Republican resistance. Transcending all else was the fact that, under the circumstances, the entire Spanish left proved unable to elude the most terrible of defeats.

Today it would likewise be unfruitful to level the accusation of "betrayal" at the French communists, and they too would be well advised to refrain from hurling the charge of "leftist adventurism" at their adversaries.

Did the French Communist party, in effect, betray the revolution because it deliberately adhered to the strategic revolutionary model which consists in placing the party both *within* and *without* the seat of power? This strategic model, set up by the international communist movement at the time of the Popular Front, was perfected after the war. It is a variation of the technique of dual power patterned after the 1917 Leninist model, to wit: instead of vainly attempting to counter the working-class tendency to be-

1. The Workers' Party of Marxist Unity, a Catalonian revolutionary party with Trotskyist sympathies which played an important role in the Spanish Civil War.—TRANS.

come integrated, a tendency based entirely on social reality, it would be better to lend support by sharing power within the framework of established society. In liberal democracies such participation takes the form of having the communists join the government whenever the electoral or parliamentary situation permits. But participation also occurs in a general way when communists are allowed to infiltrate all the structures of established society and thereby acquire a position within them—or even all the available positions. Is this a concession to the social democratic thesis which holds that one must help from the inside in order to enable the accumulation of socioeconomic gains to bring the anticapitalist revolution to an early climax? No, because participation in bourgeois power structures is necessarily accompanied by the stubborn preservation of the party's radical external activities. Instead of attenuating the foreign nature of the party, one must on the contrary intensify and emphasize it. The party, and it alone, becomes the universal external place in which the future socialist society will take root. Besides, as it gradually augments its role within the state and society, the party will also gradually but systematically effect the transfer of power into its own hands.

Now, at the very moment when success, after twenty difficult years of marking time, appeared to be around the corner, would it not have been paradoxical for the French Communist party to abandon this strategy? Early in 1968 many observers thought that a leftist victory at the polls was a genuine possibility. If they were right, such a victory would have preluded a sharing of power which, even if it were initially of rather modest proportions, might easily have turned into the hegemonic leadership—given the relative internal strength of the French left—of a pluralist government that remained in outward form a

coalition. One can see how superficial is the charge that
the communists frowned on the May movement because
they wanted to safeguard Gaullism on account of its foreign policy.

On the other hand, it is altogether human (although
this has nothing to do with political analysis) to enjoy
seeing the French Communist party flounder in the same
kind of morass into which the social democrats had fallen.
It would be a mistake, however, to view this misadventure
as an unquestionable indication of the communists' degeneration into a social democratic party. To do so would
be to confuse the situation with the nature of the party,
even though the first affects the second.

In effect, the French Communist party had two choices:
at the risk of being dragged into a catastrophe, it could
have followed the lead of the leftist groups, with an unavoidable awareness of where it was going; or it could
have held firm to its own strategy, publicly condemning
the entire undertaking and assuming full responsibility for
the even more inescapable defeat that an avant-garde,
openly subversive action would entail.

Like the social democrats of the past, the French Communist party knew that it could not resolve the dilemma
while the crisis was still raging. If it did act prematurely, it
was bound to be the loser. Accordingly, it would have to
choose between two evils: to lose moderately on two
counts, or to lose everything on one. It avoided decisive
action and thus managed to keep its head above water.

Never for a moment did it lose sight of its own strategy.
Considering its own image, it was disinclined to relinquish
the monopoly it always takes for granted in regard to the
leadership of any revolutionary alliance. In addition, under the circumstances, there was a fundamental conflict
between its strategy and that of the student movement.

Uncertain as the student movement was in some respects, it was nonetheless definite on one major point: the revolution must take place without delay. It was this attitude that accounts for all the "ifs, ands, and buts" expressed by the French Communist party. Hardly had the May movement reached its final phase when communist spokesmen began to explain why it was that the advent of the May riots was poorly timed. Of course, to no one's surprise, the party's reservations about the disturbances brought on the accusation of betrayal. But the accusation was somewhat attenuated by the fact that the party had attempted to act energetically whenever it could do something positive. Besides, as soon as things reverted to a more or less normal state, and elections were held, it could go back to its normal course of action. As for the "leftists," they were excluded from the elections by their own wish as well as because of concern over the nature, composition, and the real size of all the activist groups.

Nonetheless, the communist leaders had few illusions. The situation was serious: first, because of the loss of electoral votes; second and above all, because the relative strength of communists and noncommunists within the left was shifting too obviously in favor of the communists. The strategy of conquering power from within, paradoxically enough, became more difficult to implement because a Popular Front free from communist domination became less and less likely. A time would come when the principal concern of Waldeck Rochet would be to find militants and voters for the trade unions.

On the other hand, the party was constrained to abandon its strategy at least partially, or at any rate to go through the motions of abandoning it twice. The first time was when it unleashed working-class agitation in order to smother the student agitation. To be sure, it was careful to attribute to the social movement objectives that consisted exclusively in demands for reforms and to isolate the workers in their factories, in their homes, or in the street where the upsetting experience of May 13 would not be repeated. But the party could not prevent this traditional social movement from being viewed from a revolutionary point of view because of the fact that it had developed in conjunction with the students' revolutionary movement. The party could not prevent people from believing it was the promoter, the animator, the leader of the movement. And yet, even though of course there were risks here and there of excesses or tactical errors, neither the strike at the Renault-Cléon nor the agitation at Renault-Flins could have brought about a general strike if the party had decided otherwise (and even if the CFDT [Confédération française démocratique du travail, the Catholic trade unions] had backed it). Only if the powerful federation of railway workers had gone into action, and along with it the Paris federation of the RATP trade unions (Régie autonome des transports parisiens, or metro workers), could a general strike have materialized. For decades the railway workers have been led by the communists. Both their federations and that of the RATP unions are vital nerve centers, and they would surely have carried with them other labor organizations.

The blurring of the line of demaraction between those who didn't go to work because there was no transportation and those who failed to show up because they were on strike enhanced this certainty. All in all, and until a more definitive analysis has been made, it must be concluded that from the point of view of the communists, it was here that the harm done was held to a minimum. No matter what was said, the party, through the intermediary of the CGT, gave the impression of having solidly backed up the working class, or at least of having done so as solidly as possible in a country in which labor is traditionally underorganized. The CFDT had compromised itself unnecessarily by adopting a revolutionary attitude whose good sense or sincerity seemed open to question. This in turn weakened the dangerous power of attraction that its reputation for being modern had won for it. The economic and social platform of the trade unions differed from that of the party. This disparity, which constituted one of the principal bones of contention between the two left-wing partners, was eliminated when the Gaullist government decided to compromise the economy in order to save what for the moment had become essential: its political power. The federation could not have done less if the left had taken over the controls. Lastly, the workers will probably derive little actual benefit from this improvised battle. Without a doubt the government will attempt to preserve at least some of this benefit; however, from the social and trade union point of view, the worst that can happen is that things will remain exactly as they are. Perhaps, all things considered, this may represent a "success."

The second time the party had to partially abandon its strategy—on this occasion far more plainly—was during the four or five days immediately preceding de Gaulle's decisive speech of May 30. I do not mean to imply that the party suddenly decided to try for a direct revolutionary coup, or that it wanted to seize power by a Bolshevik-type coup d'etat more or less cleverly camouflaged as a Popular Front of democratic union. But things were taking such a turn that one could scarcely exclude the possibility that, in the absence of a direct heir, power might very well fall into the hands of whoever was prepared to receive it. In the light of this new situation, there was no longer any question of standing firm in doctrinaire fashion on an abstract position, or of sulking because it would have been better had the situation arisen a bit later. The party could not afford to leave the field free to others, even though disinclined to take over under such unfavorable conditions. And conditions were indeed unfavorable. Various groups were claiming their right to the Gaullist heritage. Their aim was either to strengthen the liberal middle classes or to form a coalition that would exclude the communists or at least keep them on the fringe of the political arena. In short, although the communists opposed a strategy contrary to their own, it did not necessarily follow that they would forgo a chance to reap the benefit should it unexpectedly become available to them. We must not think them to be more obstinate than they really are.

The party therefore was obliged to maneuver. It had to emphasize the Gaullist power crisis and bring the question of succession out into the open. It had to block ways and means of succeeding de Gaulle that did not suit its purposes. Finally, it had to assert itself as a "taker" of political power which the unusual circumstances might place in its hands.

All the party's ups and downs, its various actions, must be interpreted in the light of this threefold objective. These actions include the conversations at Grenelle on Sunday, May 26; the refusal to reach agreement—what really did happen at the Renault factory on Monday, May 27 (an interesting historical point to be cleared up!)?; the cautious game played with Mendès-France and Mitterand on Tuesday, May 28; the tremendous demonstration on Wednesday, May 29, when, as if a trump card had been tossed on the gaming table, battalions of workers were sent into the streets. All the way from the Bastille to Saint-

Lazare they marched, and they didn't look like Sunday strollers taking the fresh air for their health!

This analysis warrants the following conclusions. Those observers are correct who deny that the party deliberately, on its own initiative and as if to force the hand of fate, aimed at precipitating a very short-term revolution. But other commentators are not wrong when they say that the communists played their hand in such a way as to be in a position to exert their influence if the Gaullist regime fell and a new government seemed likely to take over. In the beginning the communist influence may have been limited and circumspect. But it was soon to be stronger and openly exerted. The exceptionally favorable international situation must be taken into account. No great power appeared to be in a position to intervene in any way whatsoever, given the fact that France, for its part, had fallen back on its own resources and its socialist experience. This reduces to their true proportions the somewhat absurd polemics about the communists' relationship to order. Are they defenders of order? Of course they are—of their own kind of order! Besides, communist order may on occasion coincide with bourgeois order. This has actually happened. Who doesn't remember the famous episode of 1945 when Maurice Thorez berated the miners for making demands and then urged them to increase the output of coal? Three years later the same Thorez uttered a no less famous remark: "We will not, we will never, wage war against the Soviet Union!"

During these weeks of crisis, the communist intellectuals protested against the attitude of their party and openly supported the student movement. If we are to believe the press releases about the arguments they advanced against their leaders, they disclosed an amazing misunderstanding of the movement to which they belonged. They also revealed an astonishing ignorance of the real problems that confront the communist movement.

Indeed, it was quite understandable that there should have been virulent opposition to the oversimplified manner in which the affair of the Union of Communist Students was "handled" not long ago—not perhaps because its left wing was cashiered, since it is plain today that this precaution enabled the French Communist party to withstand the dubious practice of "infiltration" to which the PSU (Parti socialiste unifié),[2] the UNEF (Union nationale des Etudiants français), the Movement of March 22, and the CAL succumbed. The CFTD, for its part, will probably pay dearly for this despite all initial indications to the contrary. The evil, perhaps, should have been preserved, since it was easily identified, recognized and localized. Also to be regretted is the tendency to regard the UEC (Union d'Etudiants communistes) as an end in itself. A rump UEC resulted from this operation, leaving the communists without a student audience and especially without a listening post in the student world, as was evident in the brief article written by Georges Marchais early in May. Moreover, had the party taken the trouble to investigate the real problems that caused the uneasiness which was reflected in the UEC crisis, it would probably have accepted more speedily what was known at the time as the "Italian ideas." The essence of these ideas was subsequently espoused by the party, but it took a long time to do so, and the leftist ferment benefited from the delay.

There is even more reason to question the initial tactical decision. Inspired by impatience, the decision unleashed the workers' agitation which, party leaders

2. The United Socialist Party, a small left-wing socialist party to which Mendès-France briefly belonged.—Trans.

hoped, would drown out that of the students. The maneuver not only failed; it also helped to give an additional fillip to the wave of student rebellion. If, instead, the students had been isolated, their movement's momentum would have been dissipated. This is a delicate but interesting point. In answer to such criticism one might say that *this time*, even in a limited and ambiguous way, one had to join the movement in order to expose fully the danger of leftism, its delusionary character. Once the experiment was over, once (as was to be expected) it was in a state of collapse, the cost of which the party was willing in advance to pay, it would then be easier to circumscribe leftism, to enclose it within the confines of the student world whence it sprang. Only then could it be trounced, with the help of all those—and they represented the majority—who cared about preserving a university, even a "bourgeois" one.

It is impossible, however, to reproach the communists for not having from the outset solemnly warned the student movement that it was heading toward disaster—that is, unless you expected them to behave in suicidal fashion.

Waldeck Rochet's policy during the following months, especially in regard to the drama that was being enacted in Czechoslovakia, leads one to conclude that the party leadership had already implicitly acknowledged its mistakes. These, however, were not the mistakes the communist intellectuals had in mind. All in all, the most bitter denunciations of leftism have no meaning or any chance of being heard unless they are accompanied by an active, audacious policy that tends toward a rupture with neo-Stalinism.

This last observation leads me to protest against the fatuousness that has led so many commentators to compare the French student movement with the events which occurred that winter and spring in Warsaw and Prague. Apart from the want of sensitivity displayed by those who contrasted two sets of action where the *risks* were so dissimilar, it is a "theoretical stupidity" to picture as parts of a single entity two movements whose principles are so *radically* antagonistic.

It is true, of course, that the two movements have common secondary features. First, both were student-inspired. Contrary to the notions held by some at the time that both movements had the earmarks of Third World societies, the students today, because of their numbers, their strength, and the rapid progress in science and technology, constitute the supporters or backers of change in *all* social organizations. But one must be very cautious in arriving at this hypothetical conclusion. The relative autonomy of the student world, its role as a detonator and amplifier of ideas and conflicts, the fact that it is neither the originator, the actual spearhead, nor the true beneficiary of such ideas and movements, are all very familiar. Nevertheless, we would do well to reexamine the situation more closely.

In any case, the dominance of students does bring with it sincerity, unselfishness, freshness—in short, purity. But purity is not necessarily a reassuring political virtue. The expression, "hard and pure," reminds us of something that is not exactly progressive—*syncretism,* for example. Agitational movements comprise heterogeneous elements. This is doubly true of student ferment. Here erudition is often of recent date; indirect knowledge about everything contributes to the amassing of a strange potpourri of declarations, demands, aphorisms, proscriptions, and prescriptions.

But, as everyone knows, the object of political thought is precisely to surmount apparent confusion and to identify the major, intrinsic purpose of an event. The *purpose* in Prague and Warsaw on the one hand, and in Paris on the other, stood in direct contradiction—even though some "revisionists" in Paris tended toward leftism, while in Prague (more than in Warsaw) some leftists joined the revisionist current. In effect, to believe that helping to break up political and trade union bureaucracies, especially neo-Stalinist ones, is enough to justify action, amounts to a resumption of that vicious argument used thirty-five years ago by those who were pleased for the same reasons to see the rise of fascism; they hoped for either the collapse of social democracy or for the breakup of communist parties. Of course, these bureaucracies should be broken up. But if I may say so, this has to be done in a good way, so as to promote a liberal revamping of the socialist pattern and model. The peremptory agitation against a background of anarchy that dominated Paris in May was not at all encouraging or new, or in any way similar to what was happening in Prague, except for the festive atmosphere. But even here we have to say something that may sound silly. A "carnival" is not in itself a political phenomenon—people have danced around all kinds of funeral pyres.

To be sure—and at first glance the argument is a powerful one—one might say that although the students in Prague and in Paris were facing entirely different problems because of their very different situations, they all harbored the same ultimate ambitions. The Prague students had socialism but they wanted freedom; the Paris students had freedom but they wanted socialism. Such reasoning, however, is rather dubious. Criticism of Stalinist socialism cannot be invalidated by simply adding a forgotten ingredient at the last minute—freedom. Nor can criticism of neocapitalism be invalidated by adding to established freedom a beaker of socialism. This was pre-

cisely the theoretical mistake committed by social democracy. It thought democracy and socialism could easily be
combined, whereas socialism must be regarded as a
springboard for the creative element in individuals and in
society.

We now can doubtless understand why all the analyses
of the past three years reached the following conclusions:
"The Communist party has definitely changed"; it was becoming a very acceptable partner; the best way to encourage a definitive change and "reintegrate it into the
democratic game" was to "take it out of its ghetto." We
can also understand all the vigilant solicitude displayed in
seizing upon its slightest liberal tremors, its subtlest expressions of an autonomous attitude toward Moscow, its
chattiest internal discussions ("they're talking!"). All
this left people uncertain, as if it were both true and false
that the party had changed, which was exactly the real
situation.

We can also understand why public opinion polls on
"the image of the Communist party" have shown that systematic hostility toward it, as demonstrated by the electorate's refusal to vote for any communist candidates, has
considerably diminished—to say nothing of the fact that,
according to the polls, "Frenchmen are no longer worried
about communism." Acceptance of the role of communists
in the political life of France has increased. In 1966, 40
percent, compared to 31 percent in 1964, favored admit-
ting communist ministers into the government; and more
than two-thirds (68 percent) of the French voting population believed that "they had nothing to lose if a communist regime were established in France." Yet, when the
problem became real in May-June, the answer, as we know,
was not at all ambiguous, although the communists took
advantage of the fact that the general public confused

them with the "leftists." Since there is no reason to believe that the polls, which are usually technically accurate, may have turned in an erroneous answer, and since it is hard to believe that Frenchmen change their minds so completely within the space of a few months, one can only conclude that the questions asked in the polls were mere traps.

Any consideration of communism—and of the French Communist party—must take place at two levels. These levels must not be combined if we are to avoid not only confusion but also conceptual or political ineffectiveness. Yet in order to perceive at any moment the unity of the phenomenon, one must establish certain connections and associations between the two levels. Only this kind of operation will, in the last analysis, make it possible to provide an overall diagnosis as well as to predict the future of the process.

I am not speaking here of the traditional distinction between strategy and tactics, between structure and circumstances, between maximum and minimum platforms. Nor is this a matter of dressing up the usual dichotomies in new garb. The two levels I am talking about are only metaphorically superimposed, the one being exposed to view, the other not. Actually, I am addressing myself to two forms of a single phenomenon.

The first level is not superficial but, let us say, exposed to all eyes. Here one perceives the communist plan exactly as it appears in everyday political life. It is a place of confrontation wth the objective world, where the history of its battle against established society unfolds. This battle, however constant it may be, sometimes takes the form of a relentless struggle, sometimes the form of collaboration, of more or less pronounced integration and cooperation; at other times it takes the intermediate form of a truce and almost total mutual disinterest.

Thus, the "class against class" strategy of the thirties represents a cantankerous way of confronting the world. You launch an all-out attack on the citadel even if you have no chance of succeeding because of the inequality of the contending forces. This is one aspect of the offensive spirit, within the framework of a generally defensive situation. Such a spirit finds justification in the fact that incursions and forays into enemy territory serve to take the war far from the sacred perimeter, the young Soviet Republic. Besides, these attacks can never culminate in total disaster, since it is always possible to retreat in time, and to seek refuge and security in the sanctuary of the "only country that is building socialism."

"The antifascist," "Popular Front," or "National Front" strategy of the thirties and forties represents a more subtle type of confrontation. It takes advantage of a particularly serious split in the capitalist world, a "break in the imperialist chain," to ally itself with one side against the other. The choice of partner is not a matter of indifference. Yet the Nazi-Soviet Pact, unless it was a pure and simple error, does prove that selection in and of itself is not of fundamental importance. In this kind of situation the Communist party's policy is twofold: very combative toward the other side, now the common enemy; very unitary, "unitary for two," toward the adversary who has become the ally. The advantages of this dual attitude are not merely cumulative, they snowball. The extent of the hostility toward the common enemy plus the important sacrifices made on behalf of a joint victory will seduce and convince those elements that, within the alliance, sincerely believe in the ideals defined in common. It then becomes easy to win the other side over completely.

The communists work closely with the ally, using all the techniques of social intercourse—participation, integration, collaboration, and even cooperation with the established government. Then, if an alliance has been made with the nation's majority party, the moment has come for the communists to enter the government. If the ally is a minority party, then the hour has struck for the communists to join the Resistance Front.

The strategy of the cold war, begun in 1947, is partially a step backwards, but it should not be confused with the earlier "class against class" strategy. It is less aggressive because a more equitable distribution of power has increased the cost of possible confrontations. Although less defensive, this strategy therefore attests a spirit of prudence and circumspection. It has been implemented within the framework of a policy whose major objective is to exploit and consolidate recent and still fragile gains. Tactics of isolation, of noncontact, are preferable to the strategy of the handshake. This is a period when the two worlds give the impression of being of separate derivation, immured in their mutual exclusion and ignorance.

Such are the main characteristics of the three strategies that have marked the historical, concrete evolution of the communist world in its relations with established French society. But in reality, if details are refined, we shall find that there are an infinite number of positions ranging all the way from the most radical externalization to overlapping and interpenetration, each marked by the ambiguous predominance of either hostility or cooperation.

The transition from one strategy to another is more or less unequivocal and direct. The transition from the cold war to peaceful coexistence is as sharp as a slalom turn. Even an observer outside the communist orbit cannot fail to notice it because the change affects precisely the zone between the two worlds. At this level the change is, by definition, spectacular.

On the other hand, the change by which the relations between the two worlds are readjusted can result from modifications that have occurred in either of these worlds. Since such a change occurs gradually, it is difficult to pinpoint with any degree of certainty when or how it began.

This permanent confrontation—in competition and rivalry— enables us to see that the level of the Communist party's involvement in the world is also the level that determines its remarkable capacity for adaptation. The latter, in turn, has enabled it to avoid becoming outmoded, fifty years after its establishment, even though its objective—to become the established society—has not been achieved. At the same time, it is both responsible for and affected by sectional backwardness and temporary rigidities. In short, this level resembles the element of reality in which the communist movement has its roots and which lends it its earthy, sometimes limited, circumspect, and prosaic quality. It would be quite erroneous to assume that communism suddenly became prosaic when it became "orthodox." Generally speaking, it is indeed prosaic, unless one discovers its other element, the element of make-believe that caused Lenin to say that one must dream.

The place of spectacular changes, the plan for an acculturation that stimulates the capacity for adaptation and renewal of the communist phenomenon—this is the first level, which is also the one where the party's most pressing questions are inscribed and where its variations appear. The uncertainties that have to do with the origin of change in the relations between communism and established society also have to do with their duration. It is not until afterward, after a probationary period, that the change causes the status of a temporary event to be replaced by the more noble status of a permanent structure. For example, the exclusion, both in theory and practice, of economic depression and war—long regarded as classic coupling devices of the revolutionary process—compels the Communist party to revise substantially its relations with established society. But it still remains to be seen whether this exclusion is only temporary.

Khrushchevism as such was initially the result of this revision. It was to this that the Soviets subordinated the war-revolution relationship, after the uncertainties and experimentations of the latter part of the forties and the beginning of the fifties. Even the costly Chinese threat did not convince them that they ought to reconsider. Doubtless, under the vigilant eye of Peking, they made a few minor concessions suggesting a sharp distinction between geographical sectors and the strategic problems of countries not protected by atomic power. The Soviets remained basically uncompromising, holding that even the triumph of socialism was not worth the risk of war in countries protected by atomic power.

It is precisely the principle of this position that the "leftists" impugn. France has just experienced the impact of this divergent view. The following lines were written by Waldeck Rochet and published in 1966; we must agree that they render inexcusable the illusion of those who felt that by locking itself into an impossible dilemma —betrayal or revolution—the Communist party would be forced to run the risk of a civil war:

> No one at this moment can state with exactitude how socialism will be achieved in the France of tomorrow. But the position and determination of the French Communist party are clear: all its activity is directed toward creating conditions favorable to a peaceful transition to socialism.

To be sure, the French Communist party could not exclude the possibility that *after* power had been seized, there might be armed resistance to socialism, whether on the part of Frenchmen or foreigners. This traditional hypothesis precludes the elimination of the theory of the proletarian dictatorship, despite the obstacle it would place in the way of establishing a pluralist democracy within the framework of socialism. Similarly, the support given to the brother party in Vietnam is amply justified by the fact that the war it is waging seems to be a defensive one against an imperialist aggressor.

The French Communist party, therefore, categorically rejected in advance the idea that it might, in the event of a *prior* takeover, resort to civil war, a step that would not necessarily endanger the cause of international peace, especially in Europe. One must concede the following point: those who believe that the French Communist party was guilty of "betrayal" when it accepted the electoral challenge hurled at it by de Gaulle, have failed to explain in explicit terms whether they hoped for a civil war in which "republican legality" would be adhered to by the other camp or whether they knew how to get the other camp to give up the idea of holding to such a course. This is probably a conventional question but I raise it in a manner as urgent as it is concrete.

However well-founded an analysis of the communist presence in the "real world" might be, if one were to stop here, it might never be possibe to arrive at an understanding of the communist phenomenon in its totality. "Beneath" this first level, or apart from it, or functioning under different conditions, there is indeed a second level or situation where we encounter a basic *strangeness*. It is this strangeness we have in mind when, in today's idiom, we say of the Communist party that it is not "a party like other parties." It is a strangeness in the original sense of the word: is the spirit of the party anything more than the awareness of the exteriority of the communist world in relation to established society?

This second "condition" is what I set out to describe in this book. My reason for doing so is that it is the least well known, being hidden from anyone not directly involved. It is the hidden element. Moreover, it is the element of stability. Despite adaptations and readjustments, it maintains its own identity. Lastly, this condition is a prefiguration of the future as well as something akin to paradise on earth. It is the imaginary element that informs the millenarian aspirations of a "perfect society."

Hidden, stable, imaginary—perhaps these are but ways of saying that what we have here is something absolute. This may provide the clue that explains the kind of impression a party like the French Communist party makes: it changes, and yet, no, after all, nothing has really changed. Unvarying, unshakable, it remains as it is in itself. The scene, the lights, the action shift but the party reappears looking as it always has looked. The communists themselves express this quality of permanence very simply. They say: "Ask us anything you want, but do not ask us to cease being communists!"

This also explains why it is that we have seen communist parties collapse and disappear—the German Communist party, for example. We have seen communist parties change their strategy, their tactics, policy, size, language, leaders, following—but we haven't seen any of them become social democratic parties. Not because a social democratic party is an "integrated" party, but because it is totally and completely engulfed in its own integration; in fact, it is nothing more than this integration.

Further, this explains why it is absolutely meaningless to condemn the Communist party for being "nonrevolutionary." The Communist party is in itself, as such, the bearer of a power other than that of the established regime. The only nonmetaphysical question to be asked, if not to be answered, is: "What is a revolutionary in France today?"

In addition, this explains why it is that the costliest bills are still to be paid. For it is not "we" who ask "you" not to be communists any longer. It is you yourselves who do so. Will the French Communist party remain faithful to its own condition? When the warmth of the hearth—represented by the Soviet revolution—can no longer give it life, will it become a dead planet? Will the French Communist party break with that which binds it to its own nature? Will it vomit forth the excesses of a static memory and, as the twentieth century draws to a close, keep a tight rein on what links it to the realities of that century? In this way the worldwide communist movement and the French left will rediscover a mutual attraction that has been lost. In any event, this is what Waldeck Rochet has announced, although in that circumspect style and with that shrewd prudence that characterize him—all this despite the predictable detours, returns, delays, and remorse, despite the position taken by the French party's political bureau toward the Red Army's invasion of Czechoslovakia. But things will have to move quickly. It is not enough for communism to "change"; it has to change *in time*.

Twenty-nine years after that day in August when the Nazi-Soviet Pact was made public, on another day in August, a certain kind of French communism came to life. A new chapter is about to begin. How much of the old communism will die? How much of it will survive? This book will perhaps be useful if it helps to illuminate those areas where the nodal points are fixed; if, from the outside, it furthers the birth of something that responds to the needs of a party in which socialism, freedom, and modernity are no longer scorned.

Appendix

NUMBER OF VOTES OBTAINED BY FRENCH COMMUNIST PARTY CANDIDATES
IN LEGISLATIVE ELECTIONS FROM 1924 TO 1968

	Registered voters	Votes cast	Votes for communist candidates	% communist, registered voters	% communist, votes cast
Third Republic					
1924 (May 11)	11,070,360	9,191,809	875,812	7.09	9.5
1928 (April 22, 29)	11,395,760	9,351,479	1,063,943	9.3	11.3
1932 (May 1, 8)	11,561,391	9,445,903	794,883	6.8	8.4
1936 (April 26, May 3)	11,768,491	9,687,519	1,487,336	12.7	15.3
Fourth Republic					
1945 (October 21)	24,622,862	19,189,799	5,005,336	20.3	26.0
1946 (June 2)	24,696,949	19,880,741	5,199,111	21.0	26.1
1951 (June 17)	24,530,523	19,129,547	4,910,547	20.0	25.6
1956 (January 2)	26,772,255	21,490,886	5,532,631	20.6	25.7
Fifth Republic					
1958 (November 23, 30)	27,244,729	20,492,371	3,882,204	14.2	18.9
1962 (November 18, 25)	27,535,019	18,329,986	3,992,431	14.4	21.7
1967 (March 5, 12)	28,300,936	22,389,514	5,039,032	17.7	22.5
1968 (June 23, 30)	28,171,635	22,138,657	4,435,357	15.7	20.03

The table on the opposite page was borrowed from *Est et Ouest*, no. 408 (July 1–31, 1968). It was compiled to give the voting figures for the legislative elections between the two wars (1924, 1928, 1936) and is based on the data provided by the works of Georges Lachapelle, *Elections législatives de* . . . , published by *Le Temps*.

For the postwar legislative elections the sources used were:

Raoul Husson, *Elections et referendums* (October 21, 1945, May 5 and June 2, 1946), edited by *Le Monde*.

Elections et referendums (October 13, November 10 and 24, December 8, 1946), published by *Le Monde*.

L'Année politique, PUF, (since 1945).

La Documentation française (the elections of 1951, 1956, 1958, 1962).

Association française de science politique, *Le Referendum de septembre et les élections de novembre 1958* (with a table showing the increase in communist votes from 1924 to 1958).

Cahiers du communisme, Les Elections législatives de mars 1967, supplement, January 1968.

Communiqués of the Minister of the Interior, *Le Monde*.

OFFICIAL BODIES OF THE FRENCH COMMUNIST PARTY SINCE THE LIBERATION

	The Congress
	(composed of delegates elected
	by the federal conferences)

Secretariat—Political Bureau	Central Committee
(elected by the central commit-	(elected by the national con-
tee)	gress)

	Federal Bureau—Federal Secre-
	tariat
	(elected by the federal commit-
	tee)

Federal Conference	Federal Committee
(composed of delegates elected	(elected by the federal confer-
by section conferences)	ence)

	Sectional Conference
	(composed of delegates elected
	by cell assemblies)

Sectional Bureau—Secretariat	Section Committee
of the Section	(elected by the sectional con-
(elected by the section commit-	ference)
tee)	

Street Cell   Factory Cell   Village Cell

COMMUNIST VOTES (IN THOUSANDS)
BASE: 100 IN 1945

Year	Total Votes		% Registered		% votes	
1924	876		7.0	39.4	9.5	36.5
1928	1,064		9.3	45.8	11.3	43.4
1932	795		6.8	33.4	8.4	32.3
1936	1,487		12.7	62.5	15.3	58.8
1945	5,005	100	20.3	100	26.0	100
1946 (June)	5,199	103.8	21.0	103.4	26.1	100.3
1946 (Nov.)	5,489	109.6	21.9	107.8	28.6	110.0
1951	4,910	98.0	20.0	98.5	25.6	98.4
1956	5,532	110.5	20.6	101.4	25.7	98.8
1958	3,882	77.3	14.2	69.9	18.9	72.6
1962	3,992	79.7	14.4	70.9	21.7	83.8
1967	5,039	100.6	17.7	87.1	22.5	86.5
1968	4,435	88.6	15.7	77.3	20.0	76.9

NUMBER OF SEATS

Year	Available Seats	Communists
1924	568	26
1928	593	14
1932	605	12
1936	608	72
1945	573	152
1946 (June)	586	176
1946 (Nov.)	621	169 +5
1951	627	99 +4
1956	596	144 +6
1958	465	10
1962	482	41
1967	486	73
1968	487	33 +1

THE FRENCH COMMUNIST PARTY'S CONGRESSES

Split Congress	Tours	Dec. 25–30, 1920
First	Marseille	Dec. 25–30, 1921
Second	Paris	Oct. 15–19, 1922
Third	Lyon	Jan. 20–24, 1924
Fourth	Clichy	Jan. 17–23, 1925
Fifth	Lille	June 20–26, 1926
Sixth	Saint-Denis	Mar. 31–Apr. 7, 1929
Seventh	Paris	Mar. 11–19, 1932
Eighth	Villeurbanne	Jan. 22–25, 1936
Ninth	Arles	Dec. 25–29, 1937
Tenth	Paris	June 26–30, 1945
Eleventh	Strasbourg	June 25–28, 1947
Twelfth	Gennevilliers	April 2–6, 1950
Thirteenth	Ivry	June 3–7, 1954
Fourteenth	Le Havre	July 18–21, 1956
Fifteenth	Ivry	June 24–28, 1959
Sixteenth	Saint-Denis	May 11–14, 1961
Seventeenth	Paris	May 14–17, 1964
Eighteenth	Levallois	Jan. 4–8, 1967

Communist Strength in 1967–1968

It does not seem unreasonable to assess communist membership as being within a range of 275,000 and 300,000.

We know that Jeannette Thorez-Vermeersch indicated in *l'Humanité* of November 28, 1961, that in 1959, 49,490 women were members of the French Communist party. At the Fifteenth Congress (June, 1959) Marcel Servin said that women represented 21.9 percent of the total membership of the party. Therefore, for that year the number of members were: 49,490 times 100, divided by 21.9 = 225,985 members.

We also know that from 1961 to 1967 the party added 50,000 new members which should bring the total for 1967 to 275,000.

This figure, remarkably enough, is confirmed by a different kind of calculation. We have been able to obtain the figures, in absolute terms, for the party membership in September 15, 1967, for the federations of the Nord, the Rhône, the Seine-Maritime, the Alpes-Maritimes and the Hérault.

	ABSOLUTE MEMBERSHIP[1]	% OF MEMBERSHIP[2]	TOTAL MEMBERS
Nord	2,720	21.9	12,447
Rhône	1,005	17.7	5,677
Seine-Mar.	766	25.4	3,015
Alpes-Mar.	637	13.7	4,649
Hérault	637	18.5	3,443

If we compare the membership of these federations with their membership in 1946, and if we assume that the ratio between their number of members and that of the total number of party members was stable and proportionate, we have the following figures:[3]

Nord $\quad$ $12{,}447 \times 819{,}155 \div 36{,}616 = 278{,}458$
Rhône $\quad$ $5{,}677 \times 819{,}155 \div 18{,}243 = 254{,}911$
Seine-Mar. $\quad$ $3{,}015 \times 819{,}155 \div 8{,}507 = 290{,}320$
Alpes-Mar. $\quad$ $4{,}649 \times 819{,}155 \div 14{,}134 = 269{,}369$
Hérault $\quad$ $3{,}443 \times 819{,}155 \div 10{,}064 = 280{,}241$

The reader will have to concede that the results of this calculation are too similar to be discounted as insignificant.

1. G. Marchais, *l'Humanité*, July 21, 1967.
2. *La Vie du Parti*, no. 7 (October 1967).
3. See the table of members by federation in 1946 in the central committee's report to the Eleventh Party Congress.

FLUCTUATIONS IN MEMBERSHIP NOTED DURING
YEARLY CAMPAIGNS

1955: 10,859[1]
1956: 52,000[2]
1959: 24,900[2]
1960: 23,611[3]
1961: 23,000[2]
1962: 48,100[2]
1963: 41,263[4]
1964: 38,200[5]
1965: 39,100[5]
1966: 33,000[6]
1967: 42,000[7]
1968: 51,000[8]

1. M. Servin, Fourteenth Congress, p. 208.

2. G. Marchais, National Conference of the French Communist Party, Gennevilliers, February 2–3, 1963, supplement to the *Cahiers du communisme*, nos. 1–2, January-February, 1963, p. 69, mentioned only 42,000. But Marcel Servin spoke of 45,895 new members and added that "their actual number is probably around 50,000" (at the Fourteenth Congress in July, 1956, *Cahiers du communisme*, special no., p. 208). Also, Ducoloné, in *Cahiers du communisme*, no. 12, December 1956, p. 1432, spoke of 52,000. It therefore seems likely that Marchais deliberately minimized a triumph that was due to the efforts of his predecessor in the organization.

3. G. Marchais, Report to the Sixteenth Congress of the French Communist Party, May 1961, *Cahiers du communisme*, special no. 6, June 1961, p. 217.

4. *1961–1964. Du XVIe au XVIIe congrès du PCF. Trois années de lutte*, Activity report of the central committee.

5. G. Marchais, Report to the organizational secretaries, January 7, 1966, *l'Humanité*, January 11, 1966.

6. G. Marchais, *l'Humanité*, October 29, 1966.

7. G. Marchais, report to the central committee, *l'Humanité*, October 19, 1967. According to Waldeck Rochet, January 10, 1968, 43,000.

8. G. Marchais, *l'Humanité*, August 7, 1968.

FLUCTUATIONS OF NET MEMBERSHIP GAINS SINCE 1961

1961:	stabilization[1]		
1962:	+18,000[2]		
1963:	+12,000[3]	+30,000	
1964:	+ 1,500[4]		+40,000
1965:	+ 8,000[5]		
1966:	+ 1,500[4]	+11,000	
1967:	+ 9,500[6]		

Total: from 1961 to 1967, +50,000[7]

1. G. Marchais, Report to the organizational secretaries, *l'Human-ité*, January 11, 1966: "The increase began as early as 1961." Actually, this statement seems questionable if we take into account the very low figure for new members for that year (23,000). But that was the year that Marchais became the organizational secretary, replacing Marcel Servin. He might therefore have been tempted to attribute a reversal of the membership trend to the date when he was promoted. Be that as it may, by 1962 this reversal was an accomplished fact.

2. *1961–1964. Du XVIᵉ au XVIIᵉ congrès du PCF. Trois années de lutte*, Activity report of the central committee, p. 196.

3. Ibid. Waldeck Rochet, in his report to the Seventeenth Congress of the French Communist Party, p. 91, announced that from now on (May, 1964) the party had 30,000 more members than it had at the Sixteenth Congress (May, 1961). These 30,000 new members appear in our table: 18,000 for 1962, 12,000 for 1963. Thus, the 30,000 members lost during the period 1958 to 1961 were recovered during the period 1961 to 1963. The number of party members is therefore the same for 1963 as for 1958.

4. Georges Marchais, in *l'Humanité*, September 5, 1966, wrote: "We have 40,000 more communists today than we had at the close of 1961." Therefore, during the years 1964, 1965, and 1966 the membership of the party increased by only 10,000. Of these 10,000 new members, the year 1965 accounts for 8,000. Moreover, at the Seventeenth Congress of the French Communist Party in January, 1967, Georges Marchais stated that "the party has 11,000 more members than it had at the Seventeenth Congress" in May, 1964. We therefore deduce that the net gains in 1966 were very slight, approximately 1,500.

5. G. Marchais, *l'Humanité*, Jan. 11, 1966.

6. In his report to the central committee, *l'Humanité*, October 19, 1967, G. Marchais indicated that, on the one hand, "as of now, eighty federations have more than 10,000 members compared to last year"; and, on the other hand, that "at the end of this year, sixteen federations have a net loss of 500 members." Hence the figure 9,500. Waldeck Rochet, however, gives a figure somewhat larger, 12,000 in net member-ship gains (*France nouvelle*, January 10, 1968).

7. At this juncture I must point out one difficulty. At the Eighteenth Congress in January, 1967, Waldeck Rochet and Marchais both concluded that 50,000 new members had been added since 1961. This statement does not square with the two other statements cited in note 4 above (40,000 additional members from 1961 to 1966, and 11,000 more in January, 1967, than in May, 1964). The explanation for this discrepancy is probably the following one: the new membership acquired in December, 1966, which normally should have been credited to the 1967 campaign, since it resulted from the "1967 resumption of membership cards," was credited instead to the report presented to the Eighteenth Congress in January, 1967. This being so, the figures are correct as they stand: 40,000 at the close of 1966, and 50,000 by the close of 1967.

INCREASE IN NUMBER OF COMPANY CELLS COMPARED TO TOTAL NUMBER OF CELLS

Year		Total Cells	Company Cells
	1926	3,188	1,544[1]
	1927	—	31%[2]
	1928	3,288	898[3]
	1929	—	29.2%[4]
	1930	—	660
Oct.	1934	2,725	586[5]
June	1935	3,647	738[5]
Oct.	1935	4,221	776[5]
Oct.	1936	10,736	2,898[6]
Oct.	1937	12,992	4,041[6]
Oct.	1938	12,654[7]	
Jan.	1945	16,925	3,416[8]
Mar.	1945	26,805	6,145[9]
Dec.	1946	36,283	8,363[10]
	1961	16,000	3,819[11]
End of 1962		17,297	4,691[12]
	1964	18,500[13]	
	1965	19,000	stagnation[14]
Jan.	1967	19,000	5,100[15]

1. P. Sémard, *l'Humanité*, June 16, 1926.
2. Communist Party, Sixth National Congress, Paris, 1929, *Rapport politique du comité central*, p. 98 (Paris: Bureau d'éditions, 1929).

Toward the close of 1927 (according to the report to the National Congress of January, 1928) 38,500, or 69 percent of the 56,000 members were members of local cells; of these, 17,500 or 31 percent, belonged to company cells.

3. O. Piatnitski, *Quelques problèmes urgents*, p. 26.

4. Communist Party, Sixth National Congress, Paris, 1929, *Rapport politique du comité central*, p. 98.

5. M. Gitton, *Le Parti des travailleurs de France*, p. 13 (a report presented to the Eighth National Congress of the French Communist Party, Villeurbanne, January 22–25, 1936).

6. French Communist Party, *Deux ans d'activité au service du peuple*, Central committee reports to the Ninth National Congress of the French Communist Party, Arles, December 25–29, 1936.

7. French Communist Party, *Une année pour le pain, la paix, la liberté*, Central committee's reports to the French Communist Party's national conference, Gennevilliers, December 25–27, 1938.

8. Léon Mauvais, *Le Parti de la Renaissance française*. Organizational report presented on January 22, 1945, to the central committee of the French Communist Party, Ivry.

9. French Communist Party, 1937–45. From the Congress of Arles to the Congress of Paris, *Sept ans de luttes ardentes au service du peuple contre l'hitlérisme et le fascisme, pour une France libre, démocratique et indépendente*, central committee's reports to the Tenth National Congress of the French Communist Party, Paris, June 26–30, 1945.

10. French Communist Party, 1945–47, from the Paris Congress to the Congress at Strasbourg, *Deux années d'activité pour la renaissance économique et politique de la République française*, central committee's reports to the Eleventh National Congress of the French Communist Party, Strasbourg, June 25–28, 1947.

11. Georges Marchais, *Pour le pain, la démocratie, la paix et le socialisme. Donner au Peuple de France un parti communiste encore plus grand et fort*, national conference of the French Communist Party, Gennevilliers, February 2–3, 1963.

12. Ibid.

13. Georges Marchais, Report to the Seventeenth Congress of the French Communist Party, *Cahiers du communisme*, special no., June-July, 1964, p. 327.

14. Georges Marchais, Report to the secretaries of the organization, *l'Humanité*, January 11, 1966.

15. Georges Marchais, Report to the Eighteenth Congress of the French Communist Party, *Cahiers du communisme*, special no. February-March, 1967, pp. 264, 280.

THE POLITICAL BUREAU[1]

June 1926 (Fifth Congress). Sémard, Crémet, Cachin, Thorez, Doriot, Bernard, Monmousseau, Midol, Renaud-Jean, Sellier, Dudillieux, Racamond.

April 1929 (Sixth Congress). Sémard, Cachin, Thorez, Doriot, Monmousseau, Racamond, Barbé, Ferrat, Billoux, Lozeray, Célor.[2]

June 1930. Barbé, Sémard, Frachon, Cachin, Doriot, Monmousseau, Thorez.[3]

March 1932 (Seventh Congress). Cachin, Doriot, Duclos, Ferrat, Frachon, Gitton, Marty, Midol, Monmousseau, Sémard, Thorez.

September 1932. All the preceding men plus four *substitutes:* Vassart, Tillon, Martel, Arrachart.[3]

January 1936 (Eighth Congress). Thorez, Duclos, Gitton, Cachin, Marty, Frachon, Sémard, Midol, Monmousseau. *Substitutes:* Ramette, Billoux.

December 1937 (Ninth Congress). Cachin, Thorez, Duclos, Gitton, Marty, Monmousseau, Sémard, Ramette, Billoux.

January 1945.[4] *Confirmed:* Thorez, Duclos, Marty, Frachon, Cachin, Monmousseau, Billoux, Ramette; *Elected:* Tillon, Guyot, Mauvais, Dupuy, Fajon, Rochet.

July 1945 (Tenth Congress). *Official members:* Thorez, Duclos, Marty, Cachin, Billoux, Ramette, Tillon, Guyot; *Substitutes:* Mauvais, Dupuy, Fajon, Rochet.

1. The composition of the political bureau is officially announced at the end of each congress in the official reports. On the mechanisms of selection and the role of the political bureau, see chapter 10 above.

2. The decisions of the April, 1929, congress were kept secret; this was an unusual procedure. Therefore the composition of the political bureau as I have noted it was not taken from the official list. The names were excerpted from Albert Vassart's *Mémoires*.

3. Data also contributed by Albert Vassart.

4. The reorganization of January, 1945, is detailed in Maurice Thorez's report to the Tenth Congress in July, 1945.

June 1947 (Eleventh Congress). *Official members:* Thorez, Duclos, Marty, Cachin, Billoux, Ramette, Tillon, Guyot, Fajon; *Substitutes:* Mauvais, Waldeck Rochet, Casanova, Michaut.

April 1950 (Twelfth Congress). *Official members:* Thorez, Duclos, Marty, Cachin, Billoux, Tillon, Guyot, Fajon, Mauvais, Waldeck Rochet; *Substitutes:* Casanova, Michaut, Lecoeur, Jeannette Vermeersch.

June 1954 Thirteenth Congress). *Official members:* Thorez, Duclos, Cachin, Billoux, Fajon, Guyot, Mauvais, Waldeck Rochet, Casanova, Vermeersch; *Substitutes:* Feix, Frischmann, Servin.

July 1956 (Fourteenth Congress). *Official members:* Thorez, Billoux, Cachin, Casanova, Duclos, Fajon, Feix, Frachon, Frischmann, Guyot, Mauvais, Waldeck Rochet, Servin, J. Vermeersch; *Substitutes:* Ansart, Garaudy, Seguy.

June 1959 (Fifteenth Congress). *Official members:* Thorez, Billoux, Casanova, Duclos, Fajon, Feix, Frachon, Frischmann, Guyot, Mauvais, Waldeck Rochet, Servin, J. Vermeersch; *Substitutes:* Ansart, Garaudy, Seguy, Marchais.

June 1961 (Sixteenth Congress). *Official members:* Thorez, Billoux, Duclos, Fajon, Feix, Frachon, Frischmann, Garaudy, Guyot, Marchais, Mauvais, Waldeck Rochet, J. Vermeersch; *Substitutes:* Ansart, Seguy, Laurent.

May 1964 (Seventeenth Congress). *Official members:* Thorez, Rochet, Ansart, Billoux, Duclos, Fajon, Frachon, Frischmann, Garaudy, Guyot, Laurent, Marchais, Seguy, J. Vermeersch; *Substitutes:* Leroy, Krasucki, Piquet, Plissonier.

January 1967 (Eighteenth Congress). *Official members:* Ansart, Billoux, Duclos, Fajon, Frachon, Frischmann, Garaudy, Guyot, Krasucki, Laurent, Leroy, Marchais, Piquet, Plissonnier, Waldeck Rochet, Seguy, J. Vermeersch; *Substitutes:* Besse, Vieuguet.

COMMUNIST MINISTERS

De Gaulle Government (September 5–8, 1944).
    François Billoux, Minister of Occupied Territories
    Fernand Grenier, Minister of Air

De Gaulle Government (September 9, 1944–November 6, 1945)
    Charles Tillon, Minister of Air
    François Billoux, Minister of Public Health

De Gaulle Government (November 21, 1945–January 20, 1946)
    Maurice Thorez, Minister of State
    Charles Tillon, Minister of Armaments
    François Billoux, Minister of National Economy
    Marcel Paul, Minister of Industrial Production
    Ambroise Croizat, Minister of Labor

Gouin Government (January 23–June 12, 1946)
    Maurice Thorez, Vice-President of the Council
    Charles Tillon, Minister of Armaments
    Marcel Paul, Minister of Industrial Production
    Ambroise Croizat, Minister of Labor and Social Security
    François Billoux, Minister of Reconstruction and Urbanism
    Laurent Casanova, Minister of War Veterans and Victims of the War
    Marius Patinaud, Undersecretary of State for Labor
    Auguste Lecoeur, Undersecretary of State for Industrial Production

Bidault Government (June 23–November 22, 1946)
    Maurice Thorez, Vice-president of the Council
    Charles Tillon, Minister of Armaments
    Marcel Paul, Minister of Industrial Production
    Ambroise Croizat, Minister of Labor
    René Arthaud, Minister of Public Health
    François Billoux, Minister of Reconstruction

Laurent Casanova, Minister of War Veterans, Victims of the War and Deportees

Auguste Lecoeur, Undersecretary of State for Industrial Production

Marius Patinaud, Undersecretary of State for Labor

Georges Gosnat, Undersecretary for Armaments

Ramadier Government (January 22–November 19, 1947)

Maurice Thorez, Minister of State, Vice-President of the Council

François Billoux, Minister of National Defense

Charles Tillon, Minister of Reconstruction

Ambroise Croizat, Minister of Labor and Social Security

Georges Marrane, Minister of Public Health and Population

Bibliographical Note: Historiography of French Communism

I did not think that a bibliography was a good idea. Had it been exhaustive, its very length would have overwhelmed the rest of the book; had it been selective, its usefulness would have been limited.[1] For this reason I have decided instead to provide some orientation with an eye to indicating published sources and secondary works as well as methods and directions of research that might lead to an expansion of our knowledge in this area.

Sources and Archives

The nature of the sources on which the historian must rely obviously depends on the kinds of problems that interest him. Some sort of hypothesis regarding the nature of the communist phenomenon is necessary if one is to "discover" the sources, not all of which, of course, have been assembled in one place. One should not, in any case, be content with only the conventional kinds of archives. If, for example, one thinks of the communist phenomenon as something that sees itself from a global perspective *and* also constitutes a true microcosm, then information about it cannot be limited to a strictly French or political framework.[2] French com-

1. Besides, the reader can refer to *L'Etat des travaux sur le communisme français* compiled by Nicole Racine for a colloquium organized by the Fondation nationale des sciences politiques on March 1 and 2, 1968, on the theme: "Communism in France and in Italy."
2. The reader can get a first glimpse of this global perspective by consulting the bibliographical guides compiled by British researchers: Walter Kolarz, *Books on Communism, a Bibliography*, 2d ed. (London:

munism cannot be reduced merely to the contribution that it, together with other political parties, makes to the parliamentary life of the nation.

The complex nature of the phenomenon in question is not the only reason why research should be pursued in a variety of directions. Another justification is that it compensates for the difficulties one encounters in locating the kinds of sources that should provide the central core of one's information.

Doubtless, the mass of printed material is already so extensive that anything unpublished can be used to complement the study, to provide an additional means of checking certain ambiguities as well as the overly cautious statements or equivocations inherent in texts written with the idea that they would be made public immediately.[3]

Doubtless, too, there is more "secrecy" in the history of the communist movement than in many other areas of contemporary history.[4]

Nonetheless, the historian, no matter how convinced he may be about the wealth of information to be found in printed materials, no matter how aware he may be of the impossibility of uncovering all the party's "secrets," should never abandon the idea of utilizing unpublished material, if only to accomplish the most delicate of operations: that of deciding how to divide his attention between the different elements of a policy whose public exposure is often embellished by false leads and slogans. Also, he should seek unpublished material in the hope of discovering *revelations—*

Ampersand, 1963) ; Thomas T. Hammond, *Soviet Foreign Relations and World Communism, a Selected, Annotated Bibliography of 7,000 Books in 30 Languages* (Princeton University Press, 1965) ; Witold S. Sworakowski, *The Communist International and its Front Organizations, a Research Guide and Checklist of Holdings in American and European Libraries* (The Hoover Institute: Stanford University, 1965).

3. See for example the printed sources that make it possible to estimate the fluctuations of the party's membership in A. Kriegel, "Le PCF sous la III*e* République (1920–1939). Evolution des effectifs," *Revue français de science politique*, 16, no. 1 (February 1966) : 5–35.

4. See above, chapter 13.

after all, why not? I do not mean the kind of revelations one gets from professional gossipmongers or scandal sheets, but accurate, definitely established factual information. This in turn enables the historian to select the correct hypothesis from among several suggested by the event.

Three categories of unpublished sources should serve, at least in the beginning, as mines of essential information: the archives of the Communist International, an organization of which, until 1943, the French Communist party was but a section; the archives of the French Communist party itself; French government archives.

About the first we know nothing or very little. Occasionally Soviet historians, using some vague reference system, mention this or that file or document presumably extracted from cartons in the Komintern's archives.[5] But despite the hopes aroused by the Twentieth Congress of the Soviet Communist party, no systematic inventory has been compiled, or at any rate none has been placed at the disposal of the researcher, whether Russian or foreign. It was thought that after the parties in certain of the people's democracies had heard that their files had been preserved in Moscow, the French Communist party might also conceivably obtain photocopies of documents relating to the French section (which were stored among the Komintern's papers), if not the documents themselves. Should this be the case—there has as yet been no confirmation—then the first category of archives can be combined with the second.

The second category consists in the archives of the French Communist party. If we take only the period from 1920 to 1939, three problems arise. First: how extensive are the losses due to the war? We know that the persecutions which took place between 1939 and 1944 led certain organizations as well as some militants to destroy many papers they were

5. See, for example, A. Manoussevitch, M. Birmane, A. Klevanski, J. Khrenov, *Les internationalistes, travailleurs des pays étrangers engagés dans la lutte pour le pouvoir des soviets* (Moscow: Naouka, 1967), 615 pp. (in Russian).

holding. We also know that other papers were seized by the French police or the Gestapo. But we have never known exactly how much was destroyed before the papers were seized; or how much was safeguarded despite confiscations, confiscated and definitely lost, confiscated but recovered after the war, and lastly how much is still recoverable after having been seized, since the archives in both West and East Germany have never been completely destroyed. From time to time, in some Silesian or Czech hideout, cartons abandoned by Hitler's retreating army are still being discovered.

Second: the difference between official and personal archives is much less clearly defined in the government services. This is natural enough in organizations whose members were volunteers. Such being the case, how far do the discovery and compilation of dispersed personal archives make up for the loss or disappearance of central, official archives? In a party that numbered its cadres in the tens of thousands and its members in the hundreds of thousands, it is plainly impossible to reconstitute in their entirety all the printed materials and propaganda tracts, all the records of conferences and congresses, all the brochures, leaflets, pamphlets, and propaganda "literature." It is equally impossible to assemble all the archives containing unprinted material. Nevertheless, this is now being attempted by the Maurice Thorez Institute. It would be interesting to have at least a published inventory of all the documents that have been gathered so far.[6] In order not to embark on a task that could be more diverting than substantial, one would have to be able to ascertain the decision-making centers. Here the archives can be of value. If one believes that the bureaus of cells (insofar as such cells exist), the sections, the federations, and lastly the political bureau are the vital organs of the party's apparatus at various levels, then the records of the meetings of these bodies should be significant.[7] Now we come to the third problem: the French Communist party, like any private

6. See David Diamant, "Le centre de documentation de l'Institut Maurice-Thorez," *Cahiers de l'Institut Maurice-Thorez*, 5, p. 122.
7. The formulas for the proceedings of these meetings have varied:

organization, is the legitimate owner of these archives. It is therefore entirely free to decide how they should be used.

Moreover, in support of any decision to refuse access to these archives, it can adduce the policy of the state. Unlike the Anglo-Saxon countries, where such questions are handled in a very liberal fashion, the French state archives are subject to the fifty-year rule.[8] Yet they are exceedingly rich in the field of communist history (at any rate for the 1920–35 period).

A penchant for secrecy (on the part of the state and the party) so dear to Latin countries, the traditional mistrust of workers' movements and especially of their writings—the police have often leaned heavily on this at the expense of the authors concerned—and lastly the Bolshevik thesis on the need for a clandestine sector, removed from bourgeois legality, within the communist appartus even where communist parties enjoy a legal status—all this has helped to reinforce the psychological taboos which during Stalin's era equated the activities of the historian with those of the spy. This was strange behavior at a time when the master of the Kremlin wanted to remind people that Marxism was synonymous with *historical* materialism.

Although the traditions, prejudices, and precedents in this matter of the communists' and workers' archives do not serve the interests of historical science, it should be pointed out that more recently some of the old taboos have begun to disappear. The archives now available to historians are so interesting and voluminous that nothing can be gained by stubbornly concealing everything that has not yet been revealed.

For the past ten years many specialized and nonspecialized archival collections, both private and public, have been

sometimes they are stenographic reports, sometimes analytic summaries, but most often they are merely a list of the decisions reached. This type of document has always been filed, signed, and preserved with the greatest care, at least for the most important meetings.

8. A rule that it would seem ought to be quickly made more flexible in order to liberalize the conditions under which state archives prior to 1939 could be consulted.

opened. Among these are the German public archives. They
constitute an invaluable source for all contemporary history
and therefore for communist history, both in its Soviet phase
and in its international and French aspects. There are also
the personal archives of present-day or former communist
leaders. We are therefore no longer limited to printed materials.

The first outstanding French publication from this point
of view appeared in the *Archives* series. It contains among
other things the papers of Jules Humbert-Droz, the Communist International's former secretary and delegate to Paris.[9]
In addition to their intrinsic interest, these papers make
possible some important verifications. Such documents have
no direct bearing on current political affairs but are fascinating reading for the historian. Nowhere did the pillars of
the temple collapse because the means and methods by which
the International's executive committee intervened in the life
of the French section forty years ago are herein revealed.

To the publication of the Humbert-Droz papers in their
entirety (which the International Institute of Social History
in Amsterdam is undertaking with all the scientific para-
phernalia anyone can possibly want) one may add the imminent appearance of other no less interesting items that
have already been uncovered and classified. These include the
archival materials left to the various institutions in a variety
of forms by such men as: Henri Barbusse, Marcel Cachin,
Marcel Martinet, André Marty, Pierre Monatte, Léon
Moussinac, Charles Rappoport, Boris Souvarine, Angelo
Tasca,[10] Albert Vassart. Uneven in scope and value, they
nonetheless represent an irreplaceable contribution to our
factual knowledge of the different stages the French Communist party traversed throughout its entire existence.

9. J. Humbert-Droz, *"L'Oeil de Moscou" à Paris*, Texts and foot-
notes compiled with the help of Annie Kriegel (Paris: Julliard, 1964).

10. Angelo Tasca's archives, which are considerably detailed for a
history of the Italian communist movement, are also of great interest
to students of the French section. But they have not as yet been explored for this purpose.

Testimonies, recollections, memoirs, both published and unpublished, cannot properly be called archives. Nonetheless, they constitute a major source.[11] Naturally this imposing material must be given the careful scrutiny to which data of this type are customarily subjected. Let me list the contributors in alphabetical order without regard to their coverage, their purpose, or their orthodoxy: Henri Barbé,[12] Virgile Barel,[13] Pierre Célor,[14] Marcel Body,[15] Florimond Bonte,[16] Jacques Duclos,[17] André Ferrat,[18] Roger Garaudy,[19] Pierre Hervé,[20] Auguste Lecoeur,[21] Henri Lefebvre,[22] André

11. To the list that follows should be added the evidence in such publications as the *Cahiers de l'Institut Maurice-Thorez, Unir, Le Débat communiste, Est et Ouest, La Nation socialiste*.

12. Henri Barbé, "Souvenirs de militant et de dirigeant communiste" (unpublished).

13. Virgile Barel *Cinquante années de luttes (Souvenirs)*, Pref. by Georges Cogniot (Paris: Ed. sociales, 1966).

14. Henri Barbé and Pierre Célor, "Contribution à l'histoire du parti communiste français: le groupe Barbé-Célor" (BEIPI: July 1-15, 1957).

15. Marcel Body, "Le groupe communiste français à Moscou 1919-1920," in Freymond, ed. *Contribution à l'Histoire de la IIIᵉ Internationale* (Geneva: Droz, 1965).

16. Florimond Bonte, *Le chemin de l'honneur. De la Chambre des députés aux prisons de France et aux bagnes d'Afrique* (Paris: Les Ed. français réunis, 1950) ; idem, *De l'ombre à la lumière (souvenirs)*, Pref. by François Billoux (Paris: Ed. sociales, 1965).

17. Jacques Duclos, *Mémoires, 1896-1934, Le chemin que j'ai choisi, de Verdun au parti communiste* (Paris: Fayard, 1968). Rather disappointing.

18. André Ferrat, "Naissance du PCF," *Preuves* 164 (December 1964), pp. 70-75; idem, "Contributions a l'histoire du PCF. M. Fauvet saisi par la légende," Preuves 168 (February 1965), pp. 53-61.

19. Roger Garaudy, *Peut-on être communiste aujourd'hui?* (Paris: Grasset, 1968). See especially the Introduction.

20. Pierre Hervé, *La Révolution et les Fétiches* (Paris: Table Ronde, 1956) ; idem, *Lettre à Sartre et à quelques autres par la même occasion* (Paris: Table Ronde, 1956) ; idem, *Dieu et César sont-ils communistes?* (Paris: Table Ronde, 1957).

21. Auguste Lecoeur, *L'Autocritique attendue* (Saint-Cloud: Girault, 1955) ; *Le Partisan* (Paris: Flammarion, 1963) ; *Le Parti communiste français et la Résistance, Août 1939-Juin 1941* (Paris: Plon 1968).

22. Henri Lefebvre, *La Somme et le Reste*, 2 vols. (Paris: La Nef de Paris, 1959).

Marty,[23] Edgar Morin,[24] Marcel Ollivier, Alfred Rosmer,[25] Maurice Thorez,[26] Charles Tillon.[27]

Works

During the sixties, when the archival collections became available, the historiography of French communism was suddenly enriched by three works that claimed to encompass the entire life of the French Communist party.

To be sure, they were not the first works of this nature to appear. In 1931 André Ferrat had already written an official "History" which was fated to a premature demise because of the unfortunate times.[28] Then the Popular Front witnessed a growing public curiosity regarding the communist phenomenon. T. Ferlé's book was a response to this demand. It is still useful because it contains so many names and figures.[29] In the postwar period, leaving aside sociologically oriented works,[30] G. Walter's compilation at least provided, despite its

23. André Marty, *La Révolte de la Mer noire*, 4th ed. (Paris: Ed. sociales, 1949) ; idem, *L'Affaire Marty* (Paris: Éd. des deux Rives, 1955).

24. Edgar Morin, *Autocritique* (Paris: Julliard, 1959).

25. Alfred Rosmer, *Moscou sous Lénine: les origines du communisme*, Pref. by Albert Camus (Paris: P. Horay, 1953) ; *Le Mouvement ouvrier pendant la guerre*, vol. 1, *De l'Union sacrée à Zimmerwald* (Paris: Lib. du Travail, 1936) ; vol. 2, *De Zimmerwald à la Révolution russe* (Paris: Mouton, 1959).

26. Maurice Thorez, *Fils du peuple* (Paris: ESI, 1937). See successive editions (2nd ed.: 1949; 4th ed.: 1954; edition revised and reissued: 1960).

27. Charles Tillon, *Les F.T.P., témoignage pour servir à l'histoire de la Résistance* (Paris, Julliard, 1962).

28. André Ferrat, *Historie du parti communiste français* (Paris: Bureau d'éd., 1931).

29. T. Ferlé, *Le Communisme en France. Organisation, la documentation catholique* (Paris: Bonne Presse, 1937).

30. See especially Raymond Aron, *Le Grand Schisme* (Paris: Gallimard, 1948) ; Dyonis Mascolo, *Le Communisme, Révolution et communication ou la dialectique des valeurs et des besoins* (Paris: Gallimard, 1952) ; Jules Monnerot, *Sociologie du communisme*, new and revised edition (Paris: Gallimard, 1963). Also, the important collection of the review, *Arguments*, should be consulted from this angle.

errors, a rather detailed chronology, as well as an abundance
of specific data and documents.[31] But the real work of the
historian, that of analyzing the origins, significance, impact,
and logical sequence of events rather than merely collecting
texts, still remains to be done.

The following are three books that appeared fifteen years
later.

First, the two-volume history written by Jacques Fauvet[32]
for the larger public. At first glance it gives the impression
of being the hastily composed but elegantly written work of
a seasoned journalist: short chapters, accompanied by topical
general introductions; lively narration and vivid sketches of
individuals. But on rereading it, one realizes that the author's
thinking goes deeper than initially appears. His analysis of
the 1934–39 period is particularly good. The epilogue at the
end of the first volume is forceful, and suggests that a distinction should be drawn between the success of the instrument—the party—and the failure of the object to be attained
by the instrument—the socialist revolution. But Fauvet's
evaluation, which deals primarily with the French Communist party, seems to me to be marred by a serious error in
perspective—if, from the outset, communism did represent a
worldwide undertaking. "Its efficacy," he concludes, "did not
measure up to its loyalty." I wonder! It is extremely difficult
to measure efficacity. During the early twenties, the aim of the
French section of the Communist International was to prevent
the French government, by means of sustained agitation
throughout the country, from intervening in a possible German revolution. During the thirties, the France of the Popular Front was the Soviet Union's ally against Hitler. In 1940,
this alliance gave Stalin the opportunity to suggest that a

31. Gérard Walter, *Histoire du parti communiste français* (Paris:
Somogy, 1948).

32. Jacques Fauvet, *Histoire du parti communiste français* (in collaboration with Alain Duhamel). Vol. 1, *De la guerre à la guerre (1917–
1939)* (Paris: Fayard, 1964); vol. 2: *Vingt-cinq ans de drames
(1939–1965)* (1965).

choice had to be made by him between two systems of security. And lastly, after World War II, the considerable influence exerted by French communism caused enough disturbance in the European situation to make people feel that the transformation of the Eastern European nations into people's democracies constituted the lesser evil.

All things considered, Jacques Fauvet did not write a history of the French Communist party but rather a history of its intervention in French politics or, to be more exact, in French parliamentary life. Many political parties probably find it difficult not to confuse their activities with those of the parliamentary groups that wear the party hats. But this is not true of the French Communist party for two reasons: it is part of a supranational ensemble, not secondarily but in an essential, congenital, fashion; to achieve its ends, it intends to expend its efforts, not only or even *primarily* in the parliamentary arena but in a multitude of arenas (political, economic, social, cultural) where successively or simultaneously the class struggle is taking place.

A collective work of several authors, headed by François Billoux and Jacques Duclos, appeared a few weeks later.[33] Based on criteria quite different from those of Jacques Fauvet's book, this work seems as ponderous as its predecessor seems hurried. In fact, the "manual" subtitle, which the authors employ to underscore its pedagogical purpose, suggests that if it is truly pedagogical, its pedagogy goes back to the days when science was presumed to be boring. Or perhaps the work was called a manual in order to preclude criticism rather than to warn the reader—as if there is such a thing as a true or false "pedagogy"!

All in all, a sociologist of ideologies might have found in it excellent material on how French communism viewed its own history in 1964, rather than on merely the history of the movement. In fact, the authors of this official manual were

33. *Histoire du parti communiste français (manuel)* (Paris: Ed. sociales, 1964).

writing immediately after Khrushchev's sensational denunciation of the Stalinist "cult of personality," at an exciting time when a fresh drama, the Sino-Soviet schism, was being enacted. To solve the problem, they offer abstractions—no more names, no more facts. Nothing real is allowed to pierce the surface. Faces dissolve into one another, unfortunate or uninspiring events are obscured. All that emerges is a meaningless sequence of happenings; no attempt is made at systematic periodization. Interpretations and justifications, whose validity has never been questioned by the leading groups, are strung together. No mention is made of prior points of view. The more recent attitudes, although explicitly revised, are adopted. Lastly, anything that might raise questions or that has not yet been definitely formulated is passed over in silence.

The three-volume *Histoire du PCF* was planned and written by a group of communists who belonged to the opposite camp.[34] The work was probably undertaken in an attempt to combat this kind of sterile abstractionism. The books represent an effort to clarify concrete, specific points rather than to give a coordinated interpretation of forty years of communist history. The first volume, which appeared in 1960, is rather disappointing. But the two subsequent ones, written with the help of militants who participated in the events recounted, are full of rare documents. They also provide information that is often new and always interesting, even though it does require verification.

Thus we have three histories of the French Communist party, none of which is definitive. The first fails to place French communism in its proper context; the second develops into a rhetorical discourse; the third contains valuable but disconnected material.

Is it too early to embark on a work of synthesis? The

34. *Histoire du parti communiste français.* Vol. 1, *Des origines du PCF à la guerre de 1939* (Paris: Editions Verdad, 1960); vol. 2, *De 1940 à la Libération* (ed. Unir, 1962); vol. 3, *De 1945 à nos jours* (1964).

answer is definitely yes, even though such a "premature" synthesis can have the beneficial effect of stimulating monographs. In any event, that is exactly what is happening today.

First, there are the monographs that are deliberately limited to a single theme. The theme that has attracted the greatest amount of attention from this point of view is plainly the party's relationship to the intellectuals.[35] In addition to books whose focal point is an author (Barbusse, Raymond Lefebvre, Paul Nizan, Aragon) or a movement (the movement served by the periodical *Clarté*, the Surrealist movement), two more ambitious books were composed in 1963–64. Very different in purpose, execution, and conclusions, they nonetheless complement each other, although neither singly nor together do they exhaust the subject.

The first is the work of a young British historian and writer who, noting the fascination that communism has had for intellectuals of the continent at certain periods, is concerned with delineating what the French intellectual expected his adherence to communism would bring him in regard to the exercise of his creative faculties.[36] Passing rapidly over the prewar years, David Caute concentrates on the period when Zdanovism constituted a rule of behavior or at least a point of reference for all intellectuals, researchers, writers or artists who, as members of the Communist party, attempted (in accordance with the slogan of the time) "to put themselves in the position of the working class." In a shrewdly penetrating summary, he shows both the exaltation and restraint experienced by creative communist intellectuals as a consequence of the Soviet version of Marxism.

35. See, on this point, the special number of the *Revue française de science politique*, "Le Parti communiste et les Intellectuels (1920–1939)," Pref. by J. Touchard (June 1967).

36. David Caute, *Communism and the French Intellectuals, 1914–1960* (London: Macmillan, 1964). Revised and enlarged. For the French translation: *Le Communisme et les Intellectuels français 1914–1966* (Paris: Gallimard, 1967).

Nicole Racine has adopted a different point of view.[37] She has underscored the purely political intervention of communist intellectuals, seen from the perspective of a socio-professional group that was successively pacifist, progressivist, and antifascist. Her attention is attracted by the currents and movements in which communist intellectuals play a preponderant role—theoretically or actually. She notes those currents and movements that aim to redirect this or that category of intellectuals toward political, trade unionist or cultural ends, or that, drawing their recruits from a diversity of groups, affect intellectuals in particular.

Then there are monographs deliberately confined to a specific period. The contributions made by young American historians who belong in this category are considerable.

Robert Wohl of the University of California has studied the history of French communism from 1914 to 1924, which is the period of its origins antedating the decisive turning point of "Bolshevization."[38] Daniel R. Brower of Oberlin College has written on the Communist party and the Popular Front (1934–38).[39] These two academic studies are equal to the best in American historiography. They are as extensive and as carefully written as one could wish; they provide an honest examination of the facts; they are minutely detailed, linear narratives, marked by an obvious effort to comprehend the subject and to treat it sympathetically; they present altogether moderate conclusions. These books do honor to the American school of history.

37. Nicole Racine, "Les Ecrivains communistes en France, 1920–1936" (Thesis for Fondation nationale des sciences politiques, Paris, 1936). Chapters of this thesis were revised and printed in *Le Mouvement social* (January-March, 1966), and *Revue française de science politique* (June 1967).

38. Robert Wohl, *French Communism in the Making, 1914–1924* (Stanford University Press, 1966).

39. Daniel R. Brower, *The New Jacobins. The French Communist Party and the Popular Front 1934–1938* (Cornell University Press, 1968).

More recent periods have also been studied. The five years from 1939 to 1944 are the subject of quasi permanent polemics.[40] François Fetjtö composed a detailed, honest, and judicious chronicle about the ten years that followed the Soviet Communist party's Twentieth Congress.[41]

Possibilities for Future Research

Yet all this research, deliberately limited as it is to the event or to narrative, rarely comes to grips with the deeper phenomena. This is often the case in areas where the establishment of even the most obvious facts requires considerable clarification.

What are these deeper phenomena? They might be listed under three headings.

First, what are the relations between the Communist party and the working class? In other words, to what extent is the Communist party a "working-class party?" This is a complex question that cannot be answered merely by an analysis of the party's social composition. It will also be necessary to analyze its audience, its policies and objectives, the interaction between party and class mentalities and roles. This must be done with an eye to delimiting precisely, for example, the frontiers of each social class and group on the one hand, and their political development on the other.

Second, what is the place, theoretically and practically speaking, of the Communist party in the French workers' movement? In other words, how does one define the hostility, cooperation, and hegemony that it maintains with working class or socialist groups, philosophical associations, cooperatives, trade union organizations, national defense organizations? All of these, in one way or another, address themselves to a working-class clientele and hope to participate in the promotion of a society in which capitalist exploitation will have disappeared. It is necessary, for example, to clarify the

40. See above, chapter 5, n. 12, with bibliographical notes.
41. François Fejtö, *The French Communist Party and the Crisis of International Communism* (Cambridge, Mass.: MIT Press, 1965).

modes of transition, the spiritual conversions, the mutations of thought within a single large ideological family.

Third, what are the factors at work, the modalities, the mechanisms and the consequences of the insertion of the French Communist party into the international communist movement? In dealing with this subject, it is necessary to indicate precisely the extent to which the original product of the Bolshevist stamp on the body of French socialism has taken account, in the course of its history, of its French heritage and its external model.

All things considered, these problems, grouped in this way under three headings, cannot be studied in the abstract; they call for precise, carefully documented research.

Quantitative research: the first thing to do is to count. *How many* communists were there? Or better still, compare the number of *members,* the number of press *readers,* and the number of *voters,* in order to attempt a definition of the relationship between the audience, the influence, and the structure of a political group like the Communist party. Such additional quantitative research aims to isolate the phenomenon of communist indoctrination. Our concern is no longer to add up all these figures but to descend to the level of the factory or the village and to ascertain *where* the communists are. To begin with, *who* are the communists? And what are the regional, social, and cultural variations among them? This leads us to attempt a diagnosis of *why?*

The qualitative research can begin. This will include studies of the men who have given the party its features, and such analyses will rest on the *who* and the *why.* What will emerge, in addition to enlightenment about the internal relations between leaders and their followers are the persistent features of a mentality, hence the specific characteristics of a microsociety like the French Communist party—a party whose ambition is total.

Index